Reading Freud

Reading Freud

Psychoanalysis as Cultural Theory

Tony Thwaites

SAGE Publications
Los Angeles ▪ London ▪ New Delhi ▪ Singapore

First published 2007

SAGE Publications Ltd
1 Oliver's Yard
55 City Road
London EC1Y 1SP

SAGE Publications Inc.
2455 Teller Road
Thousand Oaks, California 91320

SAGE Publications India Pvt Ltd
B 1/I 1 Mohan Cooperative Industrial Area
Mathura Road, New Delhi 110 044
India

SAGE Publications Asia-Pacific Pte Ltd
33 Pekin Street #02-01
Far East Square
Singapore 048763

British Library Cataloguing in Publication data

A catalogue record for this book is available
from the British Library

ISBN   978-0-7619-5236-7
        978-0-7619-5237-4

Library of Congress control number: 2006923439

Typeset by C&M Digitals (P) Ltd, Chennai, India
Printed on paper from sustainable resources
Printed and bound in Great Britain by TJ International, Padstow, Cornwall

For Suzanne Evered,
and for Nevil and Jane Day

CONTENTS

ACKNOWLEDGEMENTS

As well as the debts of gratitude noted in the dedication, there are others. In particular, I would like to thank my students in ENGL2420, who worked through some of this material in classes and gave me valuable feedback on the first chapter and the layout; the University of Queensland, which provided the Special Studies Program on which some of this book was written; Ian Antcliff, SAGE designer, in deep appreciation of his support and ingenuity; and, as always, Jennie, Lauren and Sam, for putting up with another bloody book.

PREFACE

Why

This book is a guide to Freud's work, the concepts he introduces and works with, and the ways in which he uses them. It is for the reader who wants an overview of Freud which will show the main concepts Freud deploys, the arguments he makes with them, where he makes them, and how they develop over the course of a long career. One of the things this book should be is a preliminary to jumping in and reading Freud, and that is one of the reasons for my insistence on Freud's own words. Everywhere, it points back to Freud's writings.

Psychoanalysis is a significant presence in much recent cultural theory, particularly that which is inflected by the work of Jacques Lacan. We find it in the highly influential and inventive work of thinkers such as Judith Butler, Ernesto Laclau, Chantal Mouffe, Joan Copjec, Slavoj Žižek, Renate Salecl, Alenka Zupančič and Alain Badiou, where it has led to things such as a reconsideration of theories of ideology and sexual difference, powerful critiques of New Historicism and Foucauldian concepts of the subject, and a powerful framework for discussing things as different as the World Trade Center attack and the logic of ethnic cleansing.[1] The intending reader of Freud today often comes to it from work such as this, wanting to read back in order to find where it has come from, and indeed this book is very much about the Freud who has found his way into those bodies of work. It does not assume any previous familiarity with them, but the reader who does have that familiarity will see their obvious imprint here.[2] A secondary aim of the book is to point forward to that work, but as there are obvious limits to what can be done in a single short book, that function is left to the endnotes, which provide brief and basic sketches of the issues and direct the reader out to other places where such things can be followed up in the detail they require.

While focusing on the Freud who has been taken up later, this book is not just a summary of Freud's main ideas, but a critical argument about them, and about Freud as a cultural theorist. What it looks for in particular are the points – and they begin with the very postulation of the unconscious – at which Freud works outside that familiar division between the individual human subject and the social world of which they are part: or, in other words, outside that disciplinary division between psychology and sociology.

Freud as a cultural theorist is a radical rethinker of that category of culture. Nevertheless, these moments are not always consistently developed in Freud's work. There is a multiplicity of Freuds, and sometimes these arguments are embedded in others which do indeed seem to observe those familiar divisions.

Sometimes Freud's most radical ideas cut across the grain of what is said around them; sometimes they get proposed, then are dropped or forgotten, to be remembered again in another context. But they are, for all that, deeply *Freudian* arguments, in that they follow from his premises with the strictest application of the logic he himself develops. It is those contours I want to trace out here.

It is not surprising that there should be many Freuds, or that which is which should not always be clear. Freud's output is huge: the Standard Edition in English, which includes only the psychoanalytic papers, takes up 24 volumes, and on top of that there are almost a dozen volumes of letters. The earliest paper in the Standard Edition dates from 1885; the last ones were left unfinished at his death in 1939. Throughout this time (more than half a century), his thought changes a great deal and in all sorts of ways. Freud's texts are always carrying on a running self-critical argument with themselves, finding new problems – some-times within the old solutions, refining their apparatus, returning to earlier questions and investigations, and revising their view of what they have been doing all along. As well as this, they enter everywhere into the push and shove of their world, persuading or polemicising, attempting to retain control of the institution that rapidly and of necessity became psychoanalysis's way of ensur-ing its existence, or refuting and combating what Freud perceives to be mistaken views.

Sometimes the changes across this half-century take the form of major revisions, with a before and after, clearly heralded and explicitly acknowledged. This is particularly the case around 1923, when an entirely new terminology heralds a radical rethinking of the way the psyche is structured and the interre-lation of its parts. This means that when a work dates from, what it is answer-ing, revising or initiating, and what its context might be, are all significant and sometimes crucial points in reading Freud. One of the tasks of this book is to track some of these developments in the principal concepts.

In other cases, though, these changes take the comparatively less notice-able form of a conceptual instability or small-scale hesitation. A concept may be defined in a number of ways, which are never quite synonymous with each other, and oscillate from one to the other according to the needs of the argu-ment and the context: the *drive*, for example, is variously referred to as belong-ing to the body (certain bodily processes which get represented in the psyche), as mental (the psychical representations of those processes, rather than the processes themselves), or as a mixture of the two (somewhere on the borderline between the mental and the physical). The hesitations and silences of an argu-ment may work in just the same way as Freud argues they do in an actual analysis – revealing an unease or uncertainty at the heart of the argument. At moments like this, the reader of Freud has the responsibility of the analyst, to read carefully and in detail.

This book addresses the inconsistencies and *non sequiturs* across Freud's work, not in order to excuse or condemn them, but to do something that, it argues, is far more interesting and profitable – simply, and in a word, to *read* them. As the Introduction points out, this is, after all, precisely what psychoanalysis does with the inconsistencies of dreams, symptoms, testimonies, and the like. By exactly the same logic, these hesitations within psychoanalysis itself are the points at which psychoanalysis – like the dream and the symptom, and whether or not despite itself or behind its own back – *cannot help but say the truth of its situation.*

How

All the above are factors behind the somewhat unusual layout of this book. There are three elements to it:

1   The **main text** is an accumulative argument about the conceptual develop-ment of Freud's thought. It is in three sub-divided chapters, focused succes-sively on the unconscious, sexuality and the social. This division does not mean that the first two chapters are merely preparation, putting together an apparatus which at last, in the final chapter, can be turned to the real topic of the book, Freud as cultural theory. As this book hopes to show, Freudian cultural theory is not simply an importation and application of Freudian psychoanalytic theory to a new domain. From the outset the most basic con-cepts of psychoanalysis and the view of the human subject it proposes are never separable from questions of culture, and this is a constant focus of all three chapters.

2   All direct citations from Freud's own writings form a separate **commentary** on the main text, interspersed among it in 'breakout' boxes. Each of these breakouts is an illustration of what is being argued in the main text when it occurs. The precise point is always cued by a large dot: •. This lets me cite more frequently and at greater length than the usual system of indented block citations in the main text would permit. Too many block citations can distract from a text's argument, fragment it, or reduce it to linkages and com-mentary. But such a frequency and length of citation are a vital part of this book: one of the things it wants to do is provide an introduction to the par-ticular procedures and flavours of Freud's *writings*, as well as to his ideas – to prepare the reader for *reading Freud.*

3   Interspersed through these chapters is a series of brief **inserts** describing each of the principal works of Freud's career. At the endpoints of the book, the first inserts deal with Freud's own introductory works and surveys, while the final ones describe the case histories and their import. Within each chapter, the inserts focus on the writings which develop the themes of that chapter.

This arrangement is meant to meet the needs of several different sorts of read-ing, so that the book can simultaneously offer: a detailed argument about Freud in the light of various recent influential uptakes of his work; a brief survey of the main texts; and a way for the new reader of Freud to find their way into that large and shifting body of work as a general acquaintance or in order to follow through the development of specific concepts.

Because a sense of chronology is so important to an understanding of Freud, I have generally given the dates of works as they are mentioned, even at the cost of repetition. Where there is a discrepancy I have favoured the date of writing [cited in square brackets] over the date of publication (cited in round brackets).

What

There are certain resources which any reader of Freud needs. The Standard Edition of Freud's psychoanalytic writings is now available in relatively cheap paperback versions in both the UK and US markets (the older Penguin editions are all drawn from the Standard Edition, though their pagination is different). The editorial notes to the Standard Edition are truly invaluable in their careful tracing-out of interrelationships across that huge corpus: the introductions and the editorial footnotes point out when concepts make their first appearance, where else they are developed, swerves and redevelopments of the argument, and the revisions made across subsequent editions of the same text. A valuable way of negotiating all this is by the New York Freudian Society's complete abstracts to the Standard Edition, free online at http://nyfreudian.org/abstracts. There are many excellent guides to Freud, some of which are to be found in the bibliography. The only one I shall mention here has been particularly indispensible in the writing of this book: Laplanche and Pontalis's *The Language of Psycho-Analysis* (1973), with its thorough and meticulous documentation of all the main Freudian concepts.

Page numbers to all of Freud's work cited in the text are from the Standard Edition. Where a work occupies two volumes of this edition, volume numbers are also given. Dates given in the main text are the years in which Freud wrote the work. Dates given in documentation are those of its publication.

Notes to Preface

[1]See the bibliography for details.

[2]A few of them: Jacques Lacan's collision of Freud with Saussure in 'The Agency of the Letter' (Lacan, 1977a), and the arguments he makes about sexuation and the Real (Lacan, 1998); Jean Laplanche's return to the jettisoned seduction theory, and his argument that this provides the roots of drive and unconscious alike (Laplanche, 1976, 1989, 1999); Slavoj Žižek's insistence on Lacan's relations to both the Kantian-Hegelian tradition of European philosophy and to social theory (everywhere throughout his work, but particularly in Žižek, 1993, 1999); and Borch-Jacobsen's (1988, 1991) and Derrida's critical readings of Freud and Lacan ('To Speculate – On "Freud"' & 'Le Facteur de la Vérité' from Derrida, 1987), in ways which for all their differences are exemplary in their meticulous eye for the multiplicity of those texts.

INTRODUCTION: BORDERS

Spilling out

Think of a key moment in your life, a moment that carries a great emotional investment, and without which everything in your life would be quite different. Think of a moment you fell in love. Perhaps there was a song playing in the background, and this song has become the soundtrack to your falling in love. From now on, you will just have to hear that song and it will bring back the intensity of that moment: not necessarily only the happiness of it, but perhaps also the fear and insecurity and vulnerability of handing yourself over to another person. This song is now your song. It is a private moment: that song may not have the same intensity of connotation even for your partner, even if he or she is feeling that moment and that commitment just as intensely. You certainly do not expect anyone outside the two of you to share the connotations that song has for you, though the fact of having such a song hardly needs to be explained to anyone. Everyone falls in love: that is why the question 'What song did you fall in love by?' can be asked as a game, around the dinner table at a party, say. It comes to your turn: you're not sure you want to answer. It's not that you doubt your falling in love, it's just that you doubt your song can really measure up. It wasn't really much of a song after all, and to link it to your falling in love seems somehow to downgrade the intensity and genuinity of what you felt, and still feel. You actually don't even like the song all that much, but you certainly don't feel like explaining that. In fact, as songs go, it's actually pretty awful, not really something that expresses your love any more than the drink coaster you also took as a souvenir. It's just a little piece of the world that was in the right place at the right time, even if outside of that context it's a rather worthless or silly one. But from that moment on it's forever your falling-in-love made material.

Psychoanalysis is about what happens when things spill-out from one place to another, even to places where there would seem to be little connection.

Little Hans is afraid of horses, to the point where he is terrified of going out into the street where a horse might bite him ('Analysis of a Phobia', 1909b). But the five-year-old has never had any experience where he has been menaced by a horse. This is a symptom, Freud suggests, of something else: what he is afraid of is really a person, his father. As his father is actually a loving parent, Hans feels guilty for the violence of his thoughts against him. And because these thoughts are next to impossible to admit directly and yet don't just go away, the only ways they have of coming out are oblique and indirect ones. As circumstances would have it – and Freud traces the paths of the logic that makes this possible – everything converges on horses. The fear the little boy has spills out onto something which is seemingly unconnected with it – and which, precisely because of that disconnection, can both express the fear and at the same time hide its true source.

*A young woman describes a dream in which she is walking through a field, cutting off ears of barley and wheat. A young man of her acquaintance comes towards her and she tries to avoid him. What has generated the dream has nothing to do with ears of grain (in German, Ähren), but a lot to do with worries about honour (Ehren in German, which is pronounced in just the same way as Ähren). The dreamwork turns the source of the worry into something without that burden, and an honourable kiss (Kuss in Ehren) into a kiss in a wheatfield (Kuss in Ähren) (*The Interpretation of Dreams, *1900, p. 406–07).*

*An infant is playing a game with a cotton spool on a string. Holding onto the string, he throws the spool away so that it cannot be seen behind the curtains around his cot, saying a long drawn-out 'o–o–o–o' as he does. Then he pulls the string and the reel comes back into view, accompanied by his joyous 'da!' (*Beyond the Pleasure Principle, *1920b, pp. 14 ff.)[1] Is this, Freud asks, a way of repeating and in some way working through another, potentially more disturbing pattern of absences and presences in the child's life – the comings and goings of the mother?*

It would be easy to multiply the examples, from the case histories and from the hundreds of clinical and anecdotal cases that underpin Freud's work and which make such encyclopedic compendia out of *The Interpretation of Dreams* and *The Psychopathology of Everyday Life*. Psychoanalysis has all sorts of names for this spilling-over and its many aspects. We shall come to some of them in the course of this book: displacement, drive, cathexis, repetition, symptom, unconscious. We could even say that, for psychoanalysis, this spilling-over in all its forms is one of the very basic mechanisms of the psyche.

And yet, we very quickly find that this is also a spilling-over of what we might imagine to be the boundaries of the psyche. What seem to be events going on purely within the privacy of a head are really also matters of things in the world, even things as modest or banal as a reel and a piece of string, as silly as an embarrassing song, as contingent as the historical accident that makes two quite separate words sound the same, or the circumstances that yoke our love affair to a song. And conversely, things in the world reveal themselves to already be part of the psyche's working-out: material objects, families, customs and law, language, and all sorts of cultural practices. If we start with the psyche, we seem in no time at all to find ourselves in a densely populated world again.

And this happens in all sorts of multiple and unexpected ways, which have little respect for the divisions we might readily want to make between private and public, individual and social, self and other, or even between the one being analysed and the one doing the analysing. The same actions seem to play at one and the same time in a number of quite different stories, on quite different and apparently autonomous levels. In the child's game with the reel of thread, for example, we know the entire setup – the game, the child, the adult remembering observing it – is a displaced version of yet another absence, and another coming to grips with loss. There is a story of grief and mourning behind it. The child in the story Freud tells is Ernst Halberstadt, his first grandchild and the son of his dearly loved daughter Sophie. Sophie died in 1920, as Freud was at work on the book that recounts the game, *Beyond the Pleasure Principle*. 'Please don't worry about me,' he writes to his concerned colleague Sandor Ferenczi two weeks after Sophie's death. '"The unvaried, still returning hour of duty", and "the dear lovely habit of living" will do their bit toward letting everything go on as before.' To another friend, Oskar Pfister, he says, 'I do as much work as I can, and am grateful for the distraction' (cited in Derrida, 1987, p. 330). The child's fretting over an absent mother is also a father's mourning for an absent daughter. In this respect, *Beyond the Pleasure Principle* is not so much a psychoanalysis *of* mourning, but psychoanalysis *as* mourning. Throwing out its endless spool of speculation, it is that very distraction, that 'hour of duty' which, among other things, brings back the beloved daughter on a thin thread of writing.

What psychoanalysis talks about is something that spills over its apparent boundaries: what seems to be internal is already out there in the world, and whatever is external stands to be already there deep within. There is a tight and intriguing knot developing here, and its shape and implications will concern us in the rest of this book. In that spilling-out and in the development of a logic that can describe it, psychoanalysis provides a framework rather different from those of the empirical human sciences of psychology and sociology. It offers ways of thinking not just of the individual, but of those dimensions which are always intimately part of the individual, though they incessantly spill over those boundaries into questions of the social, and the cultural, and the ideological. This is not even strictly speaking a matter of examining how the individual and the social are connected, for that would imply an initial separation which is then overcome. With psychoanalysis, it is a matter of thinking through how the human subject is always and already in the world, from the very outset.

And from the beginning, psychoanalysis itself spills out into all sorts of other areas. If it is most obviously a form of *therapy*, with links to the other psychotherapies – in particular to psychiatry, and thus to medicine. It has also needed, from the outset, to distinguish itself from all of these. In particular, it has always tried to keep some measure of autonomy from that huge and powerful social institution of medicine. The question of whether analysts should be required to have a medical qualification (the 'question of lay analysis' of Freud's

1926 paper of that name) is on the one hand a matter of accreditation: the fledgling institution of psychoanalysis would be more easily recognised if it insisted its members should also be medical doctors, but that would also make it into a subgroup of the medical profession, and under medical control. On the other hand, it is also a matter for internal debate: psychoanalysts themselves did not agree on the path to be taken. Freud's view was that psychoanalysis needed to keep its autonomy from medicine, and be able to determine its own affairs on professionally psychoanalytic grounds. To this day, in most countries it is possible to be a psychoanalyst without being a medical doctor. But the suspicion between psychoanalysis and medicine has always been mutual: many medical practitioners see psychoanalysis as costly and inefficient, with its need for pro-longed and regular one-to-one contact between analyst and analysand. And yet it has always been pragmatically impossible for psychoanalysis *not* to have con-nections with medicine: the two share, or even compete for, the same stock of patients, and share common governmental and social health systems. One could also say similar things about the relationships psychoanalysis has with other therapies.

As well as being a therapy, psychoanalysis also lays claim to being a legit-imate form of *knowledge*, a science. That is, it lays claim to something of the same ground covered by psychology. But here again, it seeks to distinguish itself from psychology. The French analyst Jacques Lacan would even argue that psychoanalysis is not a psychology at all (Lacan 1977a, pp. 293–94). Indeed, in the English-speaking world psychoanalysis is generally not taught in academic psychology departments, and its appearance in them is usually confined to remarks about its empirical non-verifiability or the small size of Freud's sample groups. These complaints are not simply false: psychoanalysis is not amenable to many of the quantifiable and reiterable methodologies that are the basis of scientificity. But this is not because it is an inefficient or incompetent version of those methods: we shall have cause to return to Lacan's apparent hyperbole. The aims and very approach of psychoanalysis mark it off from the positivistic sciences – those which are structured on an objectivity whose function is to sep-arate out, with as much rigour as possible, the properties of the object under investigation from those phenomena which are due to the observing subject.

What happens when the object observed is precisely a subject like that doing the observing, where the thing one is studying is subjectivity itself, and where, in order to think through it *as* subject, it is necessary to constitute it as something very different from an object? The project, and the novelty, of psy-choanalysis is its attempt to think through the consequences of this with as much rigour as possible: to provide a rigorous logic of subjectivity which is not 'purely subjective' in the derogatory sense, the one which would make it a mixture of individual whim, insight and ingenuity rather than a method. Psychoanalysis is not a psychology because what it sets for itself as the focus of its investigation is in effect all of those things which psychology must set to one side in order to constitute itself as a positivistic science.

And yet psychoanalysis cannot simply give up scientificity, to declare itself a philosophy, for example, or a belief system. As we shall see, one of Freud's frequent responses to those who argue that psychoanalysis is not a science is to take precisely those features of analysis that appear least scientific and argue that they are in fact characteristic of the most rigorous and classical forms of science. Do the concepts with which psychoanalysis starts out seem rather ill-defined and vague? Well, good, so they should! That's exactly what science does and should do: you start off with a set of vague ideas and then, once you start gathering real data and putting these ideas into collision with the real world, you refine them so that they become more precise, more capable of describing the world. Is the hypothesis of the unconscious unverifiable, in the sense that one cannot simply observe it? Well, of course it is: by definition, the unconscious is what is not and cannot be made conscious. But neither can we observe directly what goes on at the centre of the earth or in the heart of a star, and this hardly makes geology or astrophysics any the less scientific ('Instincts and Their Vicissitudes', 1915b, p. 117; *New Introductory Lectures on Psychoanalysis*, 1933a, pp. 32–33).

The unconscious is a hypothesis, like quarks and gravitation. We hypothesise it because things behave *as if* it were the case. If one assumes an unconscious, then a welter of phenomena, which have previously appeared senseless, may suddenly take on a broad and consistent pattern. Dora presents herself to Freud with a range of symptoms, including difficulty in breathing, attacks of nervous coughing, speechlessness, migraines, depression, unsociability ('Fragment of an Analysis of a Case of Hysteria', 1905a, pp. 21–23). On their own, these make little sense and have little apparent connection with each other or with anything else – certainly not with any physical cause. But to see them as a series of largely unconscious reactions to and ways of coping with the impossible situation Dora has been put in by a particularly sordid family life, is to string them together in a way which makes sense out of them, and thus offers the possibility of doing something with them. Dreams appear, for the most part, as a random montage of meaningless elements; the hypothesis of an unconscious dream-work may give them a cogent and comprehensible unity. The unconscious is not unscientific because it is a hypothesis: that is exactly what gives it a claim to scientificity. Like all scientific hypotheses, it aims at the principle of parsimony, Occam's Razor: the best hypothesis is the simplest one that explains the most.

Conversely, though, there are certain things which science demands that psychoanalysis cannot supply. The scientific observer, for example, constitutes the object she is observing as quite independent of her presence as observer, and does this through a rigorous use of scientific method; the psychoanalyst, though, is interested in subjectivity itself, the very thing which, by definition, is not an object. Where psychology stands apart, the entire possibility of psychoanalysis depends on immersion. Psychoanalysis needs both to claim scientificity and to stand apart from it. This is why it would be far too hasty to conclude that psychoanalysis is simply trying to be a positivist science like psychology, but failing. It would be to miss the very point at which psychoanalysis opens up questions of the greatest interest for philosophy and science. Psychoanalysis insistently and deliberately occupies the borders of science, partly inside and partly outside what the border encloses, neither quite one nor the other. Borders are somewhat precarious places. A well-constituted science will want to place itself as far away from these ambiguous neither-nors as possible. But it is nevertheless those borders that make a science what it is: they define it as separate from and mark it off from everything surrounding it. Something which, like psychoanalysis, insists on occupying those borders may be capable of saying something about what makes science science, and about that science's relationships with what surrounds it across those borders. That is, it may be able to say something about science's existence in the world that *science does not know about itself*.

We could say (getting ahead of ourselves) that one way of describing the unconscious would be that it is *that aspect of me which I cannot know about myself, but which nevertheless makes me what I am*. My unconscious is what lies beyond the boundaries of my knowing self – can I then even call it mine? But it is also what makes me what I am, and is therefore, at the same time, at the very heart of my being. A strange topology, indeed. Freud, as we shall see, calls it a sort of internal foreign territory (*New Introductory Lectures*, 1933a, p. 57). Lacan gives it the felicitous name of *extimacy*: the extimate is both what is closest to me and radically external to me, me and not me, *in me more than me* (Lacan, 1992, p. 139).

We can generalise: *the unconscious in general is that aspect of X which X cannot know about itself, but which nevertheless makes it what it is*. This X is the marker of a place which need not even necessarily be filled by a person. Could we not with just the same logic speak of the unconscious of an *institution*, a science, a knowledge, a grouping of any sort? A *culture*, even? What could that mean if it is not to collapse into a vaguely New Ageish or Jungian 'collective unconscious'?[2]

Introductory Lectures on Psychoanalysis (1915–17) and *New Introductory Lectures on Psychoanalysis (1932)*

The best introductions to Freud's works are his own. Throughout his career, he wrote a number of expositions of psychoanalysis aimed at a lay audience. These lectures have a lively sense of exchange with an audience written into them: they address themselves out to a 'you' and use the word 'we' inclusively more frequently than not; they anticipate objections and reservations, and respond to them; they disarm with their willingness to talk about the present limits of psychoanalysis and what is not known. They are textbook examples of popular scientific writing, offering carefully constructed and graded arguments which take the reader-listener step by step through the complexities involved. With *The Psychopathology of Everyday Life* (1901), they were the most popular, the most reprinted and the most translated of Freud's writings during his lifetime.

The first set of lectures represents Freud's thought up to the mid-1910s. They were written just months after the important series of papers on metapsychology, which mark the consolidation of the so-called 'first topography' in which the primary division of the psyche is between conscious and unconscious. The 'second topography' (ego, id and superego, in *The Ego and the Id (1923))* and the hypothesis of the death drive (in *Beyond the Pleasure Principle (1920b))* were to be introduced over the next decade.

The much shorter series of *New Introductory Lectures*, from the last decade of Freud's life, brings the series up to date with these developments. By this time, though, the cancer of the jaw which would eventually kill Freud had made public speaking impossible, and though they are written in just the same style as the earlier series (and numbered consecutively to emphasise the continuity), the new lectures were never actually delivered.

The Question of Lay Analysis: Conversations with an Impartial Person (1926)

The question of the title is whether non-medical psychoanalysts should be permitted to practice: Austrian laws meant that only holders of medical degrees could legally treat patients, and the pamphlet is part of Freud's intervention when Theodor Reik, a prominent but non-medical Viennese analyst, was charged with 'quackery'. Freud always held the view that psychoanalysis should not be brought under the sole control of the medical profession, and that forms of training other than medical were potentially of at least as much value.

Freud's defence is one of his liveliest accounts of psychoanalysis for the lay person. In it, the trading of points with the audience in the *Introductory Lectures* becomes a dialogue with an imaginary interlocutor, the 'impartial person' of the subtitle, who is not convinced of either psychoanalysis or its case for lay analysis – and who continues to the last to ask sceptical questions, without being flippant or trivial. This is the first of Freud's major expositions of psychoanalysis to take into account the new scheme of things with the second topography.

'On the History of the Psychoanalytic Movement' (1914) 'A Short Account of Psychoanalysis' (1923) 'An Autobiographical Study' (1924)

The psychoanalytic movement had undergone two painful internal schisms by 1914, with the dissension of Adler and then Jung. 'On the History of the Psychoanalytic Movement' is written from within the turmoil of these splits, with the intention of demonstrating just why these two heresies have no part in the mainstream of the movement. We find similar concerns not too far from the surface in all the major writings of this time: the key paper 'On Narcissism' and the case history of the 'Wolf Man' were both written in this year.

The 'Short Account' and 'An Autobiographical Study' date from ten years later, and are far less partisan. The 'Short Account' was commissioned by the publishers of Encyclopedia Britannica, for whom Freud would later write a brief entry for the 13th edition. The 'Autobiographical Study' is not an autobiography as such, but a contribution to a four-volume series on the recent history of medical science, whose contributors describe their roles in that history.

'An Outline of Psychoanalysis' (1938)

This is Freud's last work, left unfinished at his death and published posthumously. Unlike his other overviews, it is not intended for a lay audience, but is more like a summation and stocktaking meant for psychoanalysis itself. Its condensed but lucid style assumes a detailed knowledge of analysis and of Freud's other writings.

Notes to Introduction

1   This is the famous '*fort-da* game' called after the German words that Freud understands the child as attempting to say: *fort*, meaning 'gone,' and *da*, 'there'.
2   The Jungian 'collective unconscious' is not at all unconscious in our sense of being what a society cannot know about itself as a condition of its being a society. On the contrary, it is a content that is easily stated (the Jungian catalogue of archetypes) and that circulates everywhere as a sort of shared pop knowledge.

ONE UNCONSCIOUS

The slip

You are at a party, say, in the middle of a conversation. Suddenly, to your horror, you realise that the words that have just this moment left your lips mean something else altogether. You have just quite unwittingly said the very last thing you would want to say in this situation, to these people. And you can see from their immediate reactions that this is exactly the meaning they have taken from it. There is no covering it over, no pretending it didn't happen. You go bright red, and want to sink into the floor.

There are several different stages or layers to your mortification. First of all, you are mortified because you had no deliberate intention of saying it. Perhaps the meaning itself had not even crossed your mind before you said it. But you said it, there's no denying it: with that curious detachment of a dream, you heard your own voice saying it, felt those words forming just too late to stop them slipping out. You have witnesses too: the looks on the faces of the people you are talking with tell you that. They are going to want some explanation. This thing you least wanted to say forced its way into your mouth. It is as if something that wasn't you has just used your voice to say something you would never have permitted. This first stage of your distress is that you feel divided against yourself. You cannot trust yourself. What had only a couple of seconds ago appeared to be an easy and unproblematic clarity of intention has revealed a deep fissure – in you, in your very sense of self. Something in you is not answerable to you.

Then comes the twist. Could it be that in some sense you did desire it after all? What you'd have least wanted to say is not at all the same thing as what you'd never have thought. In fact, it's all too close to what you might actually think. Now that you've said it you do in fact recognise yourself in it, much as you'd like not to. Perhaps that divided intention has really only been working behind your back to say what you've actually thought all along, but were never willingly going to say. That is, are the two warring parts of you actually in agreement that this is indeed what you feel about whatever it was? Is the only disagreement between them a matter of whether it should have been said, here and now – and with one of them now forcing the hand of the other? Everybody has heard of Freudian slips; everyone knows that they tend to show up what's on the slipper's mind anyway. This, of course, includes the friends who have just heard you make the slip, and who know you well too. All of this reasoning is just as transparent to them as it is to you. How can your very blush not be taken as confirmation, an admission that you've read the slip in exactly the way they have? If what you've just said didn't carry the meaning everyone has now given it, why would you be so embarrassed about it? Even to talk about it and try to offer some sort of explanation that it wasn't what you really meant at all, would be to acknowledge that yes, the words you've said do in fact mean exactly what's now crossed everyone's mind, that you know what they mean and that everyone else does, that the fact of having said them makes you uneasy and you'd love to explain them away, but that every word you say from now on is going to do nothing but dig you in deeper ...

In the midst of which, another twist to the knife. You become aware of an even more ghastly possibility. It is not enough for you to admit painfully to yourself that perhaps you did, in some sense, think that after all, and that the slip has just been a matter of blurting out what you didn't ever really want to say. What if you really did want to say it? After all, the whole thing has been done with devastating timing: it couldn't be worse if it had been calculated. The horrible possibility dawns, that you – for what else could it be that spoke in your voice anyway? – might in a sense have wanted to say the unsayable, with all of the consequences of that saying, whose discomforts you have the awful feeling you are just beginning to explore, and that in some sense you might actually have wanted and even called up this mortification. Everything happens as if this fierce humiliation you are feeling carries with it a somewhat perverse enjoyment. Which is doubly mortifying. And thus – by this deeply perverse logic from which there no longer seems to be any secure exit, and in a way which is utterly inseparable from this escalating mortification – somewhere, somehow, and to this someone you dare not quite think of as yourself, even more enjoyable …

By this stage, of course, it is no longer possible to convince those who heard you of your innocence, for all of this is quite transparent to them too. It is no longer even possible to know how far round these spirals they are willing to go, and how culpable they hold you. You are caught in a double bind: if you try to explain, you only make yourself look more guilt-driven, and if you refuse to explain, you leave your friends to think the worst. You have no tenable position, nowhere you can feel at all comfortable. It is not even that the only places left for you to occupy are those you feel are quite profoundly not you – false places, places that give a false idea to others of what you really are. That would be some sort of comfort in itself. Neither is it even any longer a question of having to admit to yourself that, yes, you really were thinking that all along, yes, you really did want it to be expressed, with all of its consequences, and that in some way you were after that mortification all along. Things have got beyond that stage. The problem here is, now that you no longer know what you wished; what your motivations might have been. Nothing will confirm them one way or another. All you are left with is that acute sense of having nowhere at all to go. Oddly enough, it is precisely at moments like this that you are most aware of your own selfhood, as a series of empty positions, none of which fit.

We can plot it out:

1   *You didn't want to say it.*
2   *You did want to say it.*
3   *There's a perverse enjoyment in being skewered on the double bind of 1 and 2.*

We make slips of the tongue. We dream, and wake amazed by the strangeness of what has been passing through our minds. Ideas just come into our heads, unbidden: we can beat our heads against a problem all evening without results and then wake up in the morning knowing the answer in all its details. We perform elaborate and highly directed series of actions automatically, even when they require a good deal of alertness, such as driving a car. Our everyday experience suggests that not all thought processes are actually accessible to our consciousness, and that even those which are, are not conscious all the time. What's more, once those unconsciously-performed acts are examined, it's often easy to see in them all the detail, complexity and even lucidity we might usually associate with conscious thought. All of which suggests that we should not equate mental processes and consciousness. There would seem to be mental processes of which we are not conscious, but which nevertheless have all the complexity of those of which we are aware.

Some of these may of course be easily brought up into consciousness. Though the song 'Happy Birthday to You' isn't always in my conscious attention, I can bring it to mind without effort when the situation calls for it. Much of our day-to-day driving of a car is semi-automatic, but this state is one of smoothly implemented skill rather than unawareness. The phrase for it is exact: you *really know what you're doing* only when your actual doing of it no longer fills the centre stage of your consciousness. You start becoming a competent driver once the complex co-ordination of different tasks for all four limbs becomes automatic. A vast amount of our consciousness, our learning, our memory, is like this: not occupying the forefront of attention, but neatly packed somewhere off to one side, waiting for the moment when it's needed, when it springs out almost without bidding. Freud uses the term **preconscious** for this off-stage consciousness. Preconscious mental processes seem to exist seamlessly with conscious processes, sliding effortlessly from one to the other as required.

Of course, there are other possibilities. Sometimes that unpacking of the preconscious doesn't take place as smoothly as we believe it should, and this failure can be persistent, and even oddly *con*sistent. We may forget the name of an acquaintance or get it wrong, even when it's someone we know perfectly well and have regular dealings with. We may find ourselves doing this repeatedly, even after being embarrassed by the lapse and making a deliberate effort to remember the name the next time. We may even feel that the very repetition we make to fix it in our mind may serve to increase our confusion about which is the right version. In cases like this, there is not only the feeling that what should be a clear passage between conscious and preconscious is blocked, but that there even appears to be some sort of opposing force reinforcing the blockage. It can work the other way around too for example, if 'Happy Birthday to You' refuses to be sent back into the preconscious lumber room after the candles have been blown out, and stays around as an annoying jingle for a good part of the day. (Why is it that as often as not, the song which sticks in your mind is one you don't like – and one you certainly don't want people to hear you *singing* inadvertently?)

Not everything that is unconscious has the same easy relationship to consciousness that the preconscious has. There are blockages: some things do not slip easily from a preconscious to a conscious state, and even actively resist consciousness. Or rather, since we obviously cannot be directly aware of something that resists our awareness, it is better to say that our everyday experience of consciousness is full of *gaps*. From these gaps, we can hypothesise mental events that are not conscious.

I go to bed worrying over a problem, and I wake up to find that somehow the problem has been solved while I slept. But the fact that it has been solved, there in my own head, doesn't necessarily mean I have the slightest knowledge or memory of the processes my head used to solve it in my absence. I have been landed with the solution, perhaps even an ingenious and elegant one, but I have no idea of how it came about. Beyond doubt, *some* mental processes must have taken place, but just what they might have been remains hypothetical for the simple reason that I was not there to see them. Even to reconstruct those processes with a high degree of probability and conviction may not in itself be enough to bring them back to memory. But what a careful reconstruction can do is provide a smooth, credible and comprehensible chain of reasoning which links the problem to its solution. Without this, we are left with a solution that appears from nowhere, without explanation.

Early writings:
The Freud–Fliess correspondence (1887–1904)
'Project for a Scientific Psychology' (1887–1902)
Breuer and Freud, *Studies on Hysteria* (1893–95)

In 1881, the 25-year-old Freud graduated as a Doctor of Medicine from the University of Vienna; the next year, he began work at Vienna General Hospital, while continuing his researches in biology, physiology and neuroanatomy. Late that year, Josef Breuer, an older friend and colleague told him of a successful treatment in which an hysteric patient under hypnosis seems to have remembered a long-buried trauma, with a cathartic and curative effect. In 1885–86, after Freud had been appointed to a university lectureship in neuropathology, a travelling bursary allowed him to spend several months in Paris, studying under the great neurologist Charcot – at the Salpêtrière hospital for nervous diseases – who, at this late stage of his career, had also become interested in hysteria and the possibility of treating it with hypnosis. On his return to Vienna, Freud's work began to focus increasingly on the neuroses and their treatment, including electrotherapy and hypnosis.

In 1887, Breuer introduced Freud to Wilhelm Fliess, two years younger than Freud but already a successful Berlin ear, nose and throat specialist, whom Breuer had recommended attend Freud's lectures while carrying out further studies in Vienna. The two became close friends, and carried out a regular and voluminous correspondence over the next 14 years. In Freud's letters, one can see in gestation many of the characteristic terms, concerns and frameworks of what would become psychoanalysis, caught in the process of separating themselves from their original neuroanatomical framework. He sent Fliess a number of drafts of work in progress, including the substantial but never completed 'Project for a Scientific Psychology' in 1895.

The 'Project' draws on the recent discovery of the neuron (in 1889 by Santiago Ramón y Cajal, who would receive the Nobel Prize for the discovery in 1906), but it makes use of it in a speculative rather than strictly neurophysiological sense. Freud postulates a quantity, Q, which he does not define, but which works like a fluid or an electrical charge. This Q is *cathected* – made to flow from one point to another, to accumulate in some places and abandon others – by the neurones, which are arranged in two systems. The first system, Φ, is easily permeated by this flow of Q and retains none of it; this is the system of *perception*. By contrast, the second system, φ, is impermeable, and in holding back Q allows for the possibility of *memory*. From this, Freud builds up a conceptual system that is much closer to the outlines of the imaginary neuroanatomy, which underpin it, than any of his later and more strictly psychoanalytic work will be. Nevertheless, we can already see in it many of the concerns of that later work: cathexis and a dynamic and economic model of fluids; the subjection of these flows to a principle of constancy, which tends to keep the total quantity of excitation in a system as low as possible; the essentially biological modelling of an organism attempting to protect itself from the stimuli of a chaotic external world; structures of repression and inhibition; the aetiology of hysteria; the formation, intelligibility and functioning of dreams, and their similarity to hysteria; and the division of the psyche into primary and secondary processes according to whether psychic energies are bound or controlled.

But aside from the content, there is another dynamic at work in these letters and drafts, which makes this relationship such a crucial one for psychoanalysis. Freud and Fliess doubtless had certain commonalities, if only broad ones. Both were Jews, in a profession where, and a time when, anti-Semitism was still a major obstacle in a career path. Both were engaged in fields of research that put them somewhat at odds with the medical orthodoxy of the day. But Fliess was not an obvious ally for Freud, and oddly, this may be precisely why the relationship seemed to work so well. Fliess's concerns seem quite crankish today, and have no part to play in Freud's theories beyond the occasional footnote of approval, all part of the pact. Fliess postulated that all human life is governed by two physiological cycles, which intersect in the life of any individual, a feminine one of 28 days and a masculine one of 23. Do the calculations correctly, and one can predict optimal and crisis points in an individual's life. These cycles, he argued, are particularly evident in the mucous membrane of the nose, which has a close link to the genitals. Treat the nose, and you can treat a variety of conditions, including sexual dysfunctions and neuralgic pain. There is little here to intersect with Freud's interests, but that may be the point: given such distances between them, the two men could not easily become rivals or pose a threat to each other. That distance is quite literal too: their geographical separation meant that they met only infrequently, and this too is no doubt an essential part of the relationship: it is hard to imagine them finding much time for each other if their paths had crossed daily. The letters do not just report on or consolidate the relationship: they *are* the relationship, almost in its entirety.

Traditionally, to become a psychoanalyst, one must undergo an analysis of one's own. Analysis is not something one can do alone; it requires the distance of a third party, that largely silent listener somewhere just out of sight, who neither approves nor disapproves but simply encourages speech, without any personal stake in the outcome. Freud himself analysed all of the first generation of analysts who came to form part of his circle: Jones, Jung,

Abraham, Ferenczi, Eitingon, Adler, even – against all precepts then and since – his own daughter Anna. So if becoming a psychoanalyst requires that there already be an analyst, who analysed Freud? One of the standard answers – and one which makes perfect sense of the sheer unlikeliness of the relationship – is that the correspondence with Fliess served much of that function: a pact of listening.

*

For all of the neuroanatomical borrowings of the 'Project', during this time Freud was also working with Josef Breuer on a quite different approach to hysteria, based on the clinical practice the two of them had set up. In 1893, Freud and Breuer published a preliminary paper whose title suggested the extent of the break they were making: 'On the Psychical Mechanism of Hysterical Phenomena'. Two years later, that paper was to preface their joint *Studies on Hysteria*, which included an account of Breuer's earlier case history ('Anna O.', who provided the famous description of psychoanalysis as 'the taking cure'), a number of Freud's case histories, a theoretical chapter by Breuer, and a chapter on treatment by Freud.

The neuroses, they argue, can be seen in psychic and experiential terms quite different from those of the current medical or physiological frameworks. The particular forms of hysteria they studied all revealed themselves to have been precipitated by some sort of trauma. Because the mind had been unable to process that trauma and discharge its affect, the memory of it had been repressed and was unavailable to the sufferer, though the effects of it remained in sometimes elaborately displaced forms now left without apparent cause. '*Hysterics suffer mainly from reminiscences*' (*Studies on Hysteria* p. 7; emphasis in original).

Both authors refer to these repressed thoughts as 'unconscious'. The term seems to have been first used in such a context in 1889 by the French neurologist and psychologist Pierre Janet, though from the outset Freud and Breuer's sense of its usage is far more dynamic than Janet's. For them, the unconscious is not just a name for a region of the mind, but above all the product of conflicting forces. At this stage, Freud still sees unconsciousness largely in terms of a repression which it is the task of psychoanalysis to undo: bring the forgotten memories back into consciousness, and the patient will be cured. The treatment thus has an optimism and simplicity which psychoanalytic experience will later complicate immeasurably.

In the *Studies*, Freud and Breuer frequently refer to their procedures as 'analysis'. The term 'psychoanalysis' does not yet occur; that will happen in Freud's 1896 paper, 'Further Remarks on the Neuro-Psychoses of Defence'.

I: Unconscious and conscious

The hypothesis

If we hypothesise the existence of unconscious thoughts, then all sorts of things, which until now appeared senseless and without connection, suddenly fall into place. This ability to provide a chain of reconstruction is what Freud points out in the 1915 paper on 'The Unconscious', though he is being hyperbolic when he calls this 'incontrovertible proof'.• No scientific hypothesis is ever quite incontrovertible when one of the criteria for it to be taken as scientific is precisely that it must, in principle, be falsifiable, open

> All these conscious acts [dreams, mistaken actions and slips of the tongue, and so on] remain disconnected and unintelligible if we insist upon claiming that every mental act that occurs in us must also necessarily be experienced by us through consciousness; on the other hand, they fall into a demonstrable connection if we interpolate between them the unconscious acts which we have inferred. ... When ... it turns out that the assumption of there being an unconscious enables us to construct a successful procedure by which we can exert an effective influence upon the course of conscious processes, this success will have given us an incontrovertible proof of the existence of what we have assumed. ('The Unconscious' (1915d), p. 167)

to revision in the light of new data. Newton's theory of gravitation remains scientific even though relativity and the Riemannian geometries of curved space have since provided a more accurate and wider description of the phenomena. As we have seen, Freud is forever revising his own work, sometimes with far-reaching effect: adding material with each new edition, criticising his earlier views, placing concepts into a different framework. This controvertibility is exactly what gives it its claim to scientificity. The unconscious is *not* a fact, it is a hypothesis: a perfectly legitimate one, perhaps even a valuable one – but certainly, as we shall see, one with quite peculiar and far-reaching consequences.

The reason for taking the hypothesis seriously, Freud is saying, is first of all that everything works *as if* it were true. Without the hypothesis, we have a series of scattered phenomena that seem to make little sense, if any, when taken individually. Dreams would thus be something like the sounds produced when someone who knows nothing of music lets their fingers wander over a piano keyboard.[1] But *with* that hypothesis, everything snaps into place. As any good scientific hypothesis must, the hypothesis of an unconscious aims to do the most with the least.

The hypothesis does not, then, bring hidden material to light or make the unconscious workings conscious. Instead, it provides a series of conscious mental constructions, which, if they *were* to exist, would *produce the same effects*, point for point.• The criteria for judging the

> Every science is based on observations and experiences arrived at through the medium of our psychical apparatus. But since *our* science has as its subject that apparatus itself, the analogy ends here. We make our observations through the medium of the same perceptual apparatus, precisely with the help of the breaks in the sequence of 'psychical' events: we fill in what is omitted by making plausible inferences and translating it into conscious material. In this way we construct, as it were, a sequence of conscious events complementary to the unconscious psychical processes. The relative certainty of our psychical science is based on the binding forces of these inferences.
>
> [If] we say: 'At this point an unconscious memory intervened', what that means is: 'At this point something occurred of which we are totally unable to form a conception, but which, if it had entered our consciousness, could only have been described in such and such a way.' ('An Outline of Psychoanalysis' (1940), pp. 159,197)

explanation it offers cannot be their resemblance to the unconscious processes they depict, because by definition we can have no direct conscious knowledge of those processes to act as the basis for such a comparison. Instead, the criteria are, on the one hand, the ability of these conscious mental processes of the model to produce the same outcome, and on the other, the internal coherence of the model itself. Given these two, the sense that the bare facts take on, in light of the hypothesis of the unconscious, will be functional too. That is, it will be a practical basis for intervention, from which one can make certain predictions and produce real effects in a patient's life. Freud keeps insisting that he is not a philosopher, but a clinician, faced with real lives. Finally, that is, the hypothesis of the unconscious stands or falls on the question of whether or not it works.[2]

Freud goes on to make a number of hypotheses about the unconscious in the course of almost half a century of psychoanalytic writing. As we shall see, in the 1920s he even radically revised what he had said so far, and offered a new view of the topography of the psyche. Within each schema, though, there are a number of views of the unconscious offered, and even a certain indecision and instability• about them. In part, this is exactly what one would expect of a working hypothesis, whose function is to make itself gradually more precise as it responds to and takes into account the data experience offers it. Freud says as much, in a number of places.• But there is also something else at work in this, as we shall see – something which follows from the unusual nature of this particular hypothesis.

We have often heard it maintained that sciences should be built up on clear and sharply defined basic concepts. In actual fact no science, not even the most exact, begins with such definitions. The true beginning of scientific activity consists rather in describing phenomena and then in proceeding to group, classify and correlate them. Even at the stage of description it is not possible to avoid applying certain abstract ideas to the material in hand, ideas derived from somewhere or other but certainly not from the new observations alone. Such ideas – which will later become the basic concepts of the science – are still more indispensable as the material is further worked over. They must at first necessarily possess some degree of indefiniteness; there can be no question of any clear delimitation of their content. So long as they remain in this condition, we come to an understanding about their meaning by making repeated references to the material of observation from which they appear to have derived, but upon which, in fact, they have been imposed. Thus, strictly speaking, they are in the nature of conventions – although everything depends on their not being arbitrarily chosen but determined by their having significant relations to the empirical material, relations that we seem to sense before we can clearly recognise and demonstrate them. It is only after more thorough investigation of the field of observation that we are able to formulate its basic scientific concepts with increasing precision, and progressively so to modify them that they become serviceable and consistent over a wide area. Then, indeed, the time may have come to confine them in definitions. The advance of knowledge, however, does not tolerate any rigidity even in definitions. Physics furnishes an excellent illustration of the way in which even 'basic concepts' that have been established in the form of definitions are constantly being altered in their content. ('Instincts and Their Vicissitudes' (1915b), p. 117)

A science erected on empirical interpretation ... will not envy speculation its privilege of having a smooth, logically unassailable foundation, but will gladly content itself with nebulous, scarcely imaginable basic concepts, which it hopes to apprehend more clearly in the course of its development, or which it is even prepared to replace by others. For these ideas are not the foundation of science, upon which everything rests: that foundation is observation alone. They are not the bottom but the top of the whole structure, and they can be replaced and discarded without damaging it. The same thing is happening in our day in the science of physics, the basic notions of which as regards matter, centres of force, attraction, etc., are scarcely less debatable than the corresponding notions in psychoanalysis. ('On Narcissism: An Introduction' (1914a), p. 77)

Zoology and botany did not start from correct and adequate definitions of an animal and a plant; to this very day biology has been unable to give any certain meaning to the concept of life. ('An Autobiographical Study' (1925a), p. 58)

Cathexis

Freud's first major theoretical discussion of the unconscious is in the long seventh chapter of *The Interpretation of Dreams* (1900). Here he takes stock of the implications of the techniques for analysis that have been developed in the previous chapters, and quite explicitly phrases what he is doing in terms of a hypothesis intended for ongoing refinement.• In the very last section of that chapter, he points out how misleading it can be to see the unconscious in simply *topographical* terms, as a particular *location* within the psyche (*The Interpretation of Dreams* (1900), vol. 5, p. 610). That would be to see conscious thoughts as written in one particular place in the mind and unconscious thoughts in another, and presumably with an erasure and reinscription happening every time an unconscious thought becomes conscious or *vice versa*. Instead, he suggests it may often be

There is no possibility of *explaining* dreams as a psychical process, since to explain a thing means to trace it back to something already known, and there is at the present time no established psychological knowledge under which we could subsume what the psychological examination of dreams enables us to infer as a basis for their explanation. On the contrary, we shall be obliged to set up a number of fresh hypotheses which touch tentatively upon the structure of the apparatus of the mind and upon the play of forces operating in it. We must be careful, however, not to pursue these hypotheses too far beyond their first logical links, or their value will be lost in uncertainties. Even if we make no false inferences and take all the logical possibilities into account, the probable incompleteness of our premises threatens to bring our calculation to a complete miscarriage. No conclusion upon the construction and working methods of the mental instrument can be arrived at or at least fully proved from even the most painstaking investigation of dreams or of any other mental function taken *in isolation*. To achieve this result, it will be necessary to correlate all the established implications derived from a comparative study of a whole series of such functions. Thus the psychological hypotheses to which we are led by an analysis of the processes of dreaming must be left, as it were, in suspense, until they can be related to the findings of other enquiries which seek to approach the kernel of the same problem from another angle. (*The Interpretation of Dreams* (1900), vol. 5, p. 511; emphasis in original)

more useful to think of conscious and unconscious as agencies under whose control a given set of concepts may fall at various times depending on how they are *cathected*, or infused with psychic energy. This gives a picture of the psyche as also *economic* (this energy circulates, increasing in some places and correspondingly decreasing in others) and *dynamic* (that is, as the result of conflicting forces).•

Cathexis is a central term for Freud. He uses it throughout his career, from the early and pre-

I propose that when we have succeeded in describing a psychical process in its dynamic, topographical and economic aspects, we should speak of it as a *metapsychological* presentation. ('The Unconscious' (1915d), p. 181)'

psychoanalytic 'Project for a Scientific Psychology' to the posthumous 'An Outline of Psychoanalysis'. Or rather, it is more correct to say that his English translator, James Strachey, uses it to translate Freud's term *Besetzung*. *Cathexis* is a made-up word, not found outside psychoanalytic writings in English: it comes from the Greek word at the root of the English *cathode* and *catheter*, and so gives the idea of drawing off a current or a flow from one place to another. But the word it translates, *Besetzung*, is by contrast relatively commonplace in German, even though Freud uses it in his own very particular senses. The main meanings of *besetzen*, the verb form, involve occupying something – a place, an office, a role, or a country.

Significantly, in all of that voluminous output over almost 50 years, nowhere does Freud actually define the term. The closest he gets to it is in an early paper on 'The Neuro-Psychoses of Defence,' from 1894.• It is a transitional paper like so many of his writings of this time: not yet quite psychoanalysis, but setting up many of the concepts psychoanalysis will soon take as its own: a marginal piece of Freud. It does not even call what it is describing by the term *cathexis*, though this is clearly what it is about.

I should like, finally, to dwell for a moment on the working hypothesis which I have made use of in this exposition of the neuroses of defence. I refer to the concept that in mental functions something is to be distinguished – a quota of affect or a sum of excitation – which possesses all the characteristics of a quantity (though we have no means of measuring it), which is capable of increase, diminution, displacement and discharge, and which is spread over the memory-traces of ideas somewhat as an electric charge is spread over the surface of a body. This hypothesis ... can be applied in the same sense as physicists apply the hypothesis of a flow of electric fluid. It is provisionally justified by its utility in co-ordinating and explaining a great variety of psychical states. ('The Neuro-Psychoses of Defence' (1894) pp. 60–61)

This almost complete absence of definition is, of course, partly what Freud means by a working hypothesis, one that begins vague so that in the course of the investigation it can gradually be refined and made more precise. But there is also something else going on here. This definition, if it is that, occurs very early on, before there even is quite such a thing as psychoanalysis. It never occurs again. Contrary to what Freud suggests about the necessary initial incompleteness of scientific hypotheses, he does not return to it to make it more precise. It just remains, as if in time the accumulative weight of the edifice built on top of it will stand for this refinement and definition. Neither does it quite work as, say, 'life' does for a biologist: neither a scientific term nor amenable to definition, but the loose name for a series of phenomena science will attempt to describe exhaustively in other terms altogether – those of chemistry, physics, information theory, and so on. Cathexis remains something like a foundational metaphor, or an axiom in mathematics: something which will not be proved, but the acceptance of which allows one to deduce a wide range of conclusions which, Freud argues, are in perfect keeping with the evidence offered to us by both the clinic and everyday life.•

Cathexis has its clear antecedents in nineteenth-century physiology. The abandoned 'Project for a Scientific Psychology', after all, speaks the language of neuroanatomy, and variations on that terminology will be everywhere in Freud's later work, even if he is generally quite careful to point out that what he is proposing is not to be taken as a physical model of the brain or of cellular structure, and that the flows and currents of cathexis are not to be equated with the electrical currents which pass across the neurones.• In fact, if anything, it is a physiology that is even looking a little old-fashioned by Freud's time.

Occupying, filling, drawing off, flows: Freud's particular use for the term is clear enough from context. Cathexis is a fluid model. Freud tends to use the term to indicate both the fluid and its flows. *Cathexis* sees the psyche in terms of a series of locations, and a psychic *charge* which accumulates in those locations, seeks discharge, encounters blockages, and flows, as if under pressure, from one place to another. These accumulations and flows obey laws rather

> The concepts of 'psychical energy' and 'discharge' and the treatment of psychical energy as a quantity have become habitual in my thoughts since I began to arrange the facts of psychopathology philosophically ... To avoid misunderstanding, I must add that I am making no attempt to proclaim that the cells and nerve fibres, or the systems of neurones which are taking their place today, are these psychical paths, even though it would have to be possible in some manner to represent such paths by organic elements of the nervous system. (*Jokes and Their Relation to the Unconscious* (1905b), pp. 147–48)

> Our psychical topography has for the present nothing to do with anatomy; it has reference not to anatomical localities, but to regions in the mental apparatus, wherever they may be situated in the body. ('The Unconscious' (1915d), p. 175)

> [E]very attempt ... to discover a localisation of mental processes, every endeavour to think of ideas as stored up in nerve-cells and of excitations as migrating along nerve-fibres, has miscarried completely. The same fate would await any theory which attempted to recognise, let us say, the anatomical position of the system *Cs.* – conscious mental activity – as being in the cortex, and to localise the unconscious processes in the subcortical parts of the brain. There is a hiatus here which at present cannot be filled, nor is it one of the tasks of psychology to fill it. ('The Unconscious' (1915d), pp. 174–75)

like those which govern fluids or electricity, and form a coherent system: push the fluid out of one location, and it will have to go somewhere else.

Initially, and for a long while after, Freud argued that the accumulation of excitation (whether it be from an external stimulus or generated internally) is experienced as *displeasure*. Correspondingly, its discharge is experienced as *pleasure*. This is thus a profoundly *homeostatic* system: the psyche aims, if not at a state of no excitation, at least at a state in which excitation is minimal, distributed and stable. This is what Freud calls variously the **principle of constancy** or, more famously, the **pleasure principle**: the psyche seeks pleasure and avoids unpleasure.

But pleasure is not, of course, always an immediate option. The psyche itself may form, or try to form, such a homeostatic system, but try as it may, something remains left over. The psyche is, after all, bombarded incessantly by the stimuli of a world over which it has no direct control, but on which its own pleasure may so often depend. There may be all sorts of subterfuges to go through before pleasure can be achieved, all sorts of discomforts submitted to in the hope of an eventual pay-off. For the psyche to have any chance of establishing itself as a homeostatic system, it needs to be able to take into account a world whose pressures are unrelenting. The pleasure principle, that is, is inevitably counterbalanced by a **reality principle**. •

Between them, the pleasure and reality principles allow Freud the frequent analogy of the psyche with the imagined behaviour of a simple organism, reacting to min-

[U]nder the influence of the instructress Necessity, [the instincts] soon learn to replace the pleasure principle with a modification of it. For them the task of avoiding unpleasure turns out to be almost as important as that of obtaining pleasure. The ego discovers that it is inevitable for it to renounce immediate satisfaction, to postpone the obtaining of pleasure, to put up with a little unpleasure and to abandon certain sources of pleasure altogether. An ego thus educated has become 'reasonable'; it no longer lets itself be governed by the pleasure principle, but obeys the *reality principle*, which also at bottom seeks to obtain pleasure, but pleasure which is assured through taking account of reality, even though it is pleasure postponed and diminished.

The transition from the pleasure principle to the reality principle is one of the most important steps forward in the ego's development. (Lecture 22, 'Some Thoughts on Development and Regression – Aetiology', *Introductory Lectures on Psychoanalysis* (1916–17), vol. 16, p. 357; emphasis in original)

Let us picture a living organism in its most simplified possible form as an undifferentiated vesicle of a substance that is susceptible to stimulation. Then the surface turned towards the external world will from its very situation be differentiated and will serve as an organ for receiving stimuli. ... It would be easy to suppose, then, that as a result of the ceaseless impact of external stimuli on the surface of the vesicle, its substance to a certain depth may have become permanently modified, so that excitatory processes run a different course in it from what they run in the deeper layers. ... (*Beyond the Pleasure Principle* (1920b), p. 26)

imise and cope with the effects of the stimuli which bombard it from without and within. •

Displacement and condensation

Freud is not concerned with explaining precisely what this hypothetical cathected fluid might be, or whether or not one could find any empirical evidence for its actual existence. The test of it will be in the other direction altogether, with the questions of whether the psyche in fact behaves *as if* this were the case, and whether it allows one to weave a tight and rigorous web of inference connecting otherwise meaningless phenomena.

And indeed, the cathexis model allows one to describe a large number of features of mental behaviour.●

It describes how it may come about, for example, that an object or event can seem to carry with it a disproportionate

A man of twenty-four has preserved the following picture from his fifth year. He is sitting in the garden of a summer villa, on a small chair beside his aunt, who is trying to teach him the letters of the alphabet. He is in difficulties over the difference between *m* and *n* and he asks his aunt to tell him how to know one from the other. His aunt points out to him that the *m* has a whole piece more than then – the third stroke. There appeared to be no reason for challenging the trustworthiness of this childhood memory: it had, however, only acquired its meaning at a later date, when it showed itself suited to represent symbolically another of the boy's curiosities. For just as at that time he wanted to know the difference between *m* and *n*, so later he was anxious to find out the difference between boys and girls and would have been very willing for this particular aunt to be the one to teach him. He also discovered then that the difference was a similar one – that a boy, too, has a whole piece more than a girl; and at the time when he acquired this piece of knowledge he called up the recollection of the parallel curiosity of his childhood. (*The Psychopathology of Everyday Life* (1901), pp. 48–49)

and even quite inappropriate effect, as in phobias. Little Hans is terrified of horses, though he has never had any bad experiences with horses ('Analysis of a Phobia in a Five-Year-Old Boy' (1909b)). The real object of that affect, the one to which it was originally attached, Freud suggests, was the father whom Hans both loves and fears. Through a series of moves, which we shall not try to summarise here but whose intelligibility Freud makes clear, this affect comes to be *displaced* onto horses.

So, in general an idea or affect which arises in connection with one particular idea can be *displaced* onto another perhaps even quite distant idea.● And conversely, an idea may *condense* onto itself a number of aspects of other ideas.●

I can perhaps call up the impression [displacement] produces of going astray if I recall an anecdote. There was a blacksmith in a village, who had committed a capital offence. The Court decided that the crime must be punished; but as the blacksmith was the only one in the village and was indispensable, and as on the other hand there were three tailors living there, one of them was hanged instead. (Lecture 11, 'The Dream-Work', *Introductory Lectures on Psychoanalysis* (1916–17), vol. 15, pp. 174–75)

Between them, these two forms of cathexis, **condensation** and **displacement**, are the two

[Condensation's] results are particularly easy to demonstrate. You will have no difficulty in recalling instances from your own dreams of different people being condensed into a single one. A composite figure of this kind may look like A perhaps, but may be dressed like B, may do something that we remember C doing, and at the same time we may know that he is D. (Lecture 11, 'The Dream-Work', *Introductory Lectures on Psychoanalysis* (1916–17), vol. 15, p. 171) basic mechanisms of the unconscious.

Together, they account for the ways in which the dream is constructed, for the slips of the tongue and bungled actions of everyday life, for the workings of jokes and puns.• Slips of the tongue, such as the one we began this chapter with, tend to rely on condensation of a second set of meanings onto an otherwise innocent word or phrase; screen memories, such as the young man's memories of his governess, tend to be displaced substitutes for the memory which is actually significant. In some forms of neurosis, such as anxiety neuroses or phobias, as in the case of little Hans, displacement predominates. In other

[A displacement joke:]

A horse-dealer was recommending a saddle-horse to a customer. 'If you take this horse and get on it at four in the morning you'll be at Pressburg at half-past six.' – 'What should I be doing in Pressburg at half-past six in the morning?'

[A condensation joke:]

[A man boasts] of his relations with the wealthy Baron Rothschild, and finally says: 'And, as true as God shall grant me all good things, Doctor, I sat beside Salomon Rothschild and he treated me quite as his equal – quite famillionairely.' (*Jokes and Their Relation to the Unconscious* (1905b), pp. 54,16)

forms, such as conversion hysterias, condensation is the mechanism through which the symptoms find their focus in a particular part or system of the body, which comes to bear the full weight of the affect involved, in forms such as hysterical paralyses or contractions, tics, and the loss or intensification of sensation.

Repression

But why should affect need to be displaced in the first place? The Little Hans case gives us a simple answer: Hans is caught in a dilemma. On the one hand, he sees his father as a worrying rival for his mother's attention – the one who displaces him from his mother's bed when he is at home, and who is also somehow partly responsible for that nasty new arrival who now takes up all his mother's time, baby sister Hanna. On the other hand, Hans genuinely loves his father, whom Freud pictures as a kind and loving man. The boy's hatred for his rival will not go away, but neither will his love for his father. As a result, that hatred can be expressed only obliquely – here, through that complex set of displacements Freud traces out in detail.

Much later, with the anthropologist Gregory Bateson in the mid 1950s, the logical structure of this sort of no-win situation will become known as a *double bind*. In a double bind, you are faced with a number of contradictory demands, all of which must be obeyed, but all of which are mutually contradictory. To obey any one of them logically entails disobeying the others – but the others remain just as imperative as the one that has been obeyed, and just as dire in the consequences they threaten for disobedience.[3] The double bind is commonplace, but it does put the one caught in it in an impossible situation: there is no possible way of acting that will fulfil all of the demands being made.

It is important to emphasise that the double bind is a *logical* structure, not just a matter of an individual's fancy, or choice, or reluctance. This is why the double bind can present itself so often as something over which one does not have any control: something profoundly impersonal, into which one has fallen like a trap, and which happens to one from the outside. And yet, at the same time – and this will be familiar from our opening story – it is also a situation which is most profoundly and intimately personal. Those simultaneous and contradictory demands are not just external impositions on one's sense of self, or delusory ideas one might have about oneself: they *are* that very sense of self, in the deepest and most intimate sense. To fail any of those demands threatens the very self with collapse: hence the profound discomfort, even anguish, of the situation. And where there's a double bind, there would seem to be no option *but* to fail at least one of them.

Unless, of course, some strategy can get around this implacable logic. And that is exactly what happens with the ruses of the unconscious. If it is impossible to satisfy two mutually contradictory demands directly, it may be possible to deflect one of them onto some sort of compromise formation. 'I cannot love my father and hate him at the same time, but I can certainly love my father and be terrified of horses.' To handle it this way is not to do the impossible and resolve the contradiction; it's to try to make it appear as if there never was any contradiction in the first place. The contradiction does not go away; the contradictory demand has been met, but in a displaced, disguised way. For the ruse to work, one of the contradictory terms has gone underground, as it were, and now cannot any longer be spoken about by its own name. In effect, one of the ideas is placed under **repression**. It remains unspoken, even unspeakable, in the sense we have just suggested: not just because to speak it would be to admit to filial ingratitude or personal shortcoming, but because to speak it would be to undo that very sense of self. What can be spoken – and indeed must be spoken, under the terms of the double bind – is the deflected, displaced substitute for the repressed term.

The effect of repression is *like* that of an internal censorship. It is *as if* there were a censoring agency at the threshold of consciousness, scrutinising everything which presents itself and determining whether it can be admitted to consciousness. We should emphasise the 'like' and 'as if', because Freud is not quite satisfied with the description he gives. Indeed, the famous statement of it in the *Introductory Lectures* is followed immediately by a qualification suggesting it should not be taken too seriously: for all that it approximates to the facts, it is all too 'crude and fantastic'.•

Let us ... compare the system of the unconscious to a large entrance hall, in which the mental impulses jostle one another like separate individuals. Adjoining this entrance hall, there is a second, narrower, room – a kind of drawing-room –

in which consciousness, too, resides. But on the threshold between these two rooms a watchman performs his function: he examines the different mental impulses, acts as a censor, and will not admit them into the drawing room if they displease him. ... The impulses in the entrance hall of the unconscious are out of sight of the conscious, which is in the other room; to begin with they must remain unconscious. If they have already pushed their way forward to the threshold and have been turned back by the watchman, then they are inadmissible to consciousness; we speak of them as *repressed*. For any particular impulse, ... the vicissitude of repression consists in its not being allowed by the watchman to pass from the system of the unconscious into that of the preconscious. It is the same watchman whom we get to know as resistance when we try to lift the repression by means of the analytic treatment. ...

Now I know that you will say that these ideas are both crude and fantastic and quite impermissible in a scientific account. I know that they are crude: and more than that, I know that they are incorrect, and, if I am not very much mistaken, I already have something better to take their place.[†] Whether it will seem to you equally fantastic I cannot tell. They are preliminary working hypotheses, like Ampère's manikin swimming in the electric current,[+] and they are not to be despised in so far as they are of service in making our observations intelligible. I should like to assure you that these two hypotheses of the two rooms, the watchman at the threshold between them and consciousness as a spectator at the end of the second room must nevertheless be very far-reaching approximations to the real facts. (Lecture 19, 'Resistance and Repression', *Introductory Lectures on Psychoanalysis* (1916–17), vol.16, pp.295–96)

Footnotes added by the editors of the Standard Edition:

[+][What Freud had in mind is not obvious.]
[†][A.M. Ampère (1775–1836), one of the founders of the science of electromagnetism, made use of a magnetic metal manikin in [explaining] one of his early experiments establishing the relation between electricity and magnetism.]

Remains and the reality principle

The reality principle is a paradoxical thing. At first, it seems to be opposed to the pleasure principle, but their relationship is actually much more complex. The reality principle does not deny pleasure so much as aim at it indirectly, through a strategic rerouting. Its aims, that is, are the same as those of the pleasure principle, but deferred: the pleasure it aims at is not immediate, but some time in the future.• This future pleasure may even lie on the other side of unpleasure; with the reality principle, present unpleasure may be a

[The reality principle] does not abandon the intention of ultimately obtaining pleasure, but it nevertheless demands and carries into effect the postponement of satisfaction, the abandonment of a number of possibilities of gaining satisfaction and the temporary toleration of unpleasure as a step on the long indirect road to pleasure. (*Beyond the Pleasure Principle* (1920b), p. 10)

way of making a future pleasure come to pass. Or at least, because the psyche has no control over what happens to it from outside, as it were, it may be a way of making a future pleasure more likely. The reality principle is thus also a sort of wager: *if you do this, then you make pleasure more likely at a later date*. This makes it a series of calculations on what is strictly incalculable – calculations which are in principle endless, because at any stage they stand to be thrown into disarray at the next incursion of the unpredictable, so that the path to a promised ultimate pleasure needs to be recalculated all over again from the start. Ultimately, the reality principle is indistinguishable from the pleasure principle – it is the pleasure principle by another name, or separated from itself by the insistence and persistence of a world which is not under the control of the psyche, but which incessantly intervenes on the psyche's calculations.

This will be of tremendous importance to us later. What it amounts to is that *the reality principle divides the psyche radically from itself*. It installs the unpredictability of the external world in the very midst of the internal world of the psyche, like an irreducible foreign body at its very heart. Even more, with the reality principle, the boundaries between inside and outside are themselves no longer clear. If the outside is what remains inaccessible to the psyche and the pleasure principle, with the reality principle that outside nevertheless finds itself already at the very heart of the inside.

Though Freud does not use the actual term 'reality principle' until 1911, in the brief 'Formulations on the Two Principles of Mental Functioning', the concept itself can easily be seen as crucial everywhere in his earlier writing.•

In *The Interpretation of Dreams* (1900), for example, it is precisely one of the things which Freud argues distinguishes his project from the 'dream-book' methods of interpretation which are still familiar today.

> Instead of [hallucinatory satisfaction of needs], the psychical apparatus had to decide to form a conception of the real circumstances in the external world and to endeavour to make a real alteration in them. A new principle of mental functioning was thus introduced; what was presented in the mind was no longer what was agreeable but what was real, even if it happened to be disagreeable. This setting up of the *reality principle* proved to be a momentous step. ('Formulations on the Two Principles of Mental Functioning' (1911b), p. 219; emphasis in original)

The classic dream-book is a dictionary of symbols, in which individual elements of a dream are each given an interpretation. It treats dreaming as a content that has been disguised by a simple substitution code, one meaning for another, according to a single consistent key; once the key is known, the message underneath becomes obvious.•

For Freud, though, the matter is not so simple. The dream is not just the product of coding a desire according to regular and reversible rules. Instead, it is

> Suppose, for instance, that I have dreamt of a letter and also of a funeral. If I consult a 'dream-book', I find that 'letter' must be translated by 'trouble' and 'funeral' by 'betrothal'. It then remains for me to link together the key-words which I have deciphered in this way and ... to transpose the result into the future tense. (*The Interpretation of Dreams* (1900), pp. 97–98)

Something which is derived from our conscious life and shares its characteristics – we call it 'the day's residues' – combines with something else coming from the realm of the unconscious in order to construct a dream. The dream-work is accomplished between these two components. (Lecture 13, 'The Archaic Features and Infantilism of Dreams', *Introductory Lectures on Psychoanalysis* (1916–17), vol.15, p. 212)

the result of the collision of at least two very different things.• One of these, of course, is the unconscious material which seeks expression and strives to get through the dream-censor. The other, though, is what he calls **the day's residues**: something from the very recent waking life of the dreamer, from the waking period immediately preceding the dream. These residues may be the memory of an event which was obviously charged with some sort of importance during the day, and which the dream thus continues to work out and dwell on; but they may on the other hand just as easily be small and quite insignificant events.•

In every undertaking there must be a capitalist who covers the required outlay and an *entrepreneur* who has the idea and knows how to carry it out. In the construction of dreams, the part of the capitalist is always played by the unconscious wish alone; it provides the psychical energy for the construction of the dream. The *entrepreneur* is the day's residues, which decide how the day's outlay is to be employed. (Lecture 14, 'Wish-Fulfilment', *Introductory Lectures on Psychoanalysis* (1916–17), vol. 15, p. 226; emphasis in original)

Many writers before Freud, of course, have made the obvious point that you often dream about things you did in the previous waking day. Freud's argument, though, is something more than that. Just as the dream is not a direct coding of unconscious wishes, neither is it just a replay of earlier events. Instead, the dream emerges at the intersection of these two, where the unconscious wish meets the remains of the day. But – and here is the important point – those two series are irreducible to one another: the day throws up all sorts of events that have no relationship at all to unconscious desires. Instead of the smooth continuity of memory of the previous day or the coded expression of desire, the juxtaposition of the two produces new and unpredictable formations. This means there can be no general key to dreams: every dream pulls a wild card, something singular and unrepeatable drawn afresh from the contingencies of a specific life.

Like the dream-work, the formation of the **symptom** also comes about in the collision of two independent series. The symptom too is the sign of a repression: some sort of insistent behavioural pattern which may appear meaningless, even to the one who performs it, but which takes its meaning from something under repression. The symptom is the compromise formation which has been able to evade the censor (and thus both expresses and conceals its cause). It can do this precisely by latching onto something that seems not to be connected by any direct necessity to what is repressed. Indeed, as with the dream, the more indirect the connection, the more likely it is to be able to avoid the censor. Like the dream, the symptom uses whatever happens to be at hand, available to it in the contingent events of a world. The symptom is always something that *need not* have happened in quite that way. Hence the odd logic of analysis: we can trace the symptom back to its causes, but we cannot start from those causes and predict the symptom that results from them.• We shall have cause to return to the complex and retrospective temporality this logic sets in place.

The dream-work, the symptom and indeed psychoanalysis itself are always matters of a

> … a state of things … confronts us in many … instances in which light has been thrown by psychoanalysis on a mental process. So long as we trace the development from its final outcome backwards, the chain of events appears continuous, and we feel we have gained an insight which is completely satisfactory or even exhaustive. But if we proceed the reverse way, if we start from the premises inferred from the analysis and try to follow these up to the final result, then we no longer get the impression of an inevitable sequence of events which could not have been otherwise determined. We notice at once that there might have been another result, and that we might have been just as well able to understand and explain the latter. The synthesis is thus not so satisfactory as the analysis; in other words, from a knowledge of the premises we could not have foretold the nature of the result. ('The Psychogenesis of a Case of Homosexuality in a Woman' (1920a), p. 167)[4]

life story and its vicissitudes and contingencies. Unlike the dream-book with its general and universal methods, on the one hand, or, on the other, empirical psychology's focus on replicable phenomena, psychoanalysis is founded on the meticulous attention to the specific, the singular and the unrepeatable which makes it a sort of 'science of biography': psychoanalysis is granular. Before its focus is on the individual human being, it is on the question of how it is that such a thing as the subject can come about in a richly contingent world.

Everywhere, the psyche is invaded by contingency. This is why Freud's work on questions of culture and society can be more than a sort of psycho-sociology imagining the social world as essentially an aggregate of pre-social individuals. The events of the world are not just things which happen to the psyche, outside it and inflicted on it; they are constitutive of that psyche itself, in a way which no longer permits a simple distinction between inner and outer, or between those structures which belong to the psyche and those which are part of that already social world into which it is born. If *trauma* is the name for the wound caused when the outer invades the inner, then trauma is already at the heart of the psyche. (Figure 1.1)

What is unconscious forms an immense foreign territory whose logic Freud unravels throughout his career.• Sometimes he seems to forget the sheer strangeness of this logic, or not draw the full conclusions from it, but its repercussions run

> … the repressed is foreign territory to the ego – internal foreign territory … (Lecture 31, 'The Dissection of the Psychical Personality', *New Introductory Lectures on Psychoanalysis* (1933a), p. 57)

throughout his work from early to late. In what follows, we shall hold fast to it as a guiding thread through the labyrinths of the Freudian enterprise.

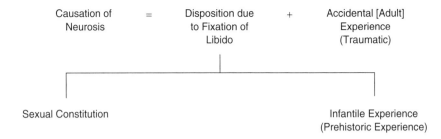

Figure 1.1   From Lecture 23, 'The Paths to the Formation of Symptoms', *Introductory Lectures on Psychoanalysis* (1916–17), vol. 16, p. 360

Opening the field:
The Interpretation of Dreams (1900)

This is the first great text of psychoanalysis, and along with the *Three Essays on The Theory of Sexuality* from five years later, its central text. Between them, these two books provided most of the material Freud was to build upon, elaborate, revise, and modify throughout his career. *The Interpretation of Dreams* ran to eight editions in Freud's lifetime, and in each of them, as psychoanalysis itself developed and Freud's views changed, the book gained new passages, footnotes, annotations, and entries in the bibliography. As a result, *The Interpretation of Dreams* is a layered, palimpsested text, whose apparatus traces out much of the subsequent development of Freud's thought. It is exhaustively documented: its first chapter is a long summary of the existing literature on dreams, popular and scientific, and the book as a whole draws on a stock of some 200 dreams, most of them carefully noted down by Freud from his patients.

As Freud points out, the interest in dreams arose directly from his work on hysteria with Josef Breuer, and took over many of the same methods and techniques.• Like the *Studies on Hysteria*, it takes phenomena that appear to be senseless, and shows an unexpected and deep intelligibility in them. But where the *studies* focused on pathological behaviour, *The Interpretation of*

My patients were pledged to communicate to me every idea or thought that occurred to them in connection with some particular subject; amongst other things they told me their dreams and so taught me that a dream can be inserted into the psychical chain that has to be traced backwards in the memory from a pathological idea. It was then only a short step to treating the dream itself as a symptom and to applying to dreams the method of interpretation that had been worked out for symptoms. (*The Interpretation of Dreams* (1900), vol. 4, pp. 100–101)

Dreams finds the workings of the unconscious in the commonplace and familiar. Much of the apparatus of the unfinished 'Project' finds itself mirrored here in a new way, cast adrift from the earlier neuroanatomical foundations. In place of a physical nervous system in which neurones bear their charges of *Q*, we now have cathexes distributed across purely psychical agencies which Freud insists should not be confused with anatomical locations.• The long final chapter of *The Interpretation of Dreams* gives the first detailed metapsychological description of these agencies, which have now taken on the names of the topography Freud continued to invoke until the 1920s: *Pcpt*, or perception; *Pcs*,

> I shall entirely disregard the fact that the mental apparatus with which we are here concerned is also known to us in the form of an anatomical preparation, and I shall carefully avoid the temptation to determine psychical locality in any anatomical fashion. I shall remain upon psychological ground, and I propose simply to follow the suggestion that we should picture the instrument which carries out our mental functions as resembling a compound microscope or a photographic apparatus, or something of the kind. On that basis, psychical locality will correspond to a point inside the apparatus at which one of the preliminary stages of an image comes into being. In the microscope and telescope, as we know, these occur in part at ideal points, regions in which no tangible part of the apparatus is situated. I see no necessity to apologise for the imperfections of this or of any similar imagery. (*The Interpretation of Dreams* (1900), vol. 5, p. 536)

or preconscious; *Cs*, or consciousness; and of course *Ucs*, the unconscious.

The concept of the unconscious is now much more complex than when it made its first appearance in the *Studies on Hysteria* (1895): Freud's analyses and his ever-growing clinical experience have shown many of the ramifications and implications of the concept. The idea of intrapsychic censorship, for example, has a couple of cursory mentions in the *Studies*, but here it becomes a key part of the apparatus, regulating as it does the commerce between conscious and unconscious. So too do the ways of avoiding that censorship: condensation and displacement become the twin mechanisms of the dream work.

The distinction between (free) primary and (bound) secondary processes is similarly developed, elaborated out in particular into the opposition between manifest content and latent dream-thoughts. The latent dream-thoughts are the material on which the profoundly unconscious dream-work can construct the manifest and generally highly disguised content remembered by the dreamer. Going the other way, it is the task of psychoanalysis to reconstruct the latent thoughts from the manifest content. Among other things, this allows Freud to argue that dreams are wish-fulfilments. Even highly disturbing dreams are unpleasant only on the manifest level of the dreamer's experience of them, and inevitably reveal some sort of wish-fulfilment – keeping in mind how ambiguous that can be – in the latent dream-thoughts. In this, we can see a version of what the 'Project' and (in passing) the *Studies on Hysteria* will have already seen as a principle of constancy, and what will by 1911 (in 'Formulations on the Two Principles of Mental Functioning') have become the pleasure principle.

With this greater complexity of concept and method, the unconscious is no longer as it was in the *Studies*, a mine of material to be brought back to consciousness in the course of a cure. At a number of points in *The*

Interpretation of Dreams, the unconscious now begins to appear as an internal and structural limit to analysis itself, as if psychoanalysis from now on will have to calculate with its own incompleteness and remainders.●

There is often a passage in even the most thoroughly interpreted dream which has to be left obscure; this is because we become aware during the work of interpretation that at that point there is a tangle of dream-thoughts which cannot be unravelled and which moreover adds nothing to our knowledge of the content of the dream. This is the dream's navel, the spot where it reaches down into the unknown. The dream thoughts to which we are led by interpretation cannot, from the nature of things, have any definite endings; they are bound to branch out in every direction into the intricate network of our world of thought. It is at some point where this meshwork is particularly close that the dream-wish grows up, like a mushroom out of its mycelium. (*The Interpretation of Dreams* (1900), vol.5, p.525

Freud had linked the infant boy's love for his mother and jealousy of his father to the Oedipus legend at least as early as 1897 (*Freud–Fliess* (1985), p. 272), but his first published comments on it occur in *The Interpretation of Dreams* (vol. 4, pp. 261–64). It was not until 1910, in an article on 'A Special Type of Object Choice Made by Men', that he would call this relation the Oedipus complex.

The Psychopathology of Everyday Life (1901) and Jokes and Their Relation to the Unconscious (1905)

The Psychopathology of Everyday Life was meant for a non-specialist audience. It was Freud's most popular book during his lifetime, in which it went through 11 German editions and was translated into ten other languages. In the process, it grew considerably: while its first published version covered some 80 pages in two instalments of a monthly journal, by the time of its appearance in the collected German edition it occupied just over four times that number. For each of these new editions, Freud added material, nearly all of it new examples of his own and from friends, colleagues, and readers. The book is essentially a compendium, whose theoretical apparatus is restricted to the discussion of examples. These range from the forgetting of words and intentions, to slips of the tongue and misreadings, from coherently and systematically bungled actions to the role of chance and belief in fate.

*

Jokes and Their Relation to the Unconscious was written at the same time as the *Three Essays on the Theory of Sexuality*, and similarly extends Freud's previous work, though in other directions. One of the letters to Fliess (22 June 1897: *Freud–Fliess* (1985), p. 254) indicates that Freud began collecting jokes ('profound Jewish stories') at roughly the same time that he began work on *The Interpretation of Dreams*. Like the *Psychopathology*, its starting point is the similarity of the phenomena it is investigating to dreams. Like dreams, jokes work by condensation, displacement, and modification, yoking dissimilar things together, with apparent nonsense capable of everting itself unexpectedly into sense. As in dreams, this nonsense is often close to unease. Like dreams, jokes have a content that is often sexual, or aggressive, or self-accusatory, and the pleasure they afford may be bound up with all of these. Like dreams, jokes provide ways of getting around restrictions on what is impermissible. Freud even calls the unconscious mechanism of joke production the *joke-work*, by analogy with the dream-work. But where the *Psychopathology* largely took over the apparatus Freud had developed in *The Interpretation of Dreams* and provided a series of examples illustrating it from other quarters, *Jokes* uses its examples to modify the theory wherever necessary.

In particular, while dreams and the parapraxes of everyday life so easily appear to be products of an individual psyche, jokes have an obvious and irreducible social – or more strictly, interpersonal – dimension. A joke is not private: it requires a teller and a listener.• Some types of tendentious joke, Freud will argue, require at least three parties: the one who makes the joke, the one who is its object, and the one who takes pleasure in the joke, and whose pleasure leads in turn to the first's.

> ... no one can be content with having made a joke for himself alone. An urge to tell the joke to someone is inextricably bound up with the joke-work; indeed, this urge is so strong that often enough it is carried through in disregard of serious misgivings. ... A joke ... must be told to someone else. The psychical process of constructing a joke seems not to be completed when the joke occurs to one: something remains over which seeks, by communicating the idea, to bring the unknown process of constructing the joke to a conclusion. (*Jokes and Their Relation to the Unconscious* (1905b), p. 143)

Freud argues that masculine 'smutty' humour works this way, forming in effect a pact in which two men pleasure each other by means of the degradation of a woman (who is the object of humour within the joke, but also the woman before whom the joke is performed). In the smutty joke, Freud proposes a mechanism behind what Eve Kosofsky Sedgwick (1990) would much later come to call *homosociality*. Like dreams, jokes are powerful disavowals. In their simultaneous expression and disavowal of hostilities, they may generate a solidarity based not on common belief, but on a common cynicism. *Jokes* thus opens up an interpersonal dialectic of a type which was then taken up in the 1913 *Totem and Taboo* and the 1921 *Group Psychology and the Analysis of the Ego*.

Metapsychological papers:
'Instincts and Their Vicissitudes' (1915), 'Repression' (1915), 'The Unconscious' (1915), 'A Metapsychological Supplement to the Theory of Dreams' (1917) and 'Mourning and Melancholia' (1917)

These are some of Freud's most concertedly theoretical writings. Where *The Interpretation of Dreams*, *The Psychopathology of Everyday Life* and *Jokes and Their Relation to the Unconscious* were rich in specific examples, these papers focus instead on the hypothetical machineries of the psyche and their principles of operation. Along with seven other papers which have not survived, they were meant to form a book, *Preliminaries to a Metapsychology*, which would have been the first full-length work of psychoanalytic theory.

We can guess some of the reasons for its incompletion and the abandonment of the other papers. Freud's paper on narcissism in the previous year had raised a number of problems for a model in which the three main agencies of the psyche were conscious, preconscious and unconscious, and this would eventually lead to his jettisoning that schema. On top of that, the *Introductory Lectures in Psychoanalysis* were written during the time the extant papers reached publication (1915–17), and although these lectures are popular rather than theoretical, they carry out many of the functions of consolidation and summation which had been planned for the series. With the incomplete metapsychological papers, Freud must have felt either that he was reworking stale territory or that the conceptual ground was shifting under his feet. In reply to Lou Andreas-Salomé's query about the missing papers in 1919, he wrote that he had decided to abandon rather than rewrite them.• Five of the lost papers were to have been on consciousness, anxiety, conversion hysteria, obsessional neurosis, and the transference neuroses;

Where is my Metapsychology? In the first place it remains unwritten. Working-over material systematically is not possible for me; the fragmentary nature of my observations and the sporadic character of my ideas will not permit it. If, however, I should live another ten years, remain capable of work during that time, not starve, not be killed, not be too deeply taken up with the misery of my family or of those around me – a little much in the way of conditions – then I promise to produce further contributions to it. A first one in this line will be contained in an essay 'Beyond the Pleasure Principle' ... (2 April 1919, *Sigmund Freud and Lou Andreas-Salomé: Letters*)

the editors of the Standard Edition guess that the other two would have been on sublimation and projection.

For all the clarity and exhaustive thoroughness of these papers, one can sense their difficulties in holding the enterprise together. What emerges so often across them is the way in which the psyche operates in such a large and only partially systematisable variety of ways. The 'vicissitudes' in the title of the first paper is entirely appropriate for the series as a whole, where it is a frequent and significant word. There is something improvisatory about the psyche: in constructing symptoms or dreams, getting around repression, managing affects and the pressures of the drives, it makes use of whatever is at hand. The unconscious is itself an experience of gaps and inconsistencies, not bound by the sequentialities and consequentialities of conscious logic, and happily entertaining contradictions. As a result, it is often difficult to derive any but the broadest general rules for its behaviour before the argument is forced to branch and meticulously follow through each of the possibilities available and their consequences for the overall picture.• Thus, for example, the paper on 'Repression' declares that there are no general rules governing the degree of disguise necessary for a repressed content to work its way through into consciousness, and that a small change in initial conditions may result in a large change in the outcome. Yet what happens to the affect connected

> Each single derivative of the repressed may have its own special vicissitude ...
>
> The extraordinary intricacy of all the factors to be taken into consideration [in repression and the formation of neurotic symptoms] leaves only one way of presenting them open to us. We must select first one and then another point of view, and follow it up through the material as long as the application of it seems to yield results. Each separate treatment of the subject will be incomplete in itself, and there cannot fail to be obscurities where it touches upon material that has not yet been treated; but we may hope that a final synthesis will lead to a proper understanding. ('Repression' (1915c),pp. 150, 157–58)

with a repressed content – whether it remains as it is, or is transformed into another sort of affect such as anxiety, or is simply suppressed ('The Unconscious' (1915d), pp. 177–78) – depends precisely on these largely unforeseeable vicissitudes. Everything is poised in a delicately chaotic system.

In the metapsychological papers, one can see the first topology straining with the task set it, as it devolves out into rich and ever more detailed complexities of description. In them, and particularly in the fifth paper on 'Mourning and Melancholia', one can also see the emergence of the new second topology, which will find its own detailed metapsychological description in 1923, with *The Ego and the Id*.

II: Ego, id and superego

Problems with the model

So far, Freud has modelled the psyche around that great split between conscious and unconscious, and the barrier separating them. But as we have seen, this split has its own paradoxical consequences: when the unconscious is an internal foreign territory with a logic which blurs insides and outsides, that topography will come to look increasingly inadequate, and altogether too simple for the phenomena it has to account for.

Though the final chapter of *The Interpretation of Dreams* (1900) had suggested that a topographical view should be replaced with a properly dynamic view,• topography does not go away quite so easily. What Freud calls a complete metapsychological

> Thus, we may speak of an unconscious thought seeking to convey itself into the preconscious so as then to be able to force its way through into consciousness. What we have in mind here is not the forming of a second thought situated in a new place, like a transcription which continues to exist alongside the original; and the notion of forcing a way through into consciousness must be kept carefully free from any idea of a change of locality. Again, we may speak of a preconscious thought being repressed or driven out and then taken over by the unconscious. These images,

derived from a set of ideas relating to a struggle for a piece of ground, may tempt us to suppose that it is literally true that a mental grouping in one locality has been brought to an end and replaced by a fresh one in another locality. Let us replace these metaphors by something that seems to correspond better to the real state of affairs, and let us say instead that some particular mental grouping has had a cathexis of energy attached to it or withdrawn from it, so that the structure in question has come under the sway of a particular agency or been withdrawn from it. What we are doing here is once again to replace a topographical way of representing things by a dynamic one. (*The Interpretation of Dreams* (1900), vol.5, p. 610)

description of any aspect of the psyche still requires not only dynamic and economic descriptions, but also topographic – even though this topography is increasingly treated as an inaccurate fiction: like the censor guarding the door between the unconscious and the preconscious, its purchase is as an aid to conceptualisation rather than strictly explanatory. Sometimes it seems logical to see the unconscious as a different psychical location from the conscious; sometimes it seems better to see it as a single location cathected differently within the two different systems. Sometimes the choice seems just a matter of convenience.• Which to choose? Perhaps the problem comes about simply because the question is actually not well phrased.

The first of the two possibilities which we considered – namely that the *Cs.* (conscious) phase of an ideal implies a fresh registration of it, which is situated in another place – is doubtless the cruder but also the more convenient. The second hypothesis – that of a merely *functional* change of state – is *a priori* more probable, but it is less plastic, less easy to manipulate ....

So for the moment we are not in a position to decide between the two possibilities that we have discussed. Perhaps later on we shall come upon factors which may turn the balance in favour of one or the other. Perhaps we shall make the discovery that our question was inadequately framed and that the difference between an unconscious and a conscious idea has to be defined in quite another way. ('The Unconscious' (1915d), pp. 175, 176; emphasis in original)

What we have permissibly called the conscious [mental] presentation of the object can now be split up into the presentation of the *word* and the presentation of the *thing*; the latter consists in the cathexis, if not of the direct memory-images of the thing, at least of remoter memory-traces derived from these. We now seem to know all at once what the difference is between a conscious and an unconscious presentation. The two are not, as we supposed, different registrations of the same content in different psychical localities, nor yet different functional states of cathexis in the same locality; but the conscious presentation comprises the presentation of the thing plus the presentation of the word, while the unconscious presentation is the presentation of the thing alone. ... A presentation which is not put into words, or a psychical act which is not hypercathected [with its word-presentation], remains thereafter in the *Ucs* [unconscious], in a state of repression. ('The Unconscious' (1915d), pp. 201–02; emphasis in original)

The 1915 paper on 'The Unconscious' attempts to act as a summation of these problems, and at the very end offers one possibility which makes just such a rephrasing of the question, if only a partial one. The difference between conscious and unconscious,• it suggests, is that conscious mental acts are connected to language, in a way in which unconscious processes are not. It is no surprise that this passage's invocation of the role of language in the psyche should find its echoes in Lacan's post-Saussurean linguistic revision of psychoanalysis from the 1950s on.

In the 1920s, Freud did away with the view that the unconscious is a system in its own right, and replaced it with another topography altogether – one which cuts across the previous division into unconscious, preconscious, and conscious.

The second topography

'Unconscious', the adjective, describes perfectly well the quality of much, even most activity of the psyche: Freud does not step back from that key insistence for a moment. Add the definite article and turn it into a substantive – *the* unconscious – and we have opened up some difficulties. There is no problem if we take care still to use the word in a strictly descriptive sense, as a term for the aggregate of all things unconscious. The problem comes once we start to follow the pull of the definite article, and think of *the* unconscious as something substantial, as some sort of system or agency in itself. That unconsciousness is a quality of certain activities of the psyche does not necessarily mean that there is some sort of agency in the psyche concerned exclusively with those activities and no others – and, of course, we can say exactly the same of consciousness. It may be that in any adequate model of the psyche, any of its systems or components may produce some unconscious effects, some conscious. 'Unconscious' and 'conscious' may be perfectly legitimate and necessary descriptions of two qualities that psychic processes have, but they are not explanations of their mechanisms, or of agencies within the psyche.

Beginning in 1923 with *The Ego and the Id*, Freud offered another tripartite division to replace that of conscious, preconscious and unconscious: **ego**, **id**, and **superego**. These are not just different names for the same thing: they are a thorough rethinking of the topography and the interrelations of its parts. Though the ego and the id may seem close to the old 'conscious' and 'unconscious,' respectively, neither of them is defined in terms of the presence or absence of consciousness – and a large part of the ego is actually not even preconscious but unconscious, in the strict descriptive sense. Even superficially, the superego is reducible to neither ego nor id; it is in effect a way of formalising certain ideas which had initially been worked out in 'On Narcissism' (1915) and *Group Psychology and the Analysis of the Ego* (1921), and of suggesting that the very nature of their functioning warrants describing them as a separate psychical agency.

And just as with the neologistic Greek of *cathexis*, the Latin forms chosen for the English translation give a rather different impression than the German terms. *Ego* translates *das Ich*, the substantive form of the German first-person pronoun – literally, *the I*. Significantly, for a writer who is always at pains to distinguish what he is doing from philosophy, *das Ich* does not carry with it the Cartesian overtones *ego* has. And *id* is similarly and simply *das Es*, where *es* is the third-person neuter

Now I think we shall gain a great deal by following the suggestion of a writer who, from personal motives, vainly asserts that he has nothing to do with the rigours of pure science. I am speaking of Georg Groddeck, who is never tired of insisting that ..., as he expresses it, we are 'lived' by unknown and uncontrollable forces. We have all had impressions of the same kind, even though they may not have overwhelmed us to the exclusion of all others, and we need feel no hesitation in finding a place for Groddeck's discovery in the structure of science. I propose to take it into account by calling the entity which starts out from the system *Pcpt.* [perception] and begins by being *Pcs.* [preconscious] the 'ego', and by following Groddeck in calling the other part of the mind, into which this entity extends and which behaves as though it were *Ucs.* [unconscious], the 'id'.*

[Freud's footnote:]
*Groddeck himself no doubt followed the example of Nietzsche, who habitually used this grammatical term for whatever in our nature is impersonal and, so to speak, subject to natural law. (*The Ego and the Id* (1923), p. 23)

pronoun, *it*. In this case, though, there is a more direct philosophical lineage. Freud notes that he is following his contemporary Georg Groddeck's usage, and through him Nietzsche.• (And significantly enough, in this case we have the writer who wishes to distinguish what he does from philosophy happy to claim his debt to a philosopher who is at pains to distinguish what he is doing from *science* ...). *Superego*, though, appears to be Freud's own coinage.

Ego is a term Freud had already used frequently throughout his writing – quite unsurprisingly, given that it was already a commonplace term in the psychology of the time. Often as not, in the early writings he uses it in a quite loose and open way, to designate nothing more than the sense of self or the personality. But from the outset, there are also times when he uses it in a much more strongly metapsychological way,• as part of thoroughly topographical, dynamic or economic descriptions, beginning with the abandoned 'Project for a Scientific Psychology' (1895).

Thus we find ourselves quite unexpectedly before the most obscure problem: the origin of the 'ego' – that is, of a complex of neurones which hold fast to their cathexis, a complex, therefore, which is for short periods at a constant level. ('Project for a Scientific Psychology' (1895), p. 369)

Throughout the *Studies on Hysteria* (1895), this ego or sense of self is the scene of conflict: the ego is variously a defence mechanism, the agency whose task is precisely to manage the double binds of the psyche, or that part of the psyche which lies beyond the censor's anteroom and must be protected from the dissension just outside it. From the outset, that is, Freud has already been thinking of the ego as something more precise and systematic than the vague sense of it as a synonym for 'self'.

Freud's first major essay in metapsychological description, however – the final chapter of *The Interpretation of Dreams* (1900) – leaves little room for following this through, with its focus on conscious, unconscious, and preconscious as agencies. Nevertheless, this more specific sense of ego as agency keeps emerging in a number of writings, mostly as the signal of a problem for the first topography, something whose mechanisms are still to be thought through. In the brief 1911 'Formulations on the Two Principles of Mental Functioning', for example, Freud suggests that there are two divergent types of drive: the sexual drives (aimed ultimately at the propagation and welfare of the species) and the ego-drives (which are concerned with self-preservation). In 'On Narcissism' (1914a), narcissism is characterised elegantly and concisely as a crossing of those boundaries: in narcissism, the ego presents itself as a love object for the sexual drives. The ego which can do that, is no longer just a broad term for the sense of self, but is now a quite specific agency in the self, a name for a *part* of the self which can offer itself for the approval and love of another part. Neither is it any longer a synonym for *the conscious* of the first topography, as consciousness is no longer a necessary part of everything it does.

The second topography is a recognition of this insistent agency of the ego, which had been so increasingly difficult to think through in the first topography's terms. This agency is largely a matter of mediation. The ego juggles the often conflicting and incommensurable demands placed on it from elsewhere• – by the other two agencies of the psyche, the id and the superego, but also by the external world, and the unforeseen and unforeseeable events the psyche has no option but to cope with. Freud often depicts the ego as that part of the psyche which is most directly in contact with, and thus most directly modified by the world. Because of this proximity, the ego is thus the seat of the reality principle.

Here are the principal characteristics of the ego. In consequence of the pre-established connection between sense perception and muscular action, the ego has voluntary movement at its command. It has the task of self-preservation. As regards *external* events, it performs that task by becoming aware of stimuli, by storing up experiences about them (in the memory), by avoiding excessively strong stimuli (through flight), by dealing with moderate stimuli (through adaptation) and finally by learning to bring about expedient changes in the external world to its own advantage (through activity). As regards *internal* events, in relation to the id, it performs that task by gaining control over the demands of the instincts, by deciding whether they are to be allowed satisfaction, by postponing that satisfaction to times and circumstances-favourable in the external world or by suppressing their excitations entirely. It is guided in its activity by consideration of the tensions produced by stimuli, whether these tensions are present in it or introduced into it. The raising of these tensions is in general felt as *unpleasure* and their lowering as *pleasure*. It is probable, however, that what is felt as pleasure or unpleasure is not the *absolute* height of this tension but something of the rhythm of the changes in them. The ego strives after pleasure and seeks to avoid unpleasure. An increase in unpleasure that is expected and foreseen is met by a *signal of anxiety*; the occasion of such an increase, whether it threaten from without or within, is known as a *danger*. From time to time the ego gives up its connection with the external world and withdraws into the state of sleep, in which it makes far-reaching changes in its organisation. It is to be inferred from the state of sleep that this organisation consists in a particular distribution of mental energy. ('An Outline of Psychoanalysis' (1940), pp. 145–46; emphasis in original)

The ego includes but is not restricted to consciousness. The **id**, by contrast, is that most deeply unconscious part of the psyche.• Furthest of all the psychic agencies from direct contact with the world, it is that

[The id] is the dark, inaccessible part of our personality; what little we know of it we have learnt from our study of the dream-work and of the construction of neurotic symptoms, and most of that is of a negative character and can be described only as a contrast to the ego. We approach the id with analogies: we call it a chaos, a cauldron full of seething excitations. ... It is filled with energy reaching it from the instincts, but it has no organisation, produces no collective will, but only a striving to bring about the satisfaction of the instinctual needs subject to the observance of the pleasure principle. The logical laws of thought do not apply in the id, and this is true above all of the laws of contradiction. Contrary impulses exist side by side, without cancelling each other out or diminishing each other: at the most they may converge to form compromises under the dominating economic pressure towards the discharge of energy. There is nothing in the id that could be compared with negation; and we perceive with surprise an exception to the philosophical theorem that space and time are necessary forms of our mental acts. There is nothing in the id that corresponds to the idea of time; there is no recognition of the passage of time, and − a thing that is most remarkable and awaits consideration in philosophical thought − no alteration in its mental processes is produced by the passage of time. Wishful impulses that have never passed beyond the id, but impressions, too, which have been sunk into the id by repression, are virtually immortal; after the passage of decades they behave as though they had just occurred. ...

The id of course knows no judgements of value: no good and evil, no morality. The economic or, if you prefer, the quantitative factor, which is intimately linked to the pleasure principle, dominates all its processes. Instinctual cathexes seeking discharge − that, in our view, is all there is in the id. It even seems that the energy of these instinctual impulses is in a state different from that in the other regions of the mind, far more mobile and capable of discharge; otherwise the displacements and condensations would not occur which are characteristic of the id and which so completely disregard the *quality* of what is cathected − what in the ego we should call an idea. You can see, incidentally, that we are in a position to attribute to the id characteristics other than that of its being unconscious, and you can recognise the possibility of portions of the ego and superego being unconscious without possessing the same primitive and irrational characteristics. (Lecture 31, 'The Dissection of the Psychical Personality', *New Introductory Lectures on Psychoanalysis* (1933a), pp. 73–75)

'internal foreign territory' whose doings seem quite out of the conscious control of the very person doing them, and source of those uncontrollable forces which live us out. If the ego is the home of the reality principle and its calculated compromise on pleasure, the id is home to the pleasure principle at its purest, with its relentless and unquenchable demands. Where the first topography saw the unconscious as made up almost entirely of repressed ideational content, repression plays a much smaller part in the id, which is primarily a repository of *libido* and *drive*, two terms about which we shall have more to say in the next chapter.

And this means that the boundary between ego and id is not the sharp line of demarcation which censorship tries to draw between conscious and unconscious in the first topography, but is somewhat blurred and shifting. Just as there is essentially no difference between the pleasure principle and the reality principle, when the latter is just the former with a knowledge of the ways of the world, Freud sometimes even goes on to suggest that there is no essential difference between id and ego other than the ego's greater proximity to the systems of perception and the stimuli of the outside world.[5] The ego is simply that part of the id closest to the surface (see Figure 1.2).

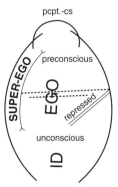

Figure 1.2   From Lecture 31, 'The Dissection of the Psychical Personality', *New Introductory Lectures* (1933), p. 78

With the ego and the id, Freud is rethinking and redistributing those qualities of consciousness and unconsciousness. Now, they are no longer the names of separate agencies, but qualities that the workings of a particular agency may have: the id is unconscious in its workings, but only some parts of the ego are conscious, with much or, perhaps even most of it, unconscious. And from about 1914 on, Freud began to focus his attention on the possibility of another agency in the psyche, one which, because it too is partly conscious and partly unconscious, does not fit well into the first topography. This is the emergence of what the second topography will eventually come to call the **superego**.

As we saw, the 1914 paper on narcissism postulated that narcissism is what happens when the ego presents itself as a love object for the sexual drives. For that to happen, though, there must be some sort of separate internal self-image, an ideal against which the psyche can measure up its own behaviour and desires. This 'ego-ideal' or 'ideal ego', as Freud calls it at this stage,[6] is formed in the course of the individual's personal history. It is what remains, stored up in the psyche, of all the demands placed on the infant from outside, by the parents and others. This ego-ideal is a loop, or a sort of cast-net, an image which tries to capture the images others have of oneself: *how I see others see me*. It is also, Freud suggests, the remains of the *primary narcissism* of the infant dominated by its own demands.• A few years later, *Group Psychology and the Analysis of the Ego* (1921) elaborated

This ideal ego is now the target of the self-love which was enjoyed in childhood by the actual ego. The subject's narcissism makes its appearance displaced onto this new ideal ego, which, like the infantile ego, finds itself possessed of every perfection that is of value. As always where the libido is concerned, man has here again shown himself incapable of giving up a satisfaction he had once enjoyed. He is not willing to forego the narcissistic perfection of his childhood; and when, as he grows up, he is disturbed by the admonitions of others and by the awakening of his own critical judgement, so that he can no longer retain that perfection, he seeks to recover it in the new form of an ego-ideal. What he projects before him as his ideal is the substitute for the lost narcissism of his childhood in which he was his own ideal. ('On Narcissism: An Introduction' (1914a), p. 94)

on the role of the ego-ideal and gave it a central role in all sorts of social and inter-personal phenomena. To *put another person in the place of one's ego-ideal*, it suggests, is the mechanism behind the fascination with another person which is at the heart of the appeal of the loved one – and of the political leader. We shall have more to say on that in Chapter 3.

This self-image implies an agency whose function is to carry out the corresponding self-scrutiny and self-criticism. While the essay on narcissism sees this as somewhat different from the ego-ideal, by the time of the first major statement of the new topography – the 1923 *The Ego and the Id* – both of these functions, the ideal and its scrutiny are part of a new hypothetical agency, the *superego*. Like the dream-censor, the super-ego is a judge or censor; but this time, it is not on the boundary between conscious and unconscious but a split within the ego itself; and its object is not forbidden thoughts which must not be allowed to enter consciousness, but self-image.

The superego is a harsh critic of how the ego appears to itself across this split; one finds it at work in things like feelings of inferiority, the murmurings of guilt or conscience, and the incessant and despairing self-criticism of depression (Freud uses the term common in his day: melancholia).• In this split, the *superego* is thus not only the possibility of identification (with myself, with an idea of myself, with myself as seen by others, with others). It is also, *and by the very same processes*, the *impossibility* of that identification.

While a melancholic can, like other people, show a greater or lesser degree of severity to himself in his healthy periods, during a melancholic attack his superego becomes over-severe, abuses the poor ego, humiliates and ill-treats it, threatens it with the direst punishment, reproaches it for actions in the remotest past which had been taken lightly at the time – as though it had spent the entire interval in collecting accusations and had only been waiting for its present access of strength in order to bring them up and make a condemnatory judgement on their basis. The superego applies the strictest moral standard to the helpless ego which is at its mercy; in general it represents the claims of morality, and we realise all at once that our moral sense of guilt is the expression of the tension between the ego and the superego. It is a most remarkable experience to see morality, which is supposed to have been given to us by God and thus deeply implanted in us, functioning [in these patients] as a periodic phenomenon. For after a certain number of months the whole moral fuss is over, the criticism of the superego is silent, the ego is rehabilitated and again enjoys all the rights of man until the next attack. In some forms of the disease, indeed, something of a contrary sort occurs in the intervals; the ego finds itself in a blissful state of intoxication, it celebrates a triumph, as though the super-ego had lost all its strength or had melted into the ego; and this liberated, manic ego permits itself a truly uninhibited satisfaction of all its appetites. Here are happenings rich in unsolved riddles! (Lecture 31, 'The Dissection of the Psychical Personality', *New Introductory Lectures* (1933a), pp. 60–61)

The superego is both a demand (*Be this*) and a prohibition (*Do not be this*) – *and on one and the same thing*.• Whatever identifications I might have are immediately caught up in a whirl

[The superego's] relation to the ego is not exhausted by the precept: 'You *ought to be* like this (like your father).' It also comprises the prohibition: 'You *may not be* like this

41

of other identifica-tions which are now, and from the outset, impossible either to complete and see the end of, or, on the other hand, to separate out from it.• The way in which I see myself is inseparable from the way in which I see myself seen by others, and the way in which I see others see myself. And all of this is in turn inseparable from – but at the same time quite irreducible to – the ways in which others see me, and the ways in which those others see me

> (like your father) – that is, you may not do all that he does; some things are his prerogative.' (*The Ego and the Id* (1923), p. 34)

> Since [the superego] goes back to the influence of parents, educators and so on, we learn still more of its significance if we turn to those who are its sources. As a rule parents and authorities analogous to them follow the precepts of their own superegos in educating children. Whatever understanding their ego may have come to with their superego, they are severe and exacting in educating children. They have forgotten the difficulties of their own childhood and they are glad to be able now to identify themselves fully with their own parents who in the past laid such severe restrictions upon them. Thus a child's superego is in fact constructed on the model not of its parents but of its parents' superego... (Lecture 31, 'The Dissection of the Psychical Personality on Psychoanalysis', *New Introductory Lectures* (1933a), p. 67)

seeing them, and see me seeing their seeing me. Once started, there is no necessary stopping point at which the reflections end – though of course there are generally all sorts of pragmatic and perfectly legitimate reasons for stopping well before vertigo.

That multiplication might seem a game with words, or at most a description of a certain paranoia. Of course, the calculations involved in those initial layers of wondering how others see us are the small change negotiated by all of us every day; we do it with practised care, but for most of the time without any great drama. Most of the time, those deeper potential layers along the lines of *seeing others seeing us seeing ourselves as seen by others* or *seeing others seeing us seeing ourselves as others see us seeing others seeing ourselves* ... barely impinge into our daily experience. Of course. But, of course, not always. We all know the moments of acute discomfort when such a vista suddenly opens up before us, as it does with the *faux pas* at the party. When identification itself is built on such a hall of mirrors, and I have no possibility of even momentarily separating *myself* out from *the way in which I see myself,* that vertigo is always there as an in-principle possibility, even if it's one realised with thankful infrequency. Just that fact that it remains as a possibility is enough to make an abyss beneath the apparently solid ground. Paying most attention to what's happening in the closest mirrors may be the most pragmatic and comfortable thing to do, but it doesn't mean you're no longer in the hall of mirrors.

Each of these agencies – ego, id, and superego – is in some way split, divided against itself. The id most obviously owes no allegiance at all to consistency, and happily harbours contradictions within itself. But the ego is only partly conscious, and is largely unknown to itself; it takes a distance from itself, offers itself as the object of love in narcissism, or of criticism by the superego, with whose imperative the very sense of self devolves into a hall of mirrors.

Far from an unmovable centre of the self, the ego is more a series of endless negotiations of conflicting demands from the other agencies and from the world itself • – demands which are ultimately irreconcilable because they share that structure of the double bind: to fulfil one is not just to ignore another, but to refuse it. At the heart of the self is irreducible dissension. And as we shall see in Chapter 3, that double-bind structure may be intimately linked to questions of ideology.

[The ego] feels hemmed in on three sides, threatened by three kinds of danger, to which, if it is hard pressed, it reacts by generating anxiety. Owing to its origin from the experiences of the perceptual system, it is earmarked for representing the demands of the external world, but it strives too to be a loyal servant of the id, to remain on good terms with it, to recommend itself to it as an object and to attract its libido to itself. In its attempts to mediate between the id and reality, it is often obliged to cloak the *Ucs.* commands of the id with its own *Pcs.* rationalisations, to conceal the id's conflicts with reality, to profess, with diplomatic disingenuousness, to be taking notice of reality even when the id has remained rigid and unyielding. On the other hand it is observed at every step it takes by the strict superego, which lays down definite standards for its conduct, without taking any account of its difficulties from the direction of the id and the external world, and which, if those standards are not obeyed, punishes it with tense feelings of inferiority and of guilt. Thus the ego, driven by the id, confined by the super ego, repulsed by reality, struggles to master its economic task of bringing about harmony among the forces and influences working in and upon it; and we can understand how it is that so often we cannot suppress a cry: 'Life is not easy!' If the ego is obliged to admit its weakness, it breaks out in anxiety, – realistic anxiety regarding the external world, moral anxiety regarding the superego and neurotic anxiety regarding the strength of the passions in the id. (Lecture 31, 'The Dissection of the Psychical Personality', *New Introductory Lectures on Psychoanalysis* (1933a), pp. 77–78)

A new topography:
The Ego and the Id (1923)

The Ego and the Id is the first detailed exploration of a new topography of the psyche. For almost a decade, Freud had been finding inadequacies in the division of the mind into conscious, preconscious, and unconscious agencies. It had been becoming increasingly clear the consciousness or unconsciousness was not the property of a single agency. The 1914 paper, 'On Narcissism', in particular, and then the fifth of the metapsychological papers, on 'Mourning and Melancholia', had taken the psychic censorship which was so central in *The Interpretation of Dreams* (1900), and elaborated it into a self-critical mechanism. This mechanism is constantly observing and judging the sense of self, and measuring it up against an *ego-ideal* – the sort of thing seen in guilt, conscience, an awareness of been watched by others, depression and paranoia. It acts as if it had a coherent program of its own, and works with what can be a considerable degree of autonomy from the other agencies: conscience can, after all, be quite severe and distressing to the ego over which it watches and judges. Yet it fits only uneasily into the previous topography. Its working is neither purely conscious nor purely unconscious, but a mixture of both; and neither is it simply latent, in the manner of the preconscious. Thus Freud gives this mechanism the status of a separate agency, the *superego*.

The new topography abandons the idea that there are separate agencies in charge of conscious, unconscious, and preconscious activities, and retains those terms purely as broad adjectival descriptions of functions carried out by the new agencies, ego, id, and superego. Where the id is profoundly unconscious, the other two agencies are a mixture of conscious and unconscious activities. What characterises them are, instead, their modes of organisation and operation. The **id** has least organisation of all: it is made up of free, unbound cathexes; has no recognition of time; and is not governed by the need to avoid contradiction. The **ego**, on the other hand, is made up of bound (though not necessarily conscious) cathexes; it has a sense of temporality, and seeks to exclude contradiction (and hence resistance is one of its functions). Freud describes the ego as that external rim of the id which has been modified by its contact with the world – a bodily ego, in the sense that it is in effect a mental representation of the body's surfaces. The **superego** is the function of watching and judging, and holds itself apart from both of the other agencies. Unlike the id, its cathexes are bound, but in its critical function it divides itself off from the ego, often fiercely.

The *Ego and the Id* traces out how these agencies might develop in the infant: we shall examine this more closely in Chapter 2.

III: The inhuman

The human machine

Go back to that image of the censor in the antechamber, vetting everything that appears at the door from the unconscious and deciding whether or not to allow it into the conscious. We may suspect that one of the reasons for the felt insufficiency of this model is that it simply does not provide what we have seen Freud characterise as a metapsychological description. It provides an imaginative basic topography, certainly, with its image of the two chambers and the censoring agency between them, but it does not describe the situation in either economic or dynamic terms, as the circulation and distribution of energy or as the conflict of forces. Instead, it provides a quite straightforward example of a *homuncular* model.

The problem with homuncular models is that they are circular: they explain the workings of their object, in this case the psyche, in terms which assume the very thing they are meant to be explaining. In this particular example, Freud is trying to give an adequate description of how it is that the psyche appears to partition itself off into two, and make decisions about what passes from one part into the other, and under what conditions. To do that, he posits a watchman to make those decisions within the psyche. But that is not an explanation so much as a repetition of the initial problem, one level down: how then does the watchman make those decisions? As Freud pictures it in this example, the watchman is itself a psyche in miniature, and thus ultimately of no use in explaining the psyche. (We should, of course, remember that the image is simply meant as an analogy to help understanding, not as a rigorous explanation. In the *Introductory Lectures*, Freud is using it to illustrate things to a partly lay audience, and pointing out to them the limits of its use as he does so. In the short metapsychological paper on 'Repression' of the previous year (1915), his argument is much more carefully metapsychological, and he does not use the analogy at all.)

We must avoid ... the distinction between 'supraconscious' and 'subconscious', which has become so popular in the recent literature of the psychoneuroses, for such a distinction seems precisely calculated to stress the equivalence of what is psychical to what is conscious. (*The Interpretation of Dreams* (1900), vol. 5, p. 615)

[W]e have to take into account the fact that analytic investigation reveals some of these latent processes as having characteristics and peculiarities which seem alien to us, or even incredible, and which run directly counter to the attributes of consciousness with which we are familiar. Thus we have grounds for modifying our inference about ourselves and saying that what is proved is not the existence of a second consciousness in us, but the existence of psychical acts which lack consciousness. We shall ... be right in rejecting the term 'subconscious' as incorrect and misleading. ('The Unconscious' (1915d), p. 170)

If someone talks of subconsciousness, I cannot tell whether he means the term topographically – to indicate something lying in the mind beneath consciousness – or qualitatively – to indicate another consciousness, a subterranean one, as it were. (*The Question of Lay Analysis* (1926b), p. 198)

With the same reasoning, we can also see just why Freud so often expresses his dislike for the term 'subconscious'•: an explanation of consciousness which relies on another hidden consciousness tucked away one level down is also a homuncular explanation, which is to say no explanation at all.

What Freud calls a metapsychology, though, sets out to do something quite different. In its emphasis on spatial organisation, the distribution and flows of energies across and within these spaces (and balances and conflicts of forces), metapsychological description aims deliberately at terms which do not simply take human consciousness for granted, but see it as something which needs to be examined and explained in other, prior terms. (What seem to be Freud's very first uses of the term, in letters to Wilhelm Fliess, suggest precisely this sense.)•

I am continually occupied with psychology – really *meta*psychology. (13 February 1897)
I am going to ask you seriously, by the way, whether I may use the name metapsychology for my psychology that leads behind consciousness. (10 March 1898, *The Complete Letters of Sigmund Freud to Wilhelm Fliess, 1887–1904*, pp. 172, 301–02)

Metapsychological description is an attempt to forestall homuncular explanations: the next level down from the conscious individual is not a person in miniature sitting in the psychic control-room, but an elaborate machinery at work. It is also an attempt to forestall the possibility that the description will really only be based on unrecognised and unexamined presuppositions about what human beings are. Instead, Freud's metapsychology rummages though and borrows from all sorts of other bodies of knowledge – the physics of forces, thermodynamics, fluid mechanics, electromagnetism, neuroanatomy, cellular biology, evolutionary biology. This ego which is no longer master of its own house is now to be described in terms which are quite simply *in*human.• The attraction the terms have is precisely in their distance from the traditional terms of the humanities – a distance which may mean they are capable of providing some new, unfamiliar and perhaps even very powerful ideas and frameworks. We should remember that '*as if*' by which Freud so often introduces his borrowings and the careful (if sometimes only initial) disclaimers: even if the terms of his descriptions are borrowed from the physical sciences, the systems he uses to describe them are

In the course of centuries the *naïve* self-love of men has had to submit to two major blows at the hands of science. The first was when they learnt that our earth was not the centre of the universe but only a tiny fragment of a cosmic system of scarcely imaginable vastness. This is associated in our minds with the name of Copernicus, though something similar had already been asserted by Alexandrian science. The second blow fell when biological research destroyed man's supposedly privileged place in creation and proved his descent from the animal kingdom and his ineradicable animal nature. This revaluation has been accomplished in our own day by Darwin, Wallace, and their predecessors, though not without the most violent contemporary opposition. But human megalomania will have suffered its third and most wounding blow from the psychological research of the present time which seeks to prove to the ego that it is not even master in its own house, but must content itself with scanty information of what is going on unconsciously in its mind. We psychoanalysts were not the first and not the only ones to utter this call to introspection; but it seems to be our fate to give it its most forcible expression and to support it with empirical material which affects every individual. (Lecture 18, 'Fixation to Traumas – 'The Unconscious', *Introductory Lectures on Psychoanalysis* (1916–17), vol.16, pp. 284–85)

nevertheless not to be confused with the physical organism itself. After the early (and abandoned) 'Project for a Scientific Psychology', at least, their purpose is to draw on bodies of knowledge which are not humanistic, and which do not start from and take for granted the human being, but seek to explain it in different terms.

Nevertheless, this is far from a complete expulsion, even with the second topography. Freud will often describe these psychic agencies in openly homuncular terms.• The superego in particular seems to invite such description, with its

As a frontier-creature, the ego tries to mediate between the world and the id, to make the id pliable to the world and, by means of its muscular activity, to make the world fall in with the wishes of the id. In point of fact it behaves like the physician during an analytic treatment: it offers itself, with the attention it pays to the real world, as a libidinal object to the id, and aims at attaching the id's libido to itself. It is not only a helper to the id; it is also a submissive slave who courts his master's love. Whenever possible, it tries to remain on good terms with

> the id; it clothes the id's *Ucs.* commands with its *Pcs.* rationalisations; it pretends that the id is showing obedience to the admonitions of reality, even when in fact it is remaining obstinate and unyielding; it disguises the id's conflicts with reality and, if possible, its conflicts with the superego too. In its position midway between the id and reality, it only too often yields to the temptation to become sycophantic, opportunist and lying, like a politician who sees the truth but wants to keep his place in popular favour. (*The Ego and the Id* (1923), p. 56).

functions of judge and critic which it so frequently exercises with harshness and cruelty. Sometimes it is hard not to slip into it. If the title of the paper on 'The Economic Problem of Masochism' (1924d, the year after the introduction of the term superego) suggests its emphasis on metapsychological description, the paper itself finds itself returning to its arresting depiction of ego and superego as themselves masochist and sadist, locked in a vicious dance around each other.

A related problem arises with the id, and the way in which Freud frequently describes in terms of a deep primordiality – that is, not as something which comes into existence in the course of an individual's development, along with the rest of the psyche, but something which is in a sense already there, a repository of the most primitive (or alternatively, most infantile), deepest and truest kernel of the self.• But to picture the id in this way is little more than a disguised version of a homuncular argument, as it finds its explanation of how the psyche comes to be in a miniature *primitive* psyche which has always been there at its heart.

> It is probable that thinking was originally unconscious, in so far as it went beyond mere ideational presentations and was directed to the relations between impressions of objects, and that it did not acquire further qualities, perceptible to consciousness, until it became bound to verbal residues.*
>
> [Freud's note:]
> *In the same way, a nation whose wealth rests on the exploitation of the produce of its soil will yet set aside certain areas for reservation in their original state and for protection from the changes brought about by civilization. (E. g. Yellowstone Park.) ('Formulations on the Two Principles of Mental Functioning' (1911b), p. 221)

Freud's metapsychology, then, is incomplete, and not consistent. One can often feel that, far from leading to a complete expulsion of homuncular explanations and humanistic presuppositions, the declaration of their expulsion is precisely what lets them continue their presence in Freud's writing, as if invisible while still in full view.

The inconstant subject

Freud is inconsistent – radically inconsistent. Side by side, at one and the same time, and with an ever-shifting balance, we find both the most radical rethinking of what the human subject might be and some of the familiar commonplaces of the time. We find declarations that a particular line of thought is to be abandoned, and yet that same line of thought continues under the cloak of invisibility that the very declaration provided. We find hypotheses introduced as speculation, and then, after repetition and development, coming to be treated as though the very familiarity they had gained were enough guarantee.

There are a number of reasons for this inconsistency, and why it is neither simply an indicator of the bankruptcy of Freud's project nor something to be explained away. On the contrary, it is central to the entire Freudian project, a point we shall miss entirely if we try to turn what he is doing into a complete and rigorously consistent system. Our task here, and precisely in order to appreciate the radicality of what Freud is doing and its implications, is neither simply to upbraid him for that inconsistency nor to try to correct it, but to focus on it as a central necessity of his project.

The most obvious thing to say about it – the weakest, too, but no less necessary for that – is that we are after all speaking about a huge body of texts produced over more than four decades. It is not only hardly surprising that Freud's views would change during this time: it is hardly likely that they wouldn't, especially given his insistence that the very business of a science is to raise and try out hypotheses; abandoning, replacing, or modifying them when needed.

But to leave it there sounds like apologetics. We can and should go further than that. More importantly, this inconsistency is *perfectly consistent with and even a necessary conclusion from his very premises*. Freud is, after all, pointing out how the data of consciousness are always necessarily inconsistent. Consciousness's attempts to explain itself in its own terms – and that cannot help but include psychology and psychoanalysis, at the very moment at which they make their different claims to scientificity – inevitably meet the blind spots, the silences and the hesitations to which Freud gives the name 'unconscious'. A consistent psychoanalysis, or any science of the psyche, is inconceivable, for the same reason that a consistent psyche is. What sets such a science apart from other branches of knowledge, as we have seen, is that its very object *is* the subject: what it studies is what is *doing* the studying, and the gaze is always on its own gazing. In such a situation, it is not only the object that is inconsistent, but the very knowing is itself based on that inconsistency, as its condition of possibility. This is why psychoanalysis is not a form of epistemological nihilism: instead of saying *All knowledge is inconsistent, so there can be no real knowledge of anything*, it says *The psyche and all it does, including its knowing, in all its accuracy and in all the concreteness of its effects, are made possible only through the radical inconsistency at its heart*.

If the ego can never quite be master of its own house, neither can psychoanalysis. The analysis always threatens to get away from the psychoanalyst, to say things about the analyst behind the analyst's back. It has often been pointed out[7] that reading a case history like 'Dora' ('Fragment of an Analysis of a Case of Hysteria' (1905a), is like reading one of those Henry James narratives in which the narrator is blissfully unaware of the real significance of what she or he is saying, and of the extent of her or his own active role in the events told: what Dora thinks of Freud seems to be clearer to Freud's reader, and even to his very narrative, than it is to Freud himself. The texts of psychoanalysis may themselves display precisely the sorts of hesitation, revision, even disarray, that

[The dream of Irma's injection carries the exculpation that] *I* was not to blame for Irma's pains, since she herself was to blame for them by refusing to accept my solution. *I* was not concerned with Irma's pains, since they were of an organic nature and quite incurable by psychological treatment. Irma's pains could be satisfactorily explained by her widowhood ... which *I* had no means of altering. Irma's pains had been caused by Otto giving her an incautious injection of an unsuitable drug – a thing *I* should never have done. Irma's pains were the result of an injection with a dirty needle ... – whereas *I* never did any harm with my injections. I noticed, it is true, that these explanations of Irma's pains (which agreed in exculpating me) were not entirely consistent with one another, and indeed they were mutually exclusive. The whole plea – for the dream was nothing else – reminded one vividly of the defence put forward by the man who was charged by one of his neighbours with having given him back a borrowed kettle in a damaged condition. The defendant asserted first, that he had given it back undamaged; secondly, that the kettle had a hole in it when he borrowed it; and thirdly, that he had never borrowed a kettle from his neighbour at all. So much the better: if only a single one of these three lines of defence were to be accepted as valid, the man would have to be acquitted. (*The Interpretation of Dreams* (1900), vol. 4, pp. 119–20)

mark secondary revision and repression in the clinical analyses they recount. The intermingling of metapsychological and homuncular description is precisely the sort of 'kettle-logic' Freud so acutely points out elsewhere, even in his own behaviour. • Footnotes can indicate the sort of material which can neither be left out nor integrated with the text in which it is embedded, and so remains hovering somewhere on the peripheries of vision,

on the margins of the text. The 'Wolf Man' case history ('From the History of an Infantile Neurosis' (1918)) is meant to be the vindication of Freud's views against the recent heresies of Jung and Rank, but the footnotes and revisions it gathers in the course of subsequent editions show that the matter is far from closed to Freud's – or, as it turns out, the Wolf Man's – satisfaction. The last of his books Freud saw through the press, *Moses and Monotheism* (1939)• has the most extraordinary structure of all, which we can

MOSES, HIS PEOPLE AND MONOTHEISTIC RELIGION
PART II
SUMMARY AND RECAPITULATION

The part of this study which follows cannot be given to the public without extensive explanations and apologies. For it is nothing other than a faithful (and often word-for-word) repetition of the first part [of the third Essay], abbreviated in some of its critical inquiries and augmented by additions relating to the problem of how the special character of the Jewish people arose. I am aware that a method of exposition such as this is no less inexpedient than it is inartistic. I myself deplore it unreservedly. Why have I not avoided it? The answer to that is not hard for me to find, but it is not easy to confess. I found myself unable to wipe out the traces of the work's origin, which was in any case unusual.

... Unluckily an author's creative power does not always obey his will: the work proceeds as it can, and often presents itself to the author as something independent or even alien. (*Moses and Monotheism: Three Essays* (1939), pp. 103, 104)

attribute only partly to the great difficulty of the personal and political circumstances in which it was written, four years during which Germany annexed

Austria and the aged and seriously ill Freud was forced to flee to England. As the editors of the Standard Edition describe it, the book is made up of 'three essays of greatly differing length, two prefaces, both situated at the beginning of the third essay, and a third preface situated half-way through that same essay, constant recapitulations and repetitions' (*Moses and Monotheism* (1939), p. 4). This is material whose recalcitrance is everywhere in the very shape of the text itself.

Such cases are, of course, partly a matter of the limits of an author's powers. Yet there is more at stake in them than this. What they point to is not just the possibility that a certain body of knowledge is not yet complete, or that it is uncompletable because of a fundamental error in the assumptions with which it began. Instead, *metapsychological description is and must be itself inconsistent – and that this, far from this being a crippling weakness, is the very thing that opens up new and quite radical possibilities.*

We must be quite clear about the implications of this. Inconsistency is not a malfunction or a sign of psychic ill health. It is not just the hysterical or neurotic subject that is inconsistent, while all around them the healthy and well-balanced have achieved that elusive psychic consistency. The *subject itself –* any subject – is inconsistent, as a condition of being a subject in the first place. What distinguishes Little Hans is not that he is caught in a double bind whereas others are not. *The double bind*, psychoanalysis suggests, *is a basic and irreducible structure of the psyche*. One does not solve double binds; one lives with them. They are not so much dissolved as managed, in a pragmatic, *ad hoc* way, with whatever happens to be at hand. What has happened in Hans's case is that by a largely fortuitous series of events, certain of the ways in which the boy has tried to manage those conflicting demands have multiplied them in ways which are less and less sustainable and functional. Rather than make the double bind bearable, they have become a panic-stricken retreat. From the earliest, what Freud offers is not the promise of some sort of psychic reconciliation, but something much more modest: the possibility of managing the irreconcilable in a bearable way.•

> When I have promised my patients help or improvement by means of a cathartic treatment I have often been faced by this objection: 'Why, you tell me yourself that my illness is probably connected with my circumstances and the events of my life. You cannot alter these in any way. How do you propose to help me, then?' And I have been able to make this reply: 'No doubt fate would find it easier than I do to relieve you of your illness. But you will be able to convince yourself that there is much to be gained if we succeed in transforming your hysterical misery into common unhappiness. With a mental life that has been restored to health you will be better armed against that unhappiness'. ('The Psychotherapy of Hysteria', *Studies on Hysteria* (1895), p. 305)

The non-existent unconscious

The new topography of ego, id, and superego emphasises that 'the unconscious' is not a name for a system. All it now names, at most, is an aggregate of things whose only common feature would be their attribute of unconsciousness. And yet in a sense, the new topography has left this substantive and systemic use of the term in tact. What it has disqualified is *the conscious*: in place of a single agency which would be the seat of consciousness, what we now have is two agencies, both of which are made up of processes which are both conscious *and* unconscious. Certain processes which the first topography happily assigned to 'the unconscious' pure and simple now get reassigned to the ego and the superego. What is left as the id is not so much a radical redefinition – as the other two agencies are – but a sort of distillation of the unconscious:• as the diagrams Freud sometimes draws show, he often conceives of it as the most deeply unconscious parts of the old unconscious.

You will not expect me to have much to tell you that is new about the id apart from its new name. (Lecture 31, 'The Dissection of the Psychical Personality', *New Introductory Lectures on Psychoanalysis* (1933a), p. 73)

It is not quite true to see the id as identical to the *Ucs.* of the old topography: if the system *Ucs.* is made up almost entirely of what has been repressed, the id is also a reservoir of libido and the energies of the drives, as we shall see in the next chapter. But these new aspects are themselves also profoundly unconscious and quite unamenable to direct representation to consciousness.

We should be clear about the very particular nature of this hypothesis of an unconscious, and about why it must remain beyond simple direct demonstration. The unconscious is not an entity, like any other except for the one fact that it is unknown. Neither is it even enough to say that it is some sort of entity which is in principle *unknowable*: something hidden, secret, existing in some transcendent realm inaccessible to our mortal logic. (That would turn the unconscious into a theological category.) Freud will state, over and over, that the unconscious is an *assumption*: one makes it because with it all sorts of data, which would otherwise be incoherent and without meaning, suddenly reveal themselves to be intelligible, and useful in the analysis.•

[The assumption of an unconscious] is *necessary* because the data of consciousness have a very large number of gaps in them; both in healthy and in sick people psychical acts often occur which can be explained only by presupposing other acts, of which, nevertheless, consciousness affords no evidence. These not only include parapraxes and dreams in healthy people, and everything described as a psychical symptom or an obsession in the sick; our most personal daily experience acquaints us with ideas that come into our head we do not know from where, and with intellectual conclusions arrived at we do not know how. All these conscious acts remain disconnected and unintelligible if we insist upon claiming that every mental act that occurs in us must also necessarily be experienced by us through consciousness; on the other hand, they fall into a demonstrable connection if we interpolate between them the unconscious acts which we have inferred. ('The Unconscious' (1915d), pp. 166–167)

[W]e call a psychical process unconscious whose existence we are obliged to assume – for some such reason as that we infer it from its effects – but of which we know nothing. (Lecture 31, 'The Dissection of the Psychical Personality', *New Introductory Lectures on Psychoanalysis* (1933a), p. 102)

There is a conclusion we can draw from this. It is one which Freud himself does not make consistently: even in the later work, where the new topography of ego, id, and superego seems designed to put to rest that tendency to turn the unconscious into something substantial, a second or deeper version of consciousness, homuncular arguments crop up frequently – if anything, with even more frequency, as if their ostensible banishment had led to a disavowed proliferation. Nevertheless, alongside those arguments, rubbing shoulders with them, we will find a different view, which is implicit in and a strictly logical consequence of Freud's very premises. To put it in its most lapidary and para-doxical form, it is simply that *the unconscious does not exist.*

The 'Wolf Man' case history ('From the History of an Infantile Neurosis' (1918)) – so called because of the centrality to Freud's analysis of a recurrent dream of wolves his patient had in childhood – is one of Freud's most impor-tant, meant as a summation of his methods and a refutation of the various here-sies which were beginning to appear in psychoanalysis. The whole analysis revolves around Freud's analytic reconstruction of a *primal scene*, which in this case is the infant's inadvertent sight of its parents engaged in sex. Like the hypothesis of the unconscious itself, the justification for the primal scene is not that it can in any way be brought into direct view or even recollection (it hap-pens, after all, in early infancy), but that it makes sense of a lot of things which without it remain scattered and with-out pattern.• In his discussion of this, Freud even goes so far as to suggest that it may not describe an actual event at all, but a later and retrospective con-struction: the point is not that it hap-pened, but that everything takes place precisely *as if* it had happened. The primal scene does not need to exist as any positive event for it to have its effect. That it may, presumably, exist is irrelevant to its effect. What has effect in the primal scene is not its existence as a documentable event on a timeline; it works in just the same way even if it should be fantasy. In as much as its effec-tivity is concerned, the primal scene does not exist.•

The view, then, that we are putting up for discussion is as follows. It maintains that scenes from early infancy, such as are brought up by an exhaustive analysis of neuroses ..., are not reproductions of real occurrences, to which it is possible to ascribe an influence over the course of the patient's later life and over the formation of his symp-toms. It considers them rather as products of the imagina-tion, which find their instigation in mature life, which are intended to serve as some kind of symbolic representa-tion of real wishes and interests, and which owe their ori-gin to a regressive tendency, to a turning-away from the tasks of the present. If that is so, we can of course spare ourselves the necessity of attributing such a surprising amount to the mental life and intellectual capacity of children of the tenderest age....

Perhaps what the child observed was not copulation between his parents but copulation between animals, which he then displaced on to his parents, as though he had inferred that his parents did things in the same way. ('From the History of an Infantile Neurosis' (1918a), p. 49, 57)

I may disregard the fact that it was not possible to put [the behaviour of the four-year-old child towards the reactivated primal scene] into words until twenty years afterwards;

for all the effects that we traced back to the scene had already been manifested in the form of symptoms, obsessions, etc., in the patient's childhood and long before the analysis. It is also a matter of indifference in this connection whether we choose to regard it as a primal *scene* or a primal *phantasy*. ('From the History of an Infantile Neurosis' (1918), p. 120, fn. 1)

Freud comes to exactly the same conclusion in another article from this time, on a sado-masochistic childhood fantasy often reported in cases of hysteria or obsessional neuroses. The final form the fantasy takes, the way it presents itself to the one who fantasises it, is that *A child is being beaten*. There is something quite impersonal and non-committal about it (who is being beaten? by whom?), and yet it is accompanied by an obvious pleasure. It is not too hard to reconstruct the first phase this final form hides, where we can see the action clearly and understand the sadistic nature of the pleasure: *My father is beating a child whom I hate because he is my rival, the one who has replaced me in my parents' affections*. But neither is there generally any difficulty for the patient to admit this level of the fantasy. Why then should it be disguised in such a non-committal way? We must suspect that there is some other emotive charge at work here as well – one which we would pass over too quickly if we see only the first and the last phase, and one which has been so well disavowed as to be all but invisible. Between these two phases, Freud argues, we must hypothesise another. That my father is beating this child gives me enjoyment; I must be bad, and in order to retain the love of my parents must be punished in turn: the missing *masochistic* second stage is *I am being beaten by my father*. But this phase is never remembered, never traceable back to a specific event or memory. It has precisely the same logic as the primal scene: an event which never took place in any historical timeline, but which is at the heart of the consistency of the fantasy and its desire.•

This second phase is the most important and the most momentous of all. But we may say of it in a certain sense that it has never had a real existence. It is never remembered, it has never succeeded in becoming conscious. It is a construction of analysis, but it is no less a necessity on that account. ('"A Child is Being Beaten": A Contribution to the Study of the Origin of Sexual Perversions', (1919), p. 185)

We may follow exactly the same logic with the unconscious. As Freud says, the unconscious is a function of the gaps in the data of consciousness. In the course of an analysis, one does not fill in those gaps and make the unconscious conscious: one constructs a different chain of conscious reasoning that would produce the same results. Far from being an entity, or even from having any sort of existence whatsoever outside of its assumption, the unconscious is, precisely, a name for the *in*consistency of what exists. The radicality of Freud's logic is that this inconsistency that is the unconscious is not only hypothesised as *not* existing, but in this very non-existence it provides the possibility of there being such a thing as a self.

For that to sound less odd, consider memory. Memory is full of holes. Even someone with eidetic memory – so-called 'photographic' memory – does not remember absolutely everything.[8] This is not an accident which happens to memory, or the flaws of a human mind which tends to forget where it should remember, but a logical and necessary property of memory itself: without it, there would be no such thing as memory.

Even mechanical memory devices have this property: a database, say, or something as simple as a card index. In order to use a database to remember anything, first of all a decision must be made about just what is to be remembered and what is not. Some things need to be remembered, others do not. I run a shop, and I am using a database to make an inventory. There are certain things I need to know about the products on the shelves: each type of product, how many I have of each, what they cost me and what I sell them for, where I got them from and where I can get more from when I run out, when I got them and how long I can stock them before they deteriorate or can no longer be sold, and so on. There are other aspects of them, just as much objectively part of them as all of these, which I am unlikely to put into a database of the products on the shelves: a spectroscopic analysis of the product, the weight and colour of the wrapping, the story of its invention, the current cost of shares in the company which manufactures them, and the name of its. If I were to add these, I would not make the database any more useful to me, and quite probably less, because it would be bigger and would take longer to find the information I *do* need among the welter of it I don't. What makes the database work is its selectiveness. It acts as a memory of some things only because it chooses deliberately to forget others, to treat them as being of no importance, accidental and irrelevant. Its remembering, in short, is posited on the possibility of forgetting. Forgetting is not just an unfortunate accident or an inadequacy external to memory: it is at the very heart of memory. Without forgetting, nothing at all gets remembered.

This is the way in which we should think of the unconscious: a profound forgetting by which consciousness is possible. We need to take the full measure of that forgetting. What is unconscious is not something that has been forgotten on the immediate surface of consciousness, but nevertheless still remembered at some deeper level, preserved for access by whoever gains the right key. That is not forgetting: it's remembering, behind a firewall. Neither is the unconscious even an obliteration, no matter how thoroughgoing, because for something to be obliterated it needs to have existed previously, even though there may now be no access to that past. What is forgotten, in contrast, in the sense in which we are trying to think it through here, is never simply present, and *never has been*. It is a thorough, radical and absolute outside to memory. This is why the unconscious is, as Freud says, a function of the gaps in consciousness, and why, indeed, the data of consciousness must always have gaps in them, as a condition of their being conscious. The unconscious is not what *fills in* those gaps: fill them in and what one has is just another conscious thought, freely available to remembrance and no longer sunk in forgetfulness. Analysis does not bring the unconscious to light; as Freud says, it constructs a conscious chain of reasoning which would produce the same result. The logic of *as if* is being used in a quite radically new sense here.

One must be careful here. In dream analysis, for example, Freud begins with what he calls the *manifest* dream, which is the dream remembered on waking or recounted for the analyst, and from that Freud proceeds to reconstruct the *latent dream thoughts* which the dream signifies – its meaning.•

Two separate functions may be distinguished in mental activity during the construction of a dream: the production of the [latent] dream-thoughts and their transformation into the [manifest] content of the dream. The dream-thoughts are entirely rational and are constructed with an expenditure of all the psychical energy of which we are capable. ... However many interesting and puzzling questions the dream-thoughts may involve, such questions have, after all, no special relation to dreams and do not call for treatment among the problems of dreams. On the other hand, the second function of mental activity during dream-construction, the transformation of the uncon-scious thoughts into the content of the dream, is peculiar to dream-life and characteristic of it. This dream-work proper diverges further from our picture of waking thought than has been supposed even by the most determined depreciator of psychical functioning during the formation of dreams. The dream-work is not simply more careless, more irrational, more forgetful and more incomplete than waking thought; it is completely different from it qualita-tively and for that reason not immediately comparable with it. It does not think, calculate or judge in any way at all; it restricts itself to giving things a new form. (*The Interpretation of Dreams* (1900), vol. 5, pp. 506–07)

But this distinction between manifest and latent is *not* simply between conscious surface and unconscious depth. The latent dream thoughts revealed by the analysis are, Freud emphasises, thoughts like any other; they may not have been conscious until their revelation by the analysis, but they are entirely rational, and con-structed in just the same way as any waking thought. Where the uncon-scious is to be found, though, is in the *dream-work*, the process by which the dream thoughts are turned into the manifest dream, and that is a very differ-ent matter. The unconscious dream-work has no content at all, it is a sheer process of transformation.

Freud will often speak of the psychoanalytic cure as a lifting of repression, a substitution of conscious material for unconscious, but, as the famous image of the draining of the Zuider Zee implies,• this is not a matter of eliminating the

Where id was, there ego shall be. It is a work of culture – not unlike the draining of the Zuider Zee. (Lecture 31, 'The Dissection of the Psychical Personality', *New Introductory Lectures on Psychoanalysis* (1933a), p. 80)

sea of the unconscious, just of relocating the shoreline. When one does this, what one finds there is land, very much like the land one already knows, and cultivatible in all the same ways; but just beyond the bound-ary of the dikes, the utter foreignness of the sea remains. We should not think of that matter which psychoanalysis draws out of the depths as actually *being* the unconscious – the unconscious, we remember, is not a thing at all, some-thing to fill a gap or appear where there was a silence: it *is* those gaps, those silences, in the very depths of their forgetting. What psychoanalysis does is not so much make the unconscious visible as *replace* unconscious thought with conscious thought.•

And the odd implication of this is that the conscious thought material which

The construction of a symptom is a substitute for *something else that did not happen.* (Lecture 18, 'Fixation to Traumas – The Unconscious', *Introductory Lectures on Psychoanalysis* (1916–17), vol.16, p. 280: emphasis added)

stands in the place of what was unconscious, and which thus represents something that remains obdurately unrepresentable, need not – indeed *cannot* – bear any real resemblance to what it represents. It too is 'entirely rational', like the latent dream thoughts one reconstructs behind the manifest dream, to which the unconscious it represents remains foreign territory, not even comparable. It is, after all, produced in and by the sophisticated and intricately rational technique of reading that is psychoanalysis, to *stand in the place of* something unconscious. Its relation to what it stands in place of is not one of any necessary resemblance (which would be impossible to determine), but of *hypothesis*: it all works *as if* this were the case.•

Should we not take this as a general description of psycho-

... so far as my experience hitherto goes, these scenes from infancy are not reproduced during the treatment as recollections, they are the products of construction. ('From the History of an Infantile Neurosis' (1918), pp. 50–51)

analysis, too, and the way *all* of its terms work? Psychoanalysis is concerned with how the psyche comes to be there, how it emerges from what it is not – and with how that is never just a single moment on a timeline or in a history, done once and for all, but a gesture that is repeated endlessly, at every instant. Psychoanalysis is concerned with the liminal, those paradoxical and impossible moments on the edge between *being* and *not being*, and the way in which that liminality is oddly at the very heart of any possible subject, as its very structure. The unconscious is both within me and yet foreign territory, thought that I do not think but is nevertheless the very possibility of what I do think. We could even go as far as to say that the thing which, above all, distinguishes psychoanalysis from psychology is that while psychology takes the subject as an object in a way which is modelled on the empiricism and positivism of the other sciences, psychoanalysis focuses instead, and uniquely, on the strange and often paradoxical logic of emergence. As we shall see, above and beyond its theory of the individual human subject, it is this logic of emergence that gives psychoanalysis its purchase on questions of the social and the cultural. Psychoanalysis is thus something other than an application of an individualist psychology to wider questions, even though those are at times precisely the terms in which Freud will phrase it. It unravels a pre-individual, inhuman logic that underpins both individual and social, as the condition for both.

Psychoanalysis deals with the moment of emergence, with the liminal and what is not quite there, not quite graspable. As a result, all of its terms are necessarily ever so slightly *wrong*. They do not resemble what they name, any more than the chain of conscious reasoning one reconstructs out of the latent dream or the symptom is the unconscious as such. Psychoanalysis does not bring the contents of the unconscious to light, like those bizarre and unknown deep-sea fish dragged up by trawlers; it constructs a chain of conscious reasoning which is nothing like the unconscious, but which produces the same effects. All the terms of psychoanalysis must obey this law, from *unconscious* on. All of them are ways of starting, as we must, on this side of consciousness, and of peering back into what we cannot ever see, those moments at which consciousness is profoundly, absolutely absent. In their very nature, what they cannot ever hope to grasp or express is that profound absence, that *not yet*, of consciousness.

The unconscious does not exist. This is a strange and seemingly fragile hypothesis, but in its very fragility it opens up possibilities of thinking the individual subject as already social, through and through. Let us follow this question of emergence in more detail: first with the emergence of the individual human subject, and then, in the final chapter, to look at how Freud turns this logic of emergence onto the social and cultural.

How is it that something like an individual subject develops, already open everywhere to the world around it? And if such a subject is already irreducibly split against and within itself, is the very idea of *the human* similarly split? These two questions will inform our next chapter.

Notes to Chapter 1

[1]Freud cites Strümpell to this effect in *Introductory Lectures on Psychoanalysis* (1916–17), p. 87.

[2]Here, we can see Freud describing circles around the then well-known work of his close contemporary, the German philosopher Hans Vaihinger (1852–1933). Vaihinger's 1911 book, *The Philosophy of 'As If'*, argues that once we get beyond the immediacy of direct feeling and sensation, knowledge is an essentially fictional series of explanatory constructions. We accept one version over another simply because it works better, or because it is more *useful* to act as if the universe did in fact work that way. Freud is, in general, fairly happy to accept this pragmatism as a description of scientific method (see, for example, *The Question of Lay Analysis* (1926b), p. 194), but is less happy with it when exactly the same reasoning is used to support religion's claims to be beyond the claims of logic and reason (in that context, in the 1927 *The Future of an Illusion* he declares it a rather desperate argument (pp. 28–29)).

[3]The double bind is thus essentially a question of the *ethical*. The example philosophy so often takes as the epitome of the ethical dilemma is the story of Abraham's sacrifice of Isaac. God demands of Abraham that he sacrifice Isaac, his only and dearly beloved son. This is not just an extreme test of Abraham's obedience: the demand is a double bind, because whatever Abraham does he is guaranteed to *disobey* God. On the one hand, he can refuse to kill Isaac, and thus disobey the explicit command God has just given him; on the other hand, he can kill Isaac, and thus disobey God's injunction against murder. And on top of that, he has to act now, without a moment's hesitation, for any delay will be seen as doubt and disobedience too. (See, for example, Jacques Derrida's *The Gift of Death* (1995), particularly Chapters Three and Four.) It is significant that this basic logical structure, which opens up the entire question and possibility of the ethical, should be also at

the very heart of Freud's model of the psyche. Lacan later argues that the status of the unconscious is ethical rather than ontological (Lacan (1977b), p. 33) or psychological (Lacan (1977a), p. 302).

[4]Freud's explanation here needs examination too. 'Even supposing,' he continues, 'that we have a complete knowledge of the aetiological factors that decide a given result, nevertheless what we know about them is only their quality, and not their relative strength. Some of them are suppressed by others because they are too weak, and they therefore do not affect the final result. But we never know beforehand which of the determining factors will prove the weaker or the stronger. We only say at the end that those which succeeded must have been the stronger' ('The Psychogenesis of a Case of Homosexuality in a Woman,' (1920a), p. 168). But this last sentence risks the logical circularity of the famous phrase, 'the survival of the fittest' (which is Spencer's rather than Darwin's), in that it attributes the success of those that succeeded to an innate strength, as if all that was contributed by the actual events which led to the success was the confirmation of what was there all along and the opportunity for it to emerge. It inverts the actual logical chain: instead of saying that we call certain factors 'strong' *because* and only because they succeed, it offers a pseudo-explanation for their success by saying that success is *due to* that 'strength'. What Freud's argument requires us to keep in mind, here and in the entire logic of the symptom and the primal scene, is that those factors which succeeded *did not have to* succeed – that their success was a contingent rather than a necessary outcome.

[5]See, for example, *The Ego and the Id* (1923), p. 24; *New Introductory Lectures on Psychoanalysis* (1933a), pp. 76–77; *The Question of Lay Analysis* (1926b), pp. 195–96; 'An Outline of Psychoanalysis' (1940), p. 145.

[6]For the most part, Freud does not make any clear distinctions among all three terms, *ideal ego*, *ego-ideal*, and *superego*. While he seems to replace *ego-ideal* with the coinage *superego* in 1923, he makes a distinction between them in the *New Introductory Lectures* of 1933. There, while both terms describe the ways in which the ego measures itself up, *superego* refers to the internalisation of authority, and is a matter of threat and fear (the superego is formed under the threat of castration during the dissolution of the Oedipus complex), but *ego-ideal*, on the other hand, is reserved for the rather different emulations which come about through love or admiration (Lecture 31, 'The Dissection of the Psychical Personality' (1933a), pp. 64–65). Later writers sometimes wanted to make clear distinctions among the three terms. For Lacan, for example, *ideal ego* refers to that specular mirror image I measure myself up against and identify with (and which is hence part of the imaginary), whereas the *ego-ideal* is the point from which I am seen and judged (and hence belongs to the symbolic order of the Law and of language): see, for example, Lacan, 1988, pp. 140–41.

[7]See, for example, Bernheimer and Kahane (1990), *In Dora's Case: Freud – Hysteria – Feminism*, and in particular Neil Hertz's contribution (Hertz (1990a), pp. 221–22).

[8]Jorge Luis Borges's story 'Funes the Memorious' asks what a perfect memory might be, and gives the answer: *paralysis*. Borges's Funes is incapacitated by an accident, and as if in compensation finds that he is now capable of remembering everything, in every detail: every movement of every leaf on the tree outside his window, every occasion on which he has remembered any movement of any leaf, every remembering of remembering. Borges's narrator concludes that, drowned in an ocean of impressions, Funes is no longer capable of very much reasoning, or of the abstract thought which requires one to select – and forget – from that welter. John Frow uses this example to make the point of the necessary relationship of memory and forgetting (Frow, 1997).

TWO **SEXUALITY**

Forgetting

I forget.

I run, I work, I see, I read, *even* I think: *in short*, I perform an action. *But* I forget? *Who could this* I *that forgets possibly be?*

First of all, the verb has to be intransitive: I forget, *not* I forget this, *or* I forget that. *As soon as I name an object, I have remembered it.*

I can say I forgot to pay the bill, *but that is in the past tense, and there is no danger of paradox*: I had *forgotten, but now, at this moment of speaking, I* certainly do remember about the bill – and I remember that I had forgotten it as well. Nevertheless, something remains opaque. What I do not remember is that forgetting itself, the act of forgetting as distinct from its consequences. I cannot catch myself in the act of forgetting, even in retrospect. Even in retrospect, my forgetting is a gap in which there is nothing, not even me. What is forgotten is also the one who forgets.

I can say I forget to pay bills, which seems at first to get us back to the present tense, but in fact does something quite different. What it says is that in the past I have forgotten to pay bills, and with such a frequency that I expect it to happen in the future too. I forget to pay bills describes a loop around the present, moving from past to future and back again without really touching on the present in which, still forgotten, some particular bill I can't quite name at the moment might be waiting to be paid.

I can even say I forget to pay the bill if it is part of a narrative in which all events are described in the present tense of their occurrence: I leave, forgetting to pay the bill. Not until I am on the other side of town do I remember. But this would really be just a past tense under the thinnest of disguises. The events themselves clearly have a succession, in which that forgetting flashes momentarily forward to a future moment in which the remembering will occur. That moment may be explicit in the narrative (Not until I am on the other side of town ...), but even that is not necessary. Even if there is no narrated point at which that recognition comes to me, the remembering which will recognise that I forgot to pay must be some time after my leaving.

So to name something as a forgetting (I forget, or I forgot this) already implies at least two instances, neither of which need be a precise instant on a timeline: there is a moment at which the forgetting occurs (there in the cafe, as I am gathering up my belongings and heading for the door), and there is a moment somewhere on the other side of town when I recognise that the first has been a forgetting. Without the first, obviously, no forgetting occurs. But without the second, in which everything is immediately contaminated by memory, the forgetting and what is forgotten are never known as such. This is why the utterance I forget this or I forget that is never really present tense, despite the grammatical status of the verb. To forget something never happens in a now; or rather, it turns that now into a fragmented serial moment, a loop reaching into the past and the future. To forget something is thus an imperfect forgetting, one which draws on an imperfect remembering to know at least something of what has been forgotten, and thus to rescue at least part of it from forgetting.

As with the something that is forgotten, so too at every point for the I who forgets. To say I forget this or I forgot this is to perform the same circuit of loss and recovery on the I. What I forget is not only a thing or event, but my having experienced it. With the forgetting, something of myself is forgotten too, to be reclaimed in small part by my knowing it as forgotten. And yet at the same time, to say I forget is to assert that I as a residue which has not been forgotten, and which takes over as its own the very forgetting which eats away at it. The I is the subject that forgets, the active subject of the verb, only to the extent that it is what remains, a precipitate formed in and by that forgetting. The looped serial time of forgetting may be the very temporality of the psyche.

But could one not say exactly the same things throughout about forgetting pure and simple, whether or not its object is named? I forget implies an object, and precisely a forgotten one. Is not forgetting itself then forever imperfect to the extent that I can posit it?

What would a perfect, absolute forgetting be? It would have to be quite uncontaminated by memory, which is to say a forgetting which is no longer a forgetting of anything at all or by anyone at all, where there is not even forgetter or forgotten. It would have to be a forgetting without even the minimal remembering that could let it know itself as forgetting. That means it would have to be a doubled forgetting, a forgetting of forgetting, a forgetting which has forgotten even that it ever forgot anything.

Is there such a thing? Does it exist? Even to say that such a thing exists is to pull it out of its forgetting into the remembering of what is or has been or could be. The only answer has to be no, it does not exist. But this is the very question we asked of the unconscious, which also does not exist; and there, that non-existence was not the refutation of a faulty hypothesis but a precise statement of the paradoxical status of the unconscious. There is unconscious in all of us, but the unconscious does not exist: that is the radicality of Freud's discovery. Can we say something similar about this pure forgetting, which does not exist?

Indeed. That perfect forgetting, where there has not even been anything or anyone to forget, lies in the past for all of us. We all come from nothing.

[S]cience has so little to tell us about the origin of sexuality that we can liken the problem to a darkness into which not so much as a ray of a hypothesis has penetrated. In quite a different region, it is true, we do meet with such a hypothesis; but it is of so fantastic a kind – a myth rather than a scientific explanation – that I should not venture to produce it here, were it not that it fulfils precisely the one condition whose fulfilment we desire. For it traces the origin of an instinct to a *need to restore* an earlier state of things.

What I have in mind is, of course, the theory which Plato put into the mouth of Aristophanes in the *Symposium*, and which deals not only with the *origin* of the sexual instinct but also with the most important of its variations in relation to its object. 'The original human nature was not like the present, but different. In the first place, the sexes were originally three in number, not two as they are now; there was man, woman, and the union of the two ...' Everything about these primaeval men was double: they had four hands and four feet, two faces, two privy parts, and so on. Eventually Zeus decided to cut these people in two, 'like a sorb-apple which is halved for pickling'. After the division had been made, 'the two parts of man, each desiring their other half, came together, and threw their arms about one another eager to grow into one'. (*Beyond the Pleasure Principle* (1920b), pp. 57–58)

Let us just add one more thing to that, very briefly. In Beyond the Pleasure Principle, *Freud cites a famous myth which is precisely about the time of a perfect forgetting, before it is even possible to remember.• He retells it in the context of a question about the origins of sexuality, and also brings into the mix the tendency of the (death) drives to restore an earlier state of things. Forgetting, and a state before existence – what links these to sexuality?*

Sexuality:
Three Essays on the Theory of Sexuality (1905)

This was the most controversial of all of Freud's writings, with its insistence on the sexual feelings and interests of infants – though its argument about the perversions and inversions of the drive is just as radical a reframing of conceptual frameworks. That it is also the book he revised the most suggests the centrality he gave it and the topic of sexuality in his work. Each of the six editions that came out in his lifetime contained new materials and revisions intended to keep its argument current with recent developments in psychoanalytic thinking. Over the next 20 years, Freud would add sections on the sexual researches of children, the phases of development of the sexual organisation (with its distinction of oral, sadistic-anal and genital phases) and libido-theory, as well as some 70 footnotes (some of them more than a page long), and revisions to almost every page of the main text.

In the first of the essays, on 'The Sexual Aberrations', the terms Freud uses here – 'aberrations', 'deviation', 'inversion' (for homosexuality, male and female), 'perversion,' 'normal' behaviour – all come from the psychiatry and sexology of the late nineteenth century, but Freud uses them in a way which defuses their normativity and moralism. He does this by means of the concept of *drive*. Where instinct (*Instinkt*) is usually imagined as an innate and purely animal tendency which seeks the survival or reproduction of the organism, drive (*Trieb*) is more oblique. Drive seeks *satisfaction*, and that may not be at all the same thing. Satisfaction may have very little, if anything, to do with reproduction or even survival. The drive is not primarily reproductive, or even self-preservative. It may, and of course often does, result in procreation, but this is not its aim: if it achieves reproduction, it is because it aims elsewhere. This has the effect of undermining the biologism implied in the concept of instinct, and with it the idea that reproductive heterosexual behaviour is the natural, innate tendency of the organism. This argument is rehearsed in more detail in the following section of the present book.

The second of the essays is on 'Infantile Sexuality', a combination of words which outraged many of Freud's contemporaries. For Freud, sexuality is not something which emerges for the first time in puberty: until about the age of four or five, infancy is intensely charged with what he famously characterises as 'polymorphously perverse' sexual activities: sensual sucking, auto-stimulation of those bodily zones which yield pleasure (the mouth, the genitals, the anus – erogenous zones, in short). Between the ages of about three and five, the child is also faced for the first time with the double question of sexual difference and where babies come from. To make sense of these, it conducts its own researches and develops what are in effect its own theories of sexuality, fantasies that nevertheless may have a great effect on its later development.

The child's sexual development is *diphasic*, in two waves. From about five-years-old, the child's intense sexual curiosity goes into a period of latency, from which it re-emerges during 'The Transformations of Puberty', the topic of the third essay. This is when sexual differences become accentuated, and the child's sexuality tends to take on its final, adult features, in its choice of both object and aim. It is also the time at which the child's relationships with the parents are transformed, and the child must negotiate its way beyond its, until now, incestuous object choices (Freud did not use the term 'Oedipus complex' until 1910, so its appearances here are all in the later footnotes, but it is quite clear that this is the drama he is describing in even the earliest edition of the book).

The three essays are followed by a summary of the present state of psychoanalytic knowledge of sexuality.

I: Drive

Drive, instinct and stimulus

Unconsciousness is empty, radically empty, to the point where topographical metaphors (including even those of fullness and emptiness) no longer describe it adequately. And yet it is also an incessant dynamism and exchange, and an interplay of forces. What is the motor energy fuelling the various processes we have seen – repression, condensation, displacement, censorship, and so on? The concept of the *drive* is an attempt to think through these dynamic, economic aspects in the light of the paradoxical logic of the unconscious.

The word Freud gives to the motoric force behind all these processes is *Trieb*, which the Standard Edition's translation generally renders as *instinct*. But that translation runs a risk of obscuring a rather significant and generally consistent distinction in Freud's German, and in his thought. Instinct renders two quite different words: *Trieb* and *Instinkt*. *Instinkt* is in many ways the simpler of the two; it is also the one most familiar from the scientific literature of the day, and the one about which Freud has least to say. *Instinkt* refers to the purely inbuilt, automatic reflex arc we associate with animal behaviour: an animal is hungry, so it seeks food; when threatened, it flees. When speaking of the psyche and human behaviour, though, Freud almost inevitably uses *Trieb*. (The paper usually referred to in English as 'Instincts and their Vicissitudes', for example, is in German '*Triebe und Triebschicksale*'.) *Trieb* corresponds quite closely to the English word **drive**, in the sense of motive power or driving force – and this is quite a different matter from the idea of automatic behaviour carried in the term *Instinkt*. To retain that distinction, much English-language commentary on Freud now refers to *Trieb* as *drive*. I shall do that here too, though I will leave the Standard Edition's translation untouched when quoting – it simply needs to be kept in mind that the Standard Edition's use of *instinct* nearly always corresponds to that sense of *Trieb* and drive rather than the reflex arc of *Instinkt*. Unlike *instinct*, the drive is not purely animal, physical or bodily, but has a complex relationship to all of these.

Freud first uses the term in the 1905 *Three Essays on the Theory of Sexuality*.• Both here and in the 1915 'Instincts and their Vicissitudes',

> By an 'instinct' [*Trieb*] is provisionally to be understood the psychical representative of an endosomatic, continuously flowing source of stimulation, as contrasted with a 'stimulus', which is set up by *single* excitations coming from *without*. The concept of instinct is thus one of those lying on the frontier between the mental and the physical. ('The Sexual Aberrations', *Three Essays on the Theory of Sexuality* (1905c), p. 168)

which sums up much of this initial work on the drives, he begins with the similarities of drives to stimuli. We have seen that Freud is fond of the biological model, so, as a first approximation: the drive is just like a stimulus, except it comes from inside rather than outside the organism. Like stimuli, drives present the psyche with impulses to which it must react.•

But we almost immediately find one highly significant way in which drives and stimuli differ. Whereas the psyche can deal with external stimuli by means of the motor apparatus, say, which allows it to flee, it cannot do this with the drives, which it carries with it. An odd paradox: where the psyche can potentially deal with the impulse which comes from outside, it is powerless against the impulse from within itself, and precisely to the extent that it *is* internal. Already, just in the

> Let us try to give a content to [the concept of instinct [*Trieb*] by approaching it from different angles.[1]
>
> First, from the angle of physiology. This has given us the concept of a 'stimulus' and the pattern of the reflex arc ....
>
> What is the relation of 'instinct' [*Trieb*] to 'stimulus'? There is nothing to prevent our subsuming the concept of 'instinct' under that of 'stimulus' and saying that an instinct is a stimulus applied to the mind. But we are immediately set on our guard against *equating* instinct and mental stimulus. There are obviously other stimuli to the mind besides those of an instinctual kind, stimuli which behave far more like physiological ones. ...
>
> We have now obtained the material necessary for distinguishing between instinctual stimuli and other (physiological) stimuli that operate on the mind. In the first place, an instinctual stimulus does not arise from the external world but from within the organism itself. For this reason it operates differently upon the mind and different actions are necessary in order to remove it. Further, all that is essential in a stimulus is covered if we assume that it operates with a single impact, so that it can be disposed of by a single expedient action. A typical instance of this is motor flight from the source of stimulation. ... An instinct, on the other hand, never operates as a force giving a momentary impact but always as a *constant* one. ('Instincts and Their Vicissitudes' (1915b), p. 118)

juxtaposition of inside and outside and the almost immediate blurring of their boundary, we can again see the characteristic logic of the unconscious.

In a number of places, Freud will suggest that the drive is precisely a border concept, somewhere between the mental and the physical.• Sometimes he will see the drive as the mental representation of bodily processes; at other times, he will see it

> If now we apply ourselves to considering mental life from a *biological* point of view, an 'instinct' appears to us as a concept on the frontier between the mental and the somatic, as the psychical representative of the stimuli originating from within the organism and reaching the mind, as a measure of the demand made upon the mind

for work in consequence of its connection with the body. ('Instincts and Their Vicissitudes' (1915b), pp. 121–122)

An instinct can never become an object of consciousness – only the idea that represents the instinct can. Even in the unconscious, moreover, an instinct cannot be represented otherwise than by an idea. If the instinct did not attach itself to an idea or manifest itself as an affective state, we could know nothing about it. ('The Unconscious' (1915d), p. 177)

as what those mental processes represent (and thus available to us only through those representations).• Whichever way we take it, the drives themselves are profoundly unconscious. Their effects and affects are quite accessible to consciousness, of course – as Freud points out several times, while thought processes themselves may be conscious or unconscious, it makes little sense to think of affect as anything other than something which is experienced, which is to say conscious. Nevertheless, the drives themselves remain well below the waterline of consciousness. And as unconscious, they are thus not purely internal, in any simple juxtaposition with the externality of the stimulus. They share with everything else unconscious that rather uncanny property of being 'internal foreign territory', with all of its consequent blurring of distinctions between inside and outside, self and not-self. The value of Freud's initial analogy of drive and stimulus may not be that one is internal and the other external, but that for all its internality, drive too shares something of the externality of the stimulus.

If drive is a mental representative of bodily processes, it is not purely bodily. Bodily processes do not intrude directly into the psyche, but only through their representatives. If there are such things as purely autonomous instincts, reflex arcs such as those we imagine animals as having, they can have in themselves that no part in the psyche. What operates there is always and already different from the stimulus that gives rise to it. And yet at the same time, drive is not purely psychic: it is an intrusion into the psyche, or the representation within the psyche, of forces and demands which are not purely psychic, and which may even threaten to disrupt the psychic economy or equilibrium. From the very outset, the psyche is a mechanism called on to cope with the unforeseen, with what happens to it from outside itself, even if this outside should be nestled at its very heart. No wonder, then, that drives present themselves as implacable, demanding, out of my control: they drive me rather than I them. Once again, the psyche is posited on what is not properly or exclusively its own, and the most basic experience of the psyche is one of radical inconsistency. The psyche is not homogeneous, consistent with itself, unified, or a synthesis. It is a tension that is in principle unresolvable: *driven*, indeed, by what does not stop. While one can flee from threatening external stimuli, there can be no escape from the drive. Drive is implacable.•

We thus arrive at the essential nature of instincts in the first place by considering their main characteristics – their origin in sources of stimulation within the organism and their appearance as a constant force – and from this we deduce one of their further features, namely, that no actions of flight avail against them. ('Instincts and Their Vicissitudes' (1915b), p. 119)

Though drives may ultimately have their source in bodily processes, they diverge from them everywhere. Think of an infant at its mother's breast. On the one hand, the infant is satisfying a purely bodily need for food – an instinctual need, in that biological sense. It is subjected to all the internal and unpleasurable stimuli of hunger, which will vanish again once it has fed. On the other hand, though, it gains a different sort of satisfaction, because the action of suckling is itself pleasurable, quite apart from the question of food. The mouth and lips and tongue are exquisitely sensitive areas, as they have to be for the whole routine of feeding to work. But that sensitivity means that they are also capable of arousal and pleasure quite independently of what is happening in the digestive tract. Look at how frequently babies remain sucking after the hunger has gone, or the comfort a pacifier provides, or the baby who discovers that a part of its own body, its thumb, is capable of giving that pleasure.• The very areas of the body involved have changed. If the strictly instinctual satisfaction of hunger belong to the stomach, these new pleasures belong to the mouth and lips: they are no longer a

> Our study of thumb-sucking has already given us the three essential characteristics of an infantile sexual manifestation. At its origin it *attaches* itself to one of the vital somatic functions; it has as yet no sexual object, and is thus *auto-erotic*; and its sexual aim is dominated by an *erotogenic zone*. ('Infantile Sexuality', *Three Essays on the Theory of Sexuality* (1905c), pp. 182–83)

matter of depths, but of a bright ring of intense sensation on the surface of the body, where body meets world. These *erotogenic zones* are generally, but not always, focused on some aperture of the body – not surprisingly, a place of exchange where that geometry of insides and outsides becomes complex and unstable.[2]

This is the very model of a drive. Drives are attached to and have their source in bodily processes, but they peel away from these processes to exceed them everywhere (Figure 2.1). In this attachment and divergence, drives generate a sort of surplus, in the form of effects which can no longer be predicted from purely bodily needs and instinctual reflexes.[3]

Aim and object

Because drives everywhere part company with the somatic, the bodily source of a drive will tell us very little about the resultant drive. As a result, psychoanalysis will nominally have very little interest in those biological, physiological aspects – though, as we have seen, Freud continues to return to them as a source of model and metaphor. When he introduces the term 'drive' at the very beginning of the first of the 1905 *Three Essays on the Theory of Sexuality*, its first characterisation is not by source but by **object** and **aim** (again, see Figure 2.1).•

The distinction between object and aim is between *desired object* and *desired act*. Each of

> Let us call the person from whom sexual attraction proceeds the *sexual object* and the act towards which the instinct tends the *sexual aim*. ('The Sexual Aberrations', *Three Essays on the Theory of Sexuality* (1905c), pp. 135–36)

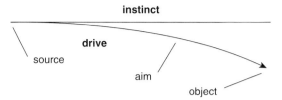

Figure 2.1

these can vary enormously. For an adult, the *object* of desire is generally an adult of the opposite or the same sex; but it may also, and less commonly, be a child, an animal, or even an inanimate object. The *act* aimed at may be the genital contact of sexual intercourse, but it may also be to see or touch (or be seen or touched by) the desired object, to punish or be punished, or to engage in sexual activity involving areas other than the genitals, such as the anus and the mouth. There may be secondary aims serving others, as with the caress that is the prelude to intercourse. Put object and aim together, each with their own possibilities for variation, and you have a good picture of the enormous variety of sexual behaviours.

Sexuality had been a burgeoning area of knowledge for medicine and psychiatry in the decade or so before the *Three Essays* – the bibliography to the Standard Edition lists many of these titles. Perhaps not surprisingly, though, the emphasis of this knowledge had been overwhelmingly on sexual pathology. The sexology of the 1890s is anchored in a firm normativity: the normal, true object is an adult of the other sex, and the normal, true aim is genital and ultimately reproductive intercourse. One does not have to look far to see a familiar moral discourse at work in this scientificity. Its standard term for variations from the heterosexual object is *inversion*; *perversions* are variations in aim. These are terms Freud takes over, too (the first of the *Three Essays* is called 'The Sexual Aberrations', after all), but we should not let that hide from us the sheer radicality and novelty of what he does with them. The framework into which he puts them, and the argument this lets him make about them, work to undermine that normativity in unexpected and radically new ways, even as he continues to use them – and at times, it even does this behind his back and against the pull of the conclusions he sometimes wishes to draw.

For a start, the distinction Freud makes between instinct and drive has at one swoop removed the possibility of a moralism of what is 'natural'. It is no longer possible to argue that a certain pattern of sexual behaviour is natural whereas others are not, when the very structure of the drive itself can no longer be reduced to the body and its needs. *All* sexual behaviour, including the most heterosexual and genitally oriented, diverges from the instinctual and 'natural'. The objects and aims of the drives are not hardwired into the organism as its nature. Instead, we get precisely the same argument Freud had used just a few years earlier, as the ground-breaking move of *The Interpretation of Dreams*: just as the dream becomes explicable only if we take into account the sheer singularity of a life (the 'residues of the day'), so too do objects and aims of the drive become established only in all the vicissitudes and twists and turns of an individual history.• In this quite contingent process, no partic-

> Throughout the entire work the various factors are placed in a particular order of precedence: preference is given to the accidental factors, while disposition is left in the background, and more weight is attached to ontogenesis than to phylogenesis. For it is the accidental factors that play the principal part in analysis: they are almost entirely subject to its influence. The dispositional ones only come to light after them, as something stirred into activity by experience: adequate consideration of them would lead far beyond the sphere of psychoanalysis. (Preface to the Third Edition (1914), *Three Essays on the Theory of Sexuality* (1905c), p. 131)

ular outcome is assured, even though some outcomes tend to occur more often than others: heterosexualities, for example, are considerably more frequent than homosexualities. When Freud talks of genital and reproductive heterosexuality as 'normal', he has thus robbed the term of its moralising, naturalising sense, and reduced it to a far weaker and purely numerical sense: what's normal is nothing more than *what happens most often*. There is nothing natural about the normal, once it is used in this sense. It does not have to come about. If it does not, it is not because some essential aspect of the process has failed, but because exactly the same processes as those involved in heterosexuality have taken other paths. This is an aetiology Freud would return to and emphasise in a number of additions to later editions of the *Three Essays*.

This is an important conclusion, and we should not let the standard psychiatric terminology of perversion and inversion hide its extraordinary novelty and liberality. With this move, the questions to be asked change completely. For nineteenth-century sexology, the question was always, 'How is it possible for the sexual instincts to be diverted away from their natural state of reproductive heterosexuality and into inversion and perversion?' In Freud's framework, though, the question is rather, 'Given that all sexuality is a process of divergence from the instinctual, how is it that reproductive heterosexuality regularly comes to be so significantly the most frequent outcome?• Why isn't there a more or less even spread of all possibilities?' In other words, with Freud, *heterosexuality, not homosexuality, is the problem*, the thing in need of explanation.

> [P]sychoanalysis considers that a choice of object independently of its sex – freedom to range equally over male and female objects – ... is the original basis from which, as a result of restriction in one direction or the other, both the normal and the inverted types develop. Thus from the point of view of psychoanalysis the exclusive sexual need felt by men for women is also a problem that needs elucidating and is not a self-evident fact based upon an attraction that is ultimately of a chemical nature. ('The Sexual Aberrations', *Three Essays on the Theory of Sexuality* (1905c), pp. 145–46, fn. 1 [added 1915])

When the aims and objects of the drive are the outcomes of a sort of adventure in the contingencies of the world, it will be impossible to make any rigorous separation between norm and its perversions and inversions *other* than frequency. A kiss – to give a famous example – is 'the bringing together of two oral erotogenic zones instead of the two genitals': should we therefore see kissing as perverse?•

There is something else that I must add in order to complete our view of sexual perversions. However infamous they may be, however sharply they may be contrasted with normal sexual activity, quiet consideration will show that some perverse trait or other is seldom absent from the sexual life of normal people. Even a kiss can claim to be described as a perverse act, since it consists in the bringing together of two oral erotogenic zones instead of the two genitals. Yet no one rejects it as perverse; on the contrary, it is permitted in theatrical performances as a softened hint at the sexual act. But precisely kissing can easily turn into a complete perversion – if, that is to say, it becomes so intense that a genital discharge and orgasm follow upon it directly, an event that is far from rare. We can learn, too, that for one person feeling and looking at the object are indispensable preconditions of sexual enjoyment, that another person will pinch or bite at the climax of sexual excitation, that the highest pitch of excitement in lovers is not always provoked by the genitals but by some other region of the object's body, and any number of similar things. There is no sense in excluding people with individual traits of this kind from the class of the normal and putting them among the perverts. On the contrary, we shall recognise more and more clearly that the essence of the perversions lies not in the extension of the sexual aim, not in the replacement of the genitals, not even always in the variant choice of the object, but solely in the exclusiveness with which these deviations are carried out and as a result of which the sexual act serving the purpose of reproduction is put on one side. In so far as the perverse actions are inserted in the performance of the normal sexual act as preparatory or intensifying contributions, they are in reality not perversions at all. The gulf between normal and perverse sexuality is of course very much narrowed by facts of this kind. It is an easy conclusion that normal sexuality has emerged out of something that was in existence before it, by weeding out certain features of that material as unserviceable and collecting together the rest in order to subordinate them to a new aim, that of reproduction. (Lecture 21, 'The Development of the Libido and the Sexual Organisations', *Introductory Lectures on Psychoanalysis* (1916–17), vol. 16, p. 322)

One answer Freud gives is that such activities are not perverse if they are secondary aims still in the service of reproduction – if the kiss is a prelude to intercourse, say, or an act which reinforces the marriage bond. They become perverse only if carried out to the exclusion of reproductive aims. Thus the question of normality or perversion becomes an essentially economic one, with its own economistic moralism not too far behind it: the normal form of behaviour is one where everything is ultimately a profit for (re)production; perversion and inversion are then forms of behaviour which refuse to put themselves in the service of production, but which squander themselves to other aims. This is the same economism we saw linking the reality and pleasure principles. Just as the reality principle is the pleasure principle taking a canny detour to make its speculation that bit more secure, so is kissing subsumed into reproductive sexuality to the extent that it is just a detour on the way to intercourse.

There are some obvious objections. We can be quite confident that there are some activities Freud would continue to see as deeply perverse even if put in the service of reproductive heterosexuality – violent sadism, or rape, or the abuse of children. We might object that his own and obviously far more innocuous example of the kiss simply does not take into account the sheer variety of kisses and the complex etiquette and mores which surround them – all those questions of whom one kisses (Immediate family? Close friends? People of the same or opposite sex?), in what circumstances (Public or private? Are different sorts of kisses exchanged in each case?), when (At what point does a relationship become one in which kisses are exchanged? Are kisses exchanged then on every occasion, or only on some? Which?), on what part of the body (The hand? The lips? The neck? The cheek? The air beside the cheek?), and so on. Kisses do not all even serve an erotic aim, let alone one whose ultimate aim is reproductive sexual activity, and it would be a social blunder of the most basic sort to work on the assumption that they did. It would not even be enough to reply that Freud is, after all, interested here only in erotic kissing, for the kiss can stand for personal social contact in general (and not only for an unstated or potential sexual act) precisely to the extent that it is a contact of two non-genital erotogenic zones which is *not* primarily subservient to reproductive aims.

But more than this, *no* drive has an aim that is that purely reproductive, and where every quota of pleasure is turned to reproductive ends. Every drive has some component which is not reproductive, and which ensures that its aim and object are somewhere slightly off to one side of reproduction. In opening up the possibility of a drive which does not depend on a biological aim, Freud has ensured that this gap cannot ever be closed again – that something always remains, left over and unassimilable. Every drive has something intractably perverse in it, even where its aims are the most thoroughly heterosexual and reproductive. We can go further: *that a drive is, by definition, not dependent on a purely biological object or aim means that perversion is the very possibility of the drive.* If perversion were not an ever-present possibility in every drive, there could be no drives.

Because the aim and object of the drive are always divergent from instinct, even if only minimally, it follows that drives cannot be satisfied in the way that bodily needs can. Bodily needs can be met in the world, but the object that meets them is never quite the same as the drive's object, which is always somewhere off to one side. The drive's object is never quite this or that object in the world at all; whatever actual object is offered to the drive will never quite satisfy it. There is something thoroughly phantasmatic about the object of the drive, which corresponds to no actual thing in the world and remains after the actual object has been exhausted.[4] Drive *cannot* be satisfied, by reproductive heterosexuality or by any other form of behaviour or object.

That the object of the drive is phantasmatic does not imply that it is some sort of illusion from which one should presumably want to wake up, or which one should want to replace with a more realistically attainable goal. *No* drive has an attainable actual thing as its object. This is why the drive opens up the entire field of *desire*, which bears precisely the same relationship to attainable need that the drive itself has to instinct. Desire is what remains unsatisfied once need is met.

In this scheme of things, reproductive heterosexuality is not a given. It is not something we all begin with, or even with an innate tendency towards. The infant's aim is not heterosexual reproductivity, but simply its own pleasure. Reproductive heterosexuality is one of the many possibilities which can emerge over a long period of development, as the result of the largely unforeseeable events which make up any given individual's history in a complex and contingent social world. It emerges from an earlier state of childhood not yet governed by the economies of reproduction. But what is not beholden to reproduction can only be, by definition, perverse. Perversion is thus not only logically prior to reproductive heterosexuality; it is chronologically prior to it as well. The only conclusion is the one which deeply shocked Freud's contemporaries on the publication of the *Three Essays*: the infant is deeply, thoroughly, irreducibly perverse. Freud's famous term for this is *polymorphous perversity*, and it remains the fundamental ground on which the child and its sexuality will develop.●

Freud is not entirely easy with the conclusions to be drawn from that, and will argue on a number of occasions – indeed, often on the same occasion – that later variations from reproductive heterosexuality amount to an *inhibition* of proper development. Yet the argument from which he began should strictly prevent any such conclusion. As he so often explains, reproductive heterosexuality itself arises only through multiple developmental inhibition and those

It is an instructive fact that under the influence of seduction children can become polymorphously perverse, and can be led into all possible kinds of sexual irregularities. This shows that an aptitude for them is innately present in their disposition. There is consequently little resistance towards carrying them out, since the mental dams against sexual excesses – shame, disgust and morality – have either not yet been constructed at all or are only in the course of construction, according to the age of the child. ('Infantile Sexuality', *Three Essays on the Theory of Sexuality* (1905), p. 191)

First and foremost, it is an untenable error to deny that children have a sexual life and to suppose that sexuality only begins at puberty with the maturation of the genitals. On the contrary, from the very first children have a copious sexual life, which differs at many points from what is later regarded as normal. What in adult life is described as 'perverse' differs from the normal in these respects: first, by disregarding the barrier of species (the gulf between men and animals), secondly, by overstepping the barrier against disgust, thirdly that against incest (the prohibition against seeking sexual satisfaction from near blood-relations), fourthly that against members of one's own sex and fifthly the transferring of the part played by the genitals to other organs and areas of the body. None of these barriers existed from the beginning; they were only gradually erected in the course of development and education. Small children are free from them. They recognise no frightful gulf between human beings and animals ... To begin with, children exhibit no disgust at excreta but acquire this slowly under the pressure of education; they attach no special importance to the distinction between the sexes, but attribute the same conformation of the genitals to both; they direct their first sexual lusts and their curiosity to those who are nearest and for other reasons dearest to them...; and finally, they show ... that they expect to derive pleasure not only from their sexual organs, but that many other parts of the body lay claim to the same sensitivity, afford them analogous feelings of pleasure and can accordingly play the part of genitals. Children may thus be described as 'polymorphously perverse'... (Lecture 13, 'The Archaic Features and Infantilism of Dreams', *Introductory Lectures on Psychoanalysis* (1916–17), vol. 15, pp. 208–209) 'mental dams' of shame, disgust and morality.• To say, then, that non-heterosexual or non-reproductive sexualities are the result of inhibitions, is not really to make any distinction at all between them and that 'normal sexuality' the argument has so effectively dismantled as a ground.• What needs explanation is, once more, how reproductive heterosexuality does in fact arise so regularly out of such a polymorphously perverse set of initial conditions.

> The time has arrived for me to attempt to summarise what I have said. ... In view of what was now seen to be the wide dissemination of tendencies to perversion we were driven to the conclusion that a disposition to perversions is an original and universal disposition of the human sexual instinct and that normal sexual behaviour is developed out of it as a result of organic changes and psychical inhibitions occurring in the course of maturation; we hoped to be able to show the presence of this original disposition in childhood. Among the forces restricting the direction taken by the sexual instinct we laid emphasis upon shame, disgust, pity and the structures of morality and authority erected by society. We were thus led to regard any established aberration from normal sexuality as an instance of developmental inhibition and infantilism. ('Summary', *Three Essays on the Theory of Sexuality* (1905c), p. 231)

> It was not possible to say what amount of sexual activity can occur in childhood without being described as abnormal or detrimental to further development. The nature of these sexual manifestations was found to be predominantly masturbatory. Experiences further showed that the further influences of seduction are capable of provoking interruptions of the latency period or even its cessation, and that in this connection the sexual instinct of children proves in fact to be polymorphously perverse; it seems, moreover, that any such premature sexual activity diminishes a child's educability. ('Summary', *Three Essays on the Theory of Sexuality* (1905c), p. 234)

Sexual drives and ego drives

In classifying the drives, Freud initially draws a distinction between *sexual drives* and *ego drives*. It appears to be quite straightforward: the ego drives are those attached to the functions of self-preservation, while the sexual drives are attached to reproduction and preservation of the species.• But we may wonder: if, as we have seen, the boundaries of that ego, that self, are far from clear, can this new distinction be any more stable? From the very outset, Freud seems oddly diffident about it. In the *Three Essays*, the text

> There is a further provisional assumption that we cannot escape in the theory of the instincts. It is to the effect that excitations of two kinds arise from the somatic organs, based upon differences of a chemical nature. One of these kinds of excitation we describe as being specifically sexual, and we speak of the organ concerned as being the 'erotogenic zone' of the sexual component instinct arising from it.
> The part played by the erotogenic zones is immediately obvious in the case of ... ('The Sexual Aberrations', *Three Essays on the Theory of Sexuality* (1905c), pp. 168–69)

which introduces the very concept of drive, his first statement of the distinction is incomplete: he suggests that there are two sorts of drive, one of which is sexual, but turns out to have nothing to say about what the other sort might be or how it differs from the sexual. In fact, it will not be until five years later, with a short paper on 'The Psychoanalytic View of Psychogenic Disturbance of Vision', that he will complete the distinction and actually give the name *ego-drives* to those other excitations. In the 1915 essay on 'Instincts and Their Vicissitudes', Freud is careful to qualify the distinction between the two by immediately playing it down as nothing more than a working hypothesis from the evidence, provisionally useful but with little consequence if new evidence should require it to be replaced.•

I have proposed that two groups of such primal instincts should be distinguished: the *ego*, or *self-preservative*, instincts and the *sexual* instincts. But this supposition has not the status of a necessary postulate ...; it is merely a working hypothesis, to be retained only so long as it proves useful and it will make little difference to the results of our work of description and classification if it is replaced by another. The occasion for this hypothesis arose in the course of the evolution of psychoanalysis, which was first employed upon the psychoneuroses, or, more precisely, upon the group described as 'transference neuroses' (hysteria and obsessional neurosis); these showed that at the root of all such affections there is to be found a conflict between the claims of sexuality and those of the ego. ('Instincts and Their Vicissitudes' (1915b), p. 124)

(One wonders how useful it could have been in the first place if it is *quite* so easily replaceable.) And while the sexual drives are central throughout Freud's output, the ego-drives play a relatively minor role: the paper on 'Psychogenic Disturbances of Vision' is one of the few places to focus on them in all of his voluminous output. Even the key paper 'On Narcissism' from 1914 – and surely narcissism is the very place one might expect to find a thorough discussion of the ego-drives – takes an ingenious twist which places the sexual drives at the forefront again: in narcissism, it argues, the ego becomes the object of the sexual drives. Where Freud does speak in passing of the ego-drives, they are often not completely distinguishable from the level of the purely somatic, as if they were not yet quite drives in the full sense generally accorded the sexual drives. At other times, they are said to be at the root of the sexual drives, though the sexual drives will inevitably form the focus of the argument.• The relation the ego-drives have to the sexual drives can seem

The sexual instincts are at the outset attached to the satisfaction of the ego-instincts; only later do they become independent of these, and even then we have an indication of that original attachment in the fact that the persons who are concerned with a child's feeding, care and protection become his earliest sexual objects: that is to say, in the first instance his mother or a substitute for her. ('On Narcissism: An Introduction' (1914), p. 87)

At their first appearance [the sexual drives] are attached to the instincts of self-preservation, from which they only gradually become separated; in their choice of object, too, they follow the paths that are indicated to them by the ego-instincts. ('Instincts and Their Vicissitudes' (1915b), p. 126)

very similar to that which instincts have to drives: some sort of necessary precursor, about which psychoanalysis can have little to say.

One conclusion it is tempting to draw from this is that *for Freud, drives are essentially sexual*. The model of the drive is the sexual drive – or, to put it another way, the sexual drives are the most drive-like of all drives, the ones furthest from the purely somatic. As we have seen, it is characteristic of the drives that they are highly mobile – and none are more mobile than those of sexuality. The regions of the body on which the sexual drives focus are not limited to the genitals; they may commonly also include – to name only the most obvious – the mouth, the anus and buttocks, the breasts, and the eyes (scopophilia and exhibitionism).● Other organs may represent the genitals, and genital pleasures may be displaced onto and eroticise other parts of the body in a complex fashion (think of the variety of kisses, from the voluptuous to the perfunctory). The sexual is at the heart of the drive.

> [In hysteria] it is quite usual for signs of stimulation, sensations and innervations, and even the processes of erection, which belong properly to the genitals, to be displaced on to other, remote regions of the body – as, for instance, by transposition upwards, to the head and face. (Lecture 21, 'The Development of the Libido and the Sexual Organizations', *Introductory Lectures on Psychoanalysis* (1916–17), vol. 16, p. 324)

Here, we can grasp some of the logic behind Freud's insistence on infantile sexuality, and indeed the centrality of sexuality to all sorts of aspects of human existence, whether or not they might be genital or reproductive.● Freud is well aware of the outrage the idea of infantile sexuality was capable of arousing, and several texts even stage the familiar objections as a pre-emptive dialogue or an interjection from the floor, as it were.● The answers he gives are generally of two sorts. On the one hand, there is the pragmatic answer, which comes from

> Its principal findings [i.e., of psychoanalysis on sexuality] are as follows:
>
> (a) Sexual life does not begin only at puberty, but starts with plain manifestations soon after birth.
> (b) It is necessary to distinguish sharply between the concepts of 'sexual' and 'genital'. The former is the wider concept and includes activities that have nothing to do with the genitals.
> (c) Sexual life includes the function of obtaining pleasure from zones of the body – a service which is subsequently brought into the service of reproduction. The two functions often fail to coincide completely.
>
> ('An Outline of Psychoanalysis' (1940), p. 152)

> 'Why', we shall be asked, 'are you so obstinate in describing as being already sexuality what on your own evidence are indefinable manifestations in childhood out of which sexual life will later develop? Why should you not be content with giving them a physiological description and simply say that in an infant at the breast we already observe activities, such as sensual sucking or holding back the excreta, which show us that he is striving for "organ-pleasure"? In that way, you would have avoided the hypothesis, so repugnant to every feeling, of the smallest babies having a sexual life.' (Lecture 21, 'The Development of the Libido and the Sexual Organizations', *Introductory Lectures on Psychoanalysis* (1916–17), vol. 16, p.323)[5]

the observations he and many others before him have made of children and their behaviour: from an early age, the young child is already familiar with the pleasures of genital stimulation, has recognised sexual difference, conducted its own 'sexual researches', and made object-choices; working backwards, the analysis arrives at these earlier pleasures only by passing through indisputably sexual materials. On the other hand, there is the answer from principle: if the drives do indeed behave as he has described them, then their very logic places sexuality at their heart, and makes it impossible to distinguish between the essentially sexual and non-sexual. When the very nature of the drive is its mobility, how could one make any meaningful distinction between a sexual pleasure and a non-sexual 'organ-pleasure'? • This blurring of the boundaries between sexual and non-sexual occurs even when Freud really does want to make a very clear and incontrovertible distinction between them.

Indeed, Gentlemen, I have no objection at all to organ-pleasure. I know that even the supreme pleasure of sexual union is only an organ-pleasure attached to the activity of the genitals. But can you tell me when this originally indifferent organ-pleasure acquires the sexual character which it undoubtedly possesses in the later phases of development? Do we know any more about 'organ-pleasure' than about sexuality? (Lecture 21, 'The Development of the Libido and the Sexual Organizations', *Introductory Lectures on Psychoanalysis* (1916–17), vol. 16, pp. 323–24)

Libido and narcissism

Freud gives a specific name to the mental energies of the sexual drives in particular: libido. Like cathexis, that other borrowing from fluid dynamics and energetics which is central to his models, the term dates from the earliest writings – the 'project' and the letters and drafts to Fliess – and is nowhere defined. Libido is, by definition, fundamentally sexual, and belongs to the sexual drives. Freud is quite insistent on this point, against Jung's rival suggestion that libido should be seen as a generalised mental energy common to all drives, and does not give any specific name to the mental energies which might be the counterpart of libido in the ego drives.

Nevertheless, this distinction gets blurred quite quickly. What if – to take as a starting point a question whose very terms we shall soon have to revise – the (sexual) drives and their libido can *take the ego as their (sexual) object*? As we have seen, this is precisely one of the explanations of narcissism Freud canvasses in his 1914 essay 'On Narcissism'. Freud suggests that there are two sorts of libido within the sexual drives: object-libido, which is directed outwards to others in the world, and ego-libido, which is directed back onto one's own ego. • This ego-libido, Freud insists, is different from the question of ego-drives. Ego-libido is libido, and thus a sexual drive, as is

... the sick man withdraws his libidinal cathexes back upon his own ego, and sends them out again when he recovers. 'Concentrated is his soul,' says Wilhelm Busch of the poet suffering from toothache, 'in his molar's narrow hole.' Here libido and ego-interest share the same fate and are once more indistinguishable from each other. ('On Narcissism' (1914a), p.82)

object-libido. Ego- and object-libido are convertible from one to the other, the sum total of both (as with Freud's homeostatic models in general) remaining constant: the more libido directed onto the self, the less there is available for external objects, and *vice versa*. Narcissism, in this preliminary model, will open up a new set of questions that will lead to the abandonment of the first topography (conscious–unconscious–perception) in favour of the ego–id–superego model.

Now the catch comes when Freud realises that it is never quite enough to declare narcissism a pathological state, a perversion or diversion from the proper processes of maturation. As we have seen, the trend of Freud's thought, from at least the 1905 *Three Essays* onwards, is away from such a progressivist and normative view of human development. In the two years or so before 'On Narcissism', Freud had already suggested on a number of occasions that narcissism might actually be a necessary stage of development: the stage in which the child is levered away from its early and undifferentiated auto-erotism, and which lays the ground for its later outward-directed affection. • Thus there would be a *primary narcissism* that the child must go through, in which

> Further study has shown that it is expedient and indeed indispensable to insert a third stage between [auto-erotism and object-choice]. ... The subject behaves as though he were in love with himself; his egoistic instincts and his libidinal wishes are not yet separable under our analysis. ('III. Animism, Magic and the Omnipotence of Thoughts', *Totem and Taboo* (1913), pp. 88–89)

its first object is itself, and which would provide the model for all of the child's subsequent investments of libido. *Secondary narcissism*, by contrast, would be the later withdrawal of libido from objects in the world to focus it instead on the ego; it depends on and assumes the success of the process of primary narcissism which has taken the child out into the world. The result of this is that, far from being a detour taken in error, narcissism, with all of its necessary blurring of the boundaries between object-libido and ego-libido, turns out to be at the heart of object-choice.•

Indeed, in a revision to the 1915 edition of the 1905 *Three Essays on Sexuality*, Freud added an entire section drawing on the recent essay on

> Recent investigations have directed our attention to a stage in the development of the libido which it passes through on the way from auto-erotism to object-love. This stage has been given the name narcissism. What happens is this. There comes a time in the development of the individual at which he unifies his sexual instincts (which have hitherto been engaged in auto-erotic activities) in order to obtain a love-object; and he begins by taking himself, his own body, as his love-object, and only subsequently proceeds from this to the choice of some person other than himself as his object. This half-way phase between auto-erotism and object-love may perhaps be indispensable normally; but it appears that many people linger unusually long in this condition, and that many of its features are carried over by them into the later stages of their development. ('Psychoanalytic Notes on an Autobiographical Account of a Case of Paranoia (Dementia Paranoides)' (1911a), pp. 60–61)

[E]go-libido is, however, only conveniently accessible to analytic study when it has been put to the use of cathecting sexual objects, that is, when it has become 'object libido'. We can then perceive it concentrating upon objects, becoming fixated to them or abandoning them, moving from one object to another and, from these situations, directing the subject's sexual activity ...

We can follow the object-libido through still further vicissitudes. When it is withdrawn from objects, it is held in suspense in peculiar conditions of tension and is finally drawn back into the ego, so that it becomes ego-libido once again. In contrast to object-libido, we also describe ego-libido as 'narcissistic' libido. From the vantage point of psychoanalysis we can look across a frontier, which we may not pass, at the activities of narcissistic libido, and may form some idea of the relation between it and object-libido. Narcissistic or ego-libido seems to be the great reservoir from which the object-cathexes are sent out and into which they are withdrawn once more; the narcissistic libidinal cathexis of the ego is the original state of things, realised in earliest childhood, and is merely covered by the later extrusions of libido, but in essentials persists behind them. ('Transformations of Puberty', *Three Essays on the Theory of Sexuality* (1905c: 1915 revision), pp. 168–69)

narcissism and its findings.• In this new section, he suggests that *ego-libido has a sort of primacy*: it is what object-libido emerges from and returns to, like a 'great reservoir'.

Now, if this were all there were to it, Freud's suggestion would be all of a piece with much of the psychology of the time. It would appear to be an assertion of something already quite familiar, the idea that we begin with the individual and move outwards from there. We would start with already-constituted individuals, already complete with their reservoirs of libido and psychical energies, and whose maturation would be a process of discovering the world beyond themselves and discovering just how their own energies can now be invested in that world. What such a model leaves out of account is the entire question we are interested in: How does that individual ego get to be there in the first place? And this is where an interesting and far-reaching complication develops, for Freud says something else as well, which shifts the argument into a very different gear.

This ego-libido, he says, is really only 'accessible to study' – that is, is really only *visible* at all – 'when it has been put to the use of cathecting sexual objects': which is to say, when it is no longer ego-libido, but has instead become object-libido. We look at ego-libido indirectly, 'across a frontier we may not pass', for whenever we may be trying to observe it, it has always and already become something else: all we have to read its existence from are the traces that this original ego-libido has left behind it. Ego-libido is no more something we can observe directly than the unconscious itself. This is familiar. Ego-libido shares the same retrospective, hypothetical logic as the unconscious.

We must take stock of the implications of this. It means that if 'the narcissistic libidinal cathexis of the ego is the original state of things, realised in earliest childhood', this original state is never accessible to us, *even at the time*. There never is a time at which we can say, *this – here, now – is ego-libido*. That moment of 'earliest childhood' at which it is realised, does not exist on any timeline. We should read that 'earliest' as meaning that it is outside the developmental timeline altogether, precisely because it is that very instant which initiates, and from which unrolls, the timeline of a life history.

This is where we have to revise the terms in which we originally posed the question, 'What happens when the (sexual) drives and their libido take the ego as their (sexual) object?' This describes *secondary* narcissism, in which there are already things such as drives and their objects, libido and egos. This form of libido is no more mysterious, reticent or indirect than any other, because it is simply a form of object-libido: the only difference between it and any other form of object-libido is that, in this particular case, the object happens to be the ego, and is thus internal rather than external. The ego-libido which is involved in this secondary narcissism is simply a derivative form of object-libido, not ego-libido as an irreducibly different form of libido, and certainly not the ego-libido which Freud talks about as being *primary*, prior to all object-libido, and to which all object-libido returns as to a great reservoir. What could such an ego-libido be which *predates* ego, the very sense of any sort of an 'I', the formation of any object – and indeed even libido, in any sense of cathexis onto an object?

Here, Freud's thought divides. There are many places in his writing in which he uses the term 'primary narcissism' to refer simply to a very early form of object-libido – the way in which the child is its own love-object before it takes an interest in external objects. This is still an object-cathexis, even if doubtless a very early one in the child's life. The only mention of a primary narcissism in 'On Narcissism' is in this sense of an object-choice.[6]• But there are also, and with no less frequency, occasions on which *primary narcissism* is used to refer to that much more paradoxical narcissism we have suggested, ego-less and object-less because predating both.

> We say that a human being has originally two sexual objects – himself and the woman who nurses him – and in doing so we are postulating a primary narcissism in everyone, which may in some cases manifest itself in a dominating fashion in his object choice. ('On Narcissism' (1914a), p. 88)

At times, Freud will refer to this as a state in which ego and object are indistinguishable; at other times, it appears as the stage in which object and ego make their appearance.•

> In a sleeper the primal state of distribution of the libido is restored – total narcissism, in which libido and ego-interest, still united and indistinguishable, dwell in the self-sufficing ego. (Lecture 26, 'The Libido 'Theory and Narcissism', *Introductory Lectures on Psychoanalysis* (1916–17), vol. 16, p. 417)

Primary narcissism in this sense thus appears as

> When, during the stage of primary narcissism, the object makes its appearance, the second opposite to loving, namely hating, also attains its development. ('Instincts and Their Vicissitudes' (1915b), p. 136).

something quite different from the first self-directed object-cathexes the child makes. It is instead something much more paradoxical, an attempt to give a name to and think through the very process by which there come to be both object and that sense of 'I' – that moment at which both emerge from indifferentiation.

But what, then, is cathected in primary narcissism, if there is not yet an object or even an 'I'? • This is often seen as an objection

> In childhood ... the sexual instinct is not unified and is at first* without an object, that is, auto-erotic. ('Summary', *Three Essays on the Theory of Sexuality* (1905c), p. 233)

*[Translator's note: The words 'not unified and is at first' were added in 1920.]

to the very concept of primary narcissism.[7] But may we not instead see it as a key to the radicality of the answer Freud is intermittently proposing with the concept? We know that the object of the drive is not that of any bodily instinct. The oral drives, for example, are not satisfied by the food that satisfies the hunger; if milk satisfies the instinctual hunger, it is the breast that is the object of the oral drive.• Drive is an originary deflection of instinct. Its objects are not objects-in-the-world. The breast that satisfies the oral drive is not limited to the actual breast of the real mother; it is also as easily the latex pacifier the infant sucks, or a thumb.[8] There is a

In all this the phylogenetic foundation has so much the upper hand over personal accidental experience that it makes no difference whether a child has really sucked at the breast or has been brought up on the bottle and never enjoyed the tenderness of a mother's care. In both cases the child's development takes the same path; it may be that in the second case its longing grows all the greater. And for however long it is fed at its mother's breast, it will always be left with a conviction after it has been weaned that its feeding was too short and too little. ('An Outline of Psychoanalysis' (1940), pp. 188–89)

sense in which the object of the drive does not pre-exist the drive, but is brought into being by and with the drive. Is this second, object-less and more tenuous version of primary narcissism not a way of describing how it is that this 'I' comes into being, as the path drive describes around a void? The 'I', in other words, is the product of drive, and once it is available, all the possibilities of object relations flow from it. This is why this sort of narcissism (if indeed one can even really call it a narcissism) is primary for Freud, even if fitfully and inconsistently; it is an impossible narcissism in which what we see is not the libido's taking the ego as its object, as a choice of object among many: it is a glimpse of the very possibility of the 'I'.

Even when Freud wants to keep ego-drives and sexual drives conceptually separate, the sexual drives and the processes which are meant to distinguish them keep turning up at the very heart of the ego drives. Just as the reality principle is inseparable from the pleasure principle, the ego drives turn out to be the sexual drives by another name.

Eros and the death drive

By 1920, Freud would admit that the phenomena of narcissism confound any strict division into ego- and sexual drives: the self-preservative drives are libidinal too.• In that year, with *Beyond the Pleasure Principle*, he would also propose a somewhat different grouping of the drives. This new hypothesis is not

The ego now [with the 1914 paper on narcissism] found its position among sexual objects and was at once given the foremost place among them. Libido which was in this way lodged in the ego was described as 'narcissistic'. This narcissistic libido was of course also a manifestation of the force of the sexual instinct in the analytical sense of those words, and it had necessarily to be identified with the self-preservative instincts whose existence had been

<blockquote>
recognised from the first. Thus the original opposition between the ego-instincts and the sexual instincts proved to be inadequate. A portion of the ego-instincts was seen to be libidinal; sexual instincts – probably alongside others – operated in the ego. (*Beyond the Pleasure Principle* (1920b), p. 52)
</blockquote>

only an attempt to resolve the impasse of the first division; it is also an attempt to incorporate a number of things that remained persistently outside the scope and explanation of that division between ego and sexual drives. Most spectacular of these were the so-called 'war neuroses', of which, like all physicians and psychiatrists in Europe in the wake of the Great War, Freud was to see many cases. In them – battle trauma, or shell shock – the sufferer repeatedly lives through the original situation, experiencing all of its trauma afresh each time. Characulsteristically, and oddly, these war neuroses seemed to occur not to those who had actually been physically wounded, but precisely to those who had otherwise escaped injury.

In *The Interpretation of Dreams*, Freud had argued that all dreams express the fulfilment of a wish. Against the obvious objection that there are such things as nightmares, he simply points out the distinction between manifest and latent: whatever the manifest dream might be, the latent dream-thoughts are working to fulfil a wish – and wishes, let us not forget, are inevitably a matter of what Freud would come to call the superego, and thus the pleasures they offer may often be harsh and self-punishing. In short, it is not at all difficult to see how dreams operate according to the pleasure principle. But war neuroses, it quickly became clear, did not work in this way. They offered no quota of wish-fulfilment, only the seemingly endless and senseless replay of the trauma in all of its horror. In their compulsive and terrifying repetition, something erupts which is resolutely beyond recuperation into the economic imperatives of the pleasure principle.

Up until this point, as we have seen, Freud had imagined the drives as dominated by the pleasure principle and its tendency to minimise excitations, which are unpleasurable. Now, however, he proposes a different organisation. One the one hand there are the **life drives** – or, to give them the collective name Freud often uses, **Eros** – which are characterised by their tendency towards an ever greater synthesis, continuity, inclusiveness, and union. These include both the sexual drives and the ego drives, which for all of their earlier opposition are, after all, both concerned with synthesis and continuity: one perpetuates the species, the other preserves the individual. On the other hand, though, Freud postulates the existence of **death drives** (sometimes – but not by Freud – called *Thanatos*, to make a matching pair). • These are blindly implacable forces of dissolution analogous to the bodily imperatives of decay and death. Life and death drives are tightly bound together, first one

<blockquote>
After long hesitancies and vacillations we have decided to assume the existence of only two basic instincts, *Eros* and the *destructive instinct*. (The contrast between the instincts of self-preservation and the preservation of the species, as well as the contrast between ego-love and object-love, falls within Eros.) The aim of the first of these basic instincts is to establish ever greater unities and to preserve them thus – in short, to bind together; the aim of the second is, on the contrary, to undo connections and so to destroy things. In the case of the destructive instinct we may suppose that its final aim is
</blockquote>

and then the other dominating. At first, the death drives arise within the organism itself; the libido may defend against them by directing them outwards onto the world and others. Together, Freud suggests, the life and death drives account for all sorts of phenomena of psychic life.

Again, Freud is drawing on the sciences of his time as a source of model and metaphor. *Beyond the Pleasure Principle* makes its first major statement of this new theory of the drives through an elaborate, famous and familiar biological analogy, in which the psyche is modelled on a single-celled animalcule and its attempts to protect itself against the threats from its environment. This is not the first time Freud had used the analogy: it is an elaboration of just the same analogy he had made five years previously, in the essay on 'Instincts and Their Vicissitudes'.[9] It is also an analogy harking back to the first topography, that of conscious–unconscious–perception, with its emphasis on the formation of the organism–psyche through its reactions to and against an environment. That is, it assumes an organism, or psyche, which is in a sense already there – the very thing the second topography of ego–id–superego was to attempt to disrupt.

The opposition is also, as Freud is well aware and as its many detractors have pointed out, a familiar and thoroughly metaphysical one, beyond the needs or limits of any scientific investigation. How could one prove or disprove that all human activity is governed by two complete abstract and oppositional principles, called by names as broad, and as empty, as 'life' and 'death'? Is it really any explanation of destructive phenomena, for example, to postulate that there is a principle of destructiveness in the human psyche – any more of an explanation than, say, the claim that addiction is caused by the addict's having an 'addictive personality', or that stamp-collecting comes about because of a drive to collect? Freud has earlier resisted such a tendency to multiply drives, and emphasised the need to accept as primal drives only those which are irreducible to others – a methodological safeguard which aims at preventing the problems of a homuncular model which would do no more than restate the problem in the guise of a solution. If he now introduces a new drive, it is presumably because it is primal in just this sense – irreducible to any of the other drives, and necessary for there to be an adequate theory of the phenomena of the drive.•

There is thus a certain caution, even reluctance, about Freud's introduction of the possibility of a death drive. The very book in which it occurs, *Beyond the Pleasure Principle*, is forever pointing out its highly speculative nature. Nevertheless, ten years later, in *Civilization and its Discontents* (1930), Freud speaks of the division into life and death drives as a habit of thought he can now scarcely do without, as if familiarity had done the work of evidence. •

Indeed, it is a distinction he will maintain throughout the rest of his work, even if that is so often accompanied, as if to disarm criticism, by acknowledgement of its speculative nature.

> The assumption of an instinct of death or destruction has met with resistance even in analytic circles ... To begin with it was only tentatively that I put forward the views I have developed here, but in the course of time they have gained such a hold upon me that I can no longer think in any other way. To my mind, they are far more serviceable from a theoretical standpoint than any other possible ones; they provide that simplification, without either ignoring or doing violence to the facts, for which we strive in scientific work. (*Civilization and its Discontents* (1930), p. 119)

The new theory comes too soon to add more than a footnote to the 1921 *Group Psychology and the Analysis of the Ego* (p. 102, fn. 2) but, as one might expect, the idea of a destructive drive that is deflected out onto the world and others informs all of the later 'The Economic Problem of Masochism' (1924d)• and *Civilization and its Discontents* (1930). The most detailed discussion occurs in *The Ego and the Id* (1923);• there, the question of life and death drives is left until the fourth of its five chapters on 'The Two Classes of Instincts', from which it returns in

> The libido has the task of making the destroying instinct innocuous, and it fulfils the task by diverting that instinct to a great extent outwards – soon with the help of a special organic system, the muscular apparatus – towards objects in the external world. The instinct is then called the destructive instinct, the instinct for mastery, or the will to power. A portion of the instinct is placed directly in the service of the sexual function, where it has an important part to play. This is sadism proper. Another portion does not share in this transposition outwards; it remains inside the organism and, with the help of the accompanying sexual excitation ... becomes libidinally bound there. It is in this portion that we recognise the original, erotogenic masochism. ('The Economic Problem of Masochism' (1924d), pp. 163–64)

> The dangerous death instincts are dealt with in the individual in various ways: in part they are rendered harmless by being fused with erotic components, in part they are diverted towards the external world in the form of aggression, while to a large extent they undoubtedly continue their internal work unhindered. (*The Ego and the Id* (1923), p. 54)

the last as the question of aggressiveness. *Civilization and Its Discontents* postulates that this is the source of the superego, which is what happens when this aggressiveness is turned back onto the ego.• These speculations will find a final expression in the 1937 paper, 'Analysis Terminable and Interminable', in which Freud speculates that the

> [The individual's] aggressiveness is introjected, internalised; it is, in point of fact, sent back to where it came from – that is, it is directed towards his own ego. There it is taken over by a portion of the ego, which sets itself over against the rest of the ego as superego, and which now, in the form of 'conscience', is ready to put into action

against the ego the same harsh aggressiveness that the ego would have liked to satisfy upon other, extraneous individuals. (*Civilization and its Discontents* (1930), p. 123) uncontrollability of the death drive may be a major factor in ensuring that some analyses can never be brought to a successful end.

Most of the time, Freud speaks of the death drive as a sort of primal destructiveness in the human psyche, even as the source of human aggression.

The death drive would thus be a *type* of drive – like Eros, the life instincts, but pointing in the opposite direction. The life drives synthesise, the death drive destroys. The death drive is largely invisible in its work, except when it manifests itself as aggression, a drive towards destructive behaviour within the world. •

There can be no question of restricting one or the other of the basic instincts to one of the provinces of the mind. They must necessarily be met with everywhere. ... At a later stage it becomes relatively easy for us to follow the vicissitudes of the libido, but this is more difficult with the destructive instinct.

So long as that instinct operates internally, as a death instinct, it remains silent; it only comes to our notice when it is diverted outwards as an instinct of destruction. It seems to be essential for the preservation of the individual that this diversion should occur; the muscular apparatus serves this purpose. When the superego is established, considerable amounts of the aggressive instinct are fixated in the interior of the ego and operate there self-destructively. This is one of the dangers to health by which human beings are faced on their path to cultural development. Holding back aggressiveness is in general unhealthy and leads to illness (to mortification). ('An Outline of Psychoanalysis' (1940), p. 149–50)

It is easy to see both the attractions of this particular view of the death drive, and the problems with it. Freud's work is marked, as it must be, by the Great War, and during the last decade of his life by the shadow of another conflagration. Much of his later work, as we shall see in the next chapter, is concerned deeply with the unparalleled violence of twentieth-century society, and the idea of a destructive drive is no doubt an attractive, if dark, way of attempting to give some psychoanalytic explanation of this. But it is, after all, a simple, polar schema, with all the mythical resonance of two eternally opposed principles at war within the human soul. (It is perhaps in this particular take on the death drive that the later Freud comes unexpectedly close to the mythicising of the banished heretic Carl Jung.) In seeing the death drive as a type of drive that produces aggression and destructiveness, is there not the danger of a too-neat, one-size-fits-all answer to all problems involving human aggression? Once one knows, already and in principle, that there is a destructive drive at work in human beings, one no longer has to look very carefully at the specifics of any particular, given situation; one would know already that, for all of the complications the situation may introduce, or for all of the triggering it may have provided, the real cause is an innate destructiveness. We only have to think of how inadequate an explanation an innate drive to destruction would be of, say, the Bush administration's foreign policy since 9/11: at one stroke, it would get rid of any need to think in terms of global geopolitics, vested interests, the fraught histories of Israel and the West's relations to Islam, and so on. All of these would vanish in a vague assertion that somehow all this is innate to human nature.

But isn't such abstraction and generalisation precisely what Freud began by countering, as early as the *Studies in Hysteria* and *The Interpretation of Dreams*? Recall Freud's earlier argument against the popular dream-book, the manual that purports to tell you the meaning of any dream by giving you the decontextualised meanings of all its components. What the dream-book doesn't take into account is precisely what Freud's methods of dream analysis insist on, the sheer specificity and singularity of any individual life history: psychoanalysis as the science of biography. From the outset, the radicality of psychoanalysis has been tied to its meticulous care for the specific, the singular, the unrepeatable; that is one of the things which has led to its problematic relationship to science (which demands the repeatasssble). To see the death drive as a type of drive among others, then, and one that offers itself as a cause for phenomena, would be to return to the sort of argument Freud began by trying to banish. We could even go so far as to suggest that it is a deeply *un*psychoanalytic move, even though we find it in the very texts of psychoanalysis. What are we to make of this anomaly? Can we think of what Freud calls the death drive as something other than an element in a typology of drives? If that typology is indeed a deeply unpsychoanalytic move, can we nevertheless discern the pull of the more psychoanalytic arguments surrounding it? Is there another logic at work, even at the very moments Freud is describing the death drive as a *type* of drive?

As we have seen, the death drive is first of all the name for what, in the drives, does not seem to be governed by the pleasure principle. We have seen also that the object of the drive is always phantasmal, somewhere off to one side of any actual object in the world. As a result, the drive can never be fully satisfied. There will always be something in the drive which does not return full-circle, and which is not accountable to the pleasure principle – a gap within the circuit, which the pleasure principle might rush to fill but will never be able to do entirely. The *drive itself*, from the outset and in its very possibility, is already beyond the pleasure principle. Far from being a new type of drive, and thus distinguishable from all other types of drive, the death drive may be a name for what is at the heart of drive itself, the very possibility of a drive, any drive at all. Freud seems to admit this at the very time he postulates a death drive: as all organisms come sooner or later to death, the life drives are not so much a refusal of death as the tendency of any organism to seek *its own* death, as against the death imposed by violence, sickness, predation. •

Where the life drives point towards an increasing

> The hypothesis of self-preservative instincts, such as we attribute to all living beings, stands in marked opposition to the idea that instinctual life as a whole serves to bring about death. Seen in this light, the theoretical importance of the instincts of self-preservation, of self-assertion and of mastery greatly diminishes. They are component instincts whose function it is to assure that the organism shall follow its own path to death, and to ward off any possible ways of returning to inorganic existence other than those which are immanent in the organism itself. We have no longer to reckon with the organism's puzzling determination (so hard to fit into any context) to maintain its own existence in the face of every obstacle. What we are left with is

the fact that the organism wishes to die only in its own fashion. Thus these guardians of life, too, were originally the myrmidons of death. Hence arises the paradoxical situation that the living organism struggles most energetically against events (dangers, in fact), which might help it to attain its life's aim rapidly – by a kind of short-circuit. (*Beyond the Pleasure Principle* (1920b), p. 39)

complexity and organisation, the death drives seek to return the organism to a simpler, pre-animate state. But in Freud's first theory,

all drives are governed by the principle of constancy, that close relative often indistinguishable from the pleasure principle: under the principle of constancy, all drives aim to minimise excitation (and thus unpleasure) by reducing it to a constant and manageable level; all drives thus repeat and take the organism back to an earlier state of affairs; ultimately, even, all drives seek death. Seen in this light, the death drive is not so much a disruption of the pleasure principle as a radically literal version of it: it aims to reduce excitation to zero, and extirpate it completely. Again, the death drive reveals itself as the very possibility of the life drives, and of drive in general. More, it makes the very concept of the *life* drives now appear curiously metaphysical and speculative, for it is not at all clear how a drive that works according to the constancy or pleasure principles could result in the sorts of sustained complexity associated with the life drives.

The death drive thus has a paradoxical position. On the one hand, it is not really a type of drive at all, to be contrasted with drives of another sort, but a name for what – in the drive, any drive – escapes any dynamic, economic, *or indeed conceptual* model whatsoever. It is a series of awkward remainders that fit nowhere. On the other hand, and for that very reason, it is the *epitome* of the drive, exhibiting in a particularly pure form all of those qualities that define a drive. Again, this shape is familiar: we have seen exactly the same logic at work in perversion. In the Freudian economy of terms, the death drive is another name for the radical and ineradicable perversion that lets the whole thing work. Freud insists that the life and death drives are in practice strictly inseparable from one another, but the situation is altogether more complex than the addition of proportions he suggests. • To be able to distinguish one proportion of aggressiveness from another would imply first of all that it is possible to distinguish an abstract something called 'aggressiveness' from everything else surrounding it, and from other similar

In biological functions the two basic instincts operate against each other or combine with each other. Thus, the act of eating is a destruction of the object with the final aim of incorporating it, and the sexual act is an act of aggression with the purpose of the most intimate union. This concurrent and mutually opposing action of the two basic instincts gives rise to the whole variegation of the phenomena of life. The analogy of our two basic instincts extends from the sphere of living things to the pairs of opposing forces – attraction and repulsion – which rule in the inorganic world.

Modifications in the proportions of the fusion between the instincts have the most tangible results. A surplus of sexual aggressiveness will turn a lover into a sex-murderer, while a sharp diminution in the aggressive factor will make him bashful or impotent. ('An Outline of Psychoanalysis' (1940), p. 149)

abstractions to which it could be opposed. But that is precisely what the logic of the death drive makes impossible, nestled as it is at the very heart of Eros and the life drives. What if, in the radical indistinction of drives, one inhabits the other as its very possibility?

This is what makes it difficult to take the hasty, if comforting, attitude that the concept of the death drive is simply incoherent – a later addition to a theory of drives which has no need of it; a speculation with neither grounding nor application in the clinical; a disguised homuncular explanation which mistakes restatement of the problem for its solution; a diversion of psychoanalysis away from its true business. It is not that the concept of the death drive is inconsistent: it is that *the death drive is a name for the inconsistency at the heart of drive itself*. Drive is not to be thought of as some sort of project, pushing on towards aims which are its own, if unknowable to those driven by them: that would perhaps be the last refuge of the homuncular, reassuring us that at base there is still a plan to drive. Drive is blind. It never forms a totality: no matter how wide we throw the net, we cannot say, *This, and only this, at last, is what drive aims at*. Drive is by definition, as we have seen, deflection and obliquity: wherever one stands, some component of drive is always pointing elsewhere. What we call the death drive, in all its paradoxicality, is no more than a name for the blindness of drive, pure and simple. The death drive does not so much add a new element to the theory, or a different type of drive to a classification, as function in true psychoanalytic fashion as a sort of *Nachträglichkeit*: the revelation, after the fact, of what has been there all along. Indeed, in a sense, the phenomena that lead Freud to a new name and a new theory are not new at all, or even unforeseen by psychoanalysis up until that point. They are simply what – after the event – one would expect from the very logic of drive. The death drive is drive in its purest form.

Let us follow the logic of these obdurate remainders, as it develops in the very question of the formation of the psyche. We shall find, at its very heart, the entire issue of sexuality. We need to go back to the beginning.

The death drive:
Beyond the Pleasure Principle (1920)

This is the work which first proposes the death drive. It is also the most sheerly speculative of Freud's major works.

The Interpretation of Dreams had found it easy to explain how the repetition of an unpleasant dream could still be in keeping with the pleasure principle: an unpleasant manifest content may still be the fulfilment of a wish on the level of the latent content. The 'return of the repressed' had been part of psychoanalysis from the outset: what is repressed is never destroyed, but is repeated in disguised fashion. The transference relationship central to psychoanalytic treatment is a way of utilising this repetition to work through some of the effects of the trauma.

Yet there are also traumatic experiences which cannot be explained quite as easily. Like most of the physicians of Europe after the Great War, Freud was to see many cases of battle neurosis, in which, characteristically, the victim would vividly and helplessly relive the original trauma, as if under some sort of compulsion. Even after one takes into account that what the ego perceives as unpleasure may be perceived as pleasure by the superego, Freud argues, in cases like this we are left with the perplexing repetition of an unpleasure which offers no quotient of pleasure at all, in complete contradiction to the pleasure principle. Does such a 'compulsion to repeat', even without any payoff in pleasure, indicate the existence of another principle at work, beyond, behind or even before the pleasure principle?

Freud's answer is to postulate a 'death drive', the innate tendency of every organism to return to its initial inorganic state. In the absence of accident or illness and left to its own devices, every organism moves towards what Freud calls 'its own' death, from the purely internal causes of its own ageing. Against this, the task of the libido – Eros, the life drives – is to diffuse this death drive, deflecting it out into the external world. At this point, what had been the pure interiority of the death drive, and which had made it so hard to see, becomes visible in often spectacular fashion as an apparent drive to destruction.

The hypothesis of the death drive will have immense effects on Freud's work after this point. For a start, it immediately offers the possibility of new explanations of psychological phenomena such as sadism and masochism (as the title of the 1924 paper on 'The Economic Problem of Masochism' states) and anxiety (*Inhibitions, Symptoms and Anxiety* (1926a)). In the outward deflection of the death drive into destructiveness, it also opens the way for Freud's later social critiques (in particular, *The Future of an Illusion* (1927b) and *Civilization and its Discontents* (1930); the 1921 *Group Psychology and the Analysis of the Ego* has few marks of its immediate predecessor beyond a single footnote). And in its seeking to return the organism to an earlier state, the death drive becomes the drive *par excellence*, or rather the aspect shared by all drives. This has profound implications for philosophy, Freudian metapsychology, and the direction of the analytic treatment (*The Ego and the Id* (1923), 'Analysis Terminable and Interminable' (1937)).

II: Development

Beginnings

Infantile amnesia is one of the first things Freud mentions in the essay on infantile sexuality in the *Three Essays on Sexuality*.● Despite all of the vast developments going on in the first four or more years of a child's life, and the lasting effects

[W]e learn from other people that during those years, of which at a later date we retain nothing in our memory but a few unintelligible and fragmentary recollections, we reacted in a lively manner to impressions, that we were capable of expressing joy and pain in a human fashion, that we gave

these have in later life, most people simply cannot recall anything of this time.

Freud links this to the sort of amnesia one finds in hysterics. Hysterical amnesia, he argues, is actually made possible by this massive childhood forgetting. Childhood amnesia lays down a rich store of memory traces whose associative links act as a strong *anti-cathectic* attraction on the contents which hysteria tries to expel from consciousness. Infantile amnesia, in other words, is primary. It is not an amnesia or repression just like any others except for the sole fact that it occurs earlier; it is a forgetting unlike any later forgetting. When the individual subject is still in the process of formation, we have the paradoxical situation that the one who does the forgetting, or to whom the forgetting happens, is not yet quite *there* to do the forgetting or for it to happen to. •

> evidence of love, jealousy and other passionate feelings by which we were strongly moved at the time, and even that we gave utterance to remarks which were regarded by adults as good evidence of our possessing insight and the beginnings of a capacity for judgement. And of all this we, when we are grown up, have no knowledge of our own! Why should our memory lag so far behind the other activities of our minds? We have, on the contrary, good reason to believe that there is no period at which the capacity for receiving and reproducing impressions is greater than precisely during the years of childhood.
>
> On the other hand we must assume, or we can convince ourselves by a psychological examination of other people, that the very same impressions that we have forgotten have none the less left the deepest traces on our minds and have had a determining effect upon the whole of our later development, ('Infantile Sexuality', *Three Essays on the Theory of Sexuality* (1905c), pp. 174–75)

The logic of that is important: it is retrospective, and retroactive. It means it is going to be very difficult, if not downright impossible, to say just when subjectivity arrives: when it arrives, it is in the mode of *having already been there*. That is, it is not a sudden sense of an *I* now being experienced for the very first time, here where just a moment ago there was no *I* at all. Instead, it is experienced as an oddly retrospective continuity: *I recognise now that I already am, and have been for some time.*

> Further reflection tells us that the adult's ego-feelings cannot have been the same from the beginning. It must have gone through a process of development, which cannot, of course, be demonstrated but which admits of being constructed with a fair degree of probability. An infant at the breast does not yet distinguish his ego from the external world as the source of the sensations flowing in upon him. (*Civilization and its Discontents* (1930), pp. 66–67)

When Freud speaks of early childhood he nearly always means a stage at which this arrival of subjectivity has already occurred. That is, what he imagines is a state in which there is already some sort of rudimentary sense of a separate individuality distinguished from a world whose stimuli it receives. Even when he uses his frequent analogy of the psyche to a single-celled organism, the argument will generally begin from a differentiation that has already been, or is about to be made, between inside and outside, between self and

Let us imagine ourselves in the situation of an almost entirely helpless living organism, as yet unorientated in the world, which is receiving stimuli in its nervous substance. This organism will very soon be in a position to make a first distinction and a first orientation. On the one hand, it will be aware of stimuli which can be avoided by muscular action (flight); these it ascribes to an external world. On the other hand, it will be aware of stimuli against which such action is of no avail and whose character of constant pressure persists in spite of it; these stimuli are the signs of an internal world, the evidence of instinctual needs. The perceptual substance of the living organism will thus have found in the efficacy of its muscular activity a basis for distinguishing between an 'outside' and an 'inside'. ('Instincts and Their Vicissitudes' (1915b), p. 119)

world.• Apart from the oblique but nevertheless insistent and repeated suggestions we have seen, he has very little to say on what might have happened before that, and for good reason. It is an impossible state, something of which there can be no direct observation. Everything is oblique, a tracing back of what remains, which will allow us to reconstruct that impossible moment (which is really no single moment at all) of emergence. In that prehistory in which there is not yet any sense of self or differentiation of objects, we have something like that perfect forgetting which resists remembering, a forgetting so deep that there is not even yet anyone there to forget.

Let us try to reconstruct some of what this must entail, extrapolating out the logic of those oblique suggestions that keep emerging in Freud's work. It is hard for us to imagine the strangeness of such a stage. We cannot, for a start, have recourse to pronouns or nouns, as those endpoints they stand for, from which or to which things happen, have not yet emerged. There are only events, things which happen, in something like what linguistics calls a middle voice, neither passive nor active because the question of whom this happens to or who performs these actions is one which cannot even yet be asked: *an appearing, a disappearing; a hungering, a distressing, a satisfying; a noising, a touching.*

Thus when we speak, as Freud often does, of the child's relation to various aspects of the maternal body, we have to keep in mind that, at this earliest of all stages, this is really no more than a shorthand for the barely imaginable.• In its way, it is as inaccurate a figure as that of the censor sitting between conscious and unconscious chambers and regulating the passage of thoughts between them. This is not a

A child's first erotic object is the mother's breast that nourishes it; love has its origin in attachment to the satisfied need for nourishment. There is no doubt that, to begin with, the child does not distinguish between the breast and its own body; when the breast has to be separated from the body and shifted to the 'outside' because the child so often finds it absent, it carries with it as an 'object' a part of the original narcissistic cathexis. ('An Outline of Psychoanalysis' (1940), p. 188)

relationship that would begin with two already differentiated bodies, here the child and there the mother, between which we could then trace out some interconnection. It is instead a matter of extreme indifferentiation, and thus barely even a relationship at all. The maternal body is not even really just the actual body of the woman who is the child's mother, though she of course will, in most cases and most of the time, fill that function for the child. It is the vast phantasmatic body from which the infant's awareness of itself emerges and into which it sinks back, the indifferentiation of what is not yet even the world. The maternal body in this sense is also the breast of the nursemaid;[10] the arms of the father, the sibling, the stranger; the bottle's nipple, the warmth of baby formula; even the warmth and comfort of the cot, the enveloping of the bedclothes. At the very moment of satiation and contentment, folded back into the arms of this phantasmatic body, the child no more experiences it than one experiences the moment of falling asleep, and for just the same reason: at that moment, there is not quite anyone there to experience it. This maternal body is what is immediately lost when there is any awareness of self, because it is the background against which that self-awareness appears, and thus can be experienced only as what has already been lost. Beyond and behind that, though, there is a further and more profound reason, a forgetting more absolute and irretrievable: at the very basis of desire, drive itself is split, inconsistent, divided against itself. Drive is from the very first also an aiming-elsewhere.

A distress: It may be anything – something an adult could recognise as hunger, wind, or the chaffing of a nappy, perhaps, but there are no names for it yet, no causes and effects. Neither is there even (quite, yet) anyone to feel this distress: it is just there, happening, an event, a blind unpleasure which suffers. It is also a noise, that wail of distress which does not even (quite, yet) respond to the distress because it is inseparable from it.

Perhaps that distress invokes a response in turn. Another voice makes altogether different noises: soft, regular, soothing. There is a touch. Unlike the gripe of the distress, this one is pleasurable. Perhaps it is a rhythmic stroking – which is fitting, as there is already a rhythm set up here in that call and response. There is an enfolding: an enveloping touch, a different smell. There is a breast, and milk: a drinking, which is also an embracing. The distress, and the noise of the distress, change in answer: not because there is anything like a decision to answer, made by a someone we cannot even (quite, yet) say is there, but because the milk prevents it, or the distress changes with the touch. Without being aware of it (or simply, without the need of being aware at all), the child is taking part in an exchange. And to signal the exchange, the voice changes: *yes, that's all right, it's all right*. Call has set up response; that response engenders in its turn another response, the calming of the child; and that response too generates response, in words of encouragement.

From the outset, the infant is bathed in a sea of utterances, gestures, gazes and demands, washing over and across it. To begin with, doubtless, the child cannot yet distinguish any of these from any of the hungerings, appearings, and disappearings that make up the blooming, buzzing confusion around it. To begin with, there is not even really *quite* a child, after all. But even so, these events have all sorts of dimensions to which the child is not party, and within which, without its even yet knowing – indeed, without there even yet being a self to know this – it is already embedded. Adults talk to, touch, feed, clean, play with, attend to, react to babies. Even though the infant may not yet offer any but the most instinctual response, it is treated from the very outset as capable of response, addressed in the expectation of response, and encouraged when it does respond. To babble babytalk with a child is a game whose aim is to get the baby to respond. Something is said: mere noise. Sooner or later, when something is said, there will be a noise in response, whether or not there is any intentionality on the child's part. Another noise happens, and in following on from the first, it is treated as having been triggered by the first. Something has been said back. Now there is a unit that can be repeated: call and response. These utterances and gestures washing over and across the child have as yet no content. They are not vehicles for any conveyed thought or meaning outside the gesture of address and the provoking of response: that will come later. Here, now, in this babble which is nothing more than empty address and counter-address, we already have a conversation which, from this point on, will never end.

(We should note, briefly and in passing, that this is precisely the dimension the analyst listens for in the course of the analysis. What the analyst pays attention to is not, first of all, the literal truth of what is being said, but the implications of the simpler, prior fact that *this is being addressed*: that the analysand is saying it, to the analyst. In that call and response, we have the basic mechanism of *transference*, the key to the analysis. In the transference relation, the analyst finds herself already playing a role in the drama the analysand is repeating in the very analytic situation. • This drama will inevitably be an inquiry about where the subject, the analysand, fits into this world into which they have been thrown. Just as there are some

... it is a perfectly normal and intelligible thing that the libidinal cathexis of someone who is partly unsatisfied, a cathexis which is held ready in anticipation, should be directed as well to the figure of the doctor. ... the cathexis will introduce the doctor into one of the psychical 'series' which the patient has already formed. ('The Dynamics of Transference' (1912), p. 100)

events which cannot be brought to conscious memory, but which are re-enacted in the analysis through transference, so too does psychoanalysis itself not so much recall that impossible forgotten early infancy, as replay it, with the very mechanism of call and response by which there comes to be a subject.)

There is an enormously important point here, to which we shall return in the third chapter. The child may not have differentiated itself from the world, but in a sense it does not have to – *that differentiation has already been made*. It is there in the very possibility of drive and its deep inconsistency with itself. The child lives in a world that already knows perfectly well its own separateness from the child. This is where Freud's analogy of the psyche with an animalcule is profoundly misleading. The world into which a child is born is never just the chaos of brute, impinging external stimuli the analogy implies. It is already, always, and irreducibly, a human world already traversed by human meaning, and inhabited by others who are already just like what the child will become. All of this happens on another stage, as it were; one which will only gradually become accessible to the child, as the unfolding of where it has been all along. Once we recognise that, the peculiar temporal paradox by which the infant is not yet what it already is vanishes. What the child *will be* is already in a sense there, in what it does not yet know is the world outside it. There is a simple word for this already-there: *culture*.

These noises, words, babblings, which pass across and around the baby, are, and have been from the outset, responses, and responses-to-responses, responses-to-responses-to-responses. This is not communication, in the classical sense in which that word implies the transferral of content from one person to another, and for the simple reason that *person* is the very category we are trying to explain. It is more like a vertigo where everything is already, at the moment of utterance and even for the first time, a response, and a response to a response, and so on. And in this exchange, from the outset, the child is addressed *as if it were already a subject.*

(Here too, let us get ahead of ourselves just briefly. This function of *address*, set up here right at the very moment of the child's entry into conscious existence in the world, is something we shall return to. As *interpellation*, it will be at the heart of that relationship between the social and the individual, the way in which, to cite a famous formulation of it, we are hailed as subjects.[11] But more on that in Chapter 3.)

Already, then, we have a sort of dialogue. But from the very outset, difference intervenes and multiples. Such a dialogue is never *just* a dialogue, a closed exchange between mother and child. It is much more a matter of the child's rhythmic emergence from and submergence back into that indifferentiation for which the shorthand is *the maternal body*. The child's emergence from this is a process in which differences come to mark out and internally divide the maternal body. From the outset, there are other voices, different in all sorts of ways: in sound and texture, in the situations in which, and to which, they respond, in the frequency and nature of that response. Even one voice is divided against itself, now sounding this way, now that. The attention, the very *address* of any voice is also, or stands to be, elsewhere. There are different touches and smells, different ways of responding (with speech, with milk, with touch, with a different milk, with all sorts of combinations of these). The voices do not only engage in exchanges with the child, but with each other, and in ways quite different from those involving the child. The infant may interrupt these exchanges, drawing them to itself; at other times, they continue as if ignoring its call, or interrupt the response to that call. From the very moment it can be known, the maternal body is itself differentiated. What appears to be a dialogue reveals itself to have been already, from before the start, a polylogue in which the child has already been only one party.

Now much of what goes on in this bustling world in which the infant arrives is of course not directed at the infant; there is a lot going on in it which appears to have nothing to do with the infant, and even more which is simply quite unintelligible. And yet, as that infant will find out, and not stop finding out in the course of a life, that world is not just chaotic: the order that runs through it is deep and persistent, even if it may never seem fully consistent or complete. As we know from the first chapter, there is an unconscious dimension to all of these exchanges. What the adults who surround the child are saying to it, what they mean by that, what they want from it, are things not known in their entirety even to those who say them. We do not have to agree at all with Freud's notorious diagnosis of 'penis envy' to know that the very existence of a baby is itself a complex and unforeseeable response to all sorts of parental desires and wishes, many of which are not at all obvious to the parents.• Laplanche gives the example of breast-feeding: for the child, the breast may simply be a source of nutrition and comfort, but for the mother, the breast is already also invested as an erogenous zone, in ways which the child cannot comprehend[12].

If we penetrate deeply enough into the neurosis of a woman, we not infrequently meet with the repressed wish to possess a penis like a man. We call this wish 'envy for a penis' and include it in the castration complex. ... In other women we find no evidence of this wish for a penis; it is replaced by the wish for a baby, the frustration of which in real life can lead to the outbreak of a neurosis. ('On Transformations of Instinct as Exemplified in Anal Eroticism' (1917c) p. 129)

Maternal body and paternal voice

Drive itself is deeply and necessarily inconsistent. From this, everything follows.

From the very first moment, because of this inconsistency, the maternal body can be experienced only as divided. The child's need is never quite just an absence that comes to be filled by a plenitude: the gap remains, and is at the heart of everything that comes to fill it. That is the first enigma of the child's existence, and what follows from it is the child's first attempt to provide an answer for that enigma. The mother, that real, flesh-and-blood woman who actually answers the child's call, is no more plenitude than the child, for it will become evident that she too always answers to elsewhere. The mother does things other than feed and comfort the child; that warm sweet body comes and goes elsewhere, turns its gaze elsewhere, is itself the object of calls from elsewhere. Who calls? Where does the mother go when she is not with the child? What else demands her attention? This is the 'other stage' we spoke about earlier: the stage on which, while the child may not yet know itself to be separate from the world, the world already knows itself separate from the child. If *maternal body* is a shorthand for that undifferentiated body of comfort, then it is tempting to give the 'elsewhere' that comes to (be seen already to) divide it a similar shorthand: *the paternal voice*.[13]

We must be clear about the status of this paternal voice. It is not the *cause* of differentiation (which is already there in the drive's blind inconsistency); it is already *the child's attempt to make sense* of the differentiation and inconsistency that is the very motor of drive. It has the same status as those fantasies Freud calls the 'sexual theories of children', and to which we shall shortly return. In fact, it is the form and model for these. Where the child's sexual theories are attempts to make sense of the enigma of sexual difference and why there seem to be two very different sorts of person, this ur-fantasy is an attempt to answer the enigma of *why there is difference*: why there is an unpleasure at the heart of the comfort of the maternal body itself, why there is no pleasure that is complete and closed in on itself. The answer this fantasy of the paternal voice provides is one whose form we shall see again. If the mother cannot provide that complete and unalloyed pleasure, the fantasy says, it is not because that satisfaction is impossible in the very structure of drive, it is simply because she is *called elsewhere*. In principle, the fantasy insists, she could provide that comfort, if only she were not called elsewhere. The fantasy takes what is an impossibility, and turns it into accident, contingency or – and here we see the whole family drama beginning to unfold – rivalry. *Mother does not give me that perfect comfort because she is giving it to another.*

The paternal voice is no more the real voice of the man, who happens to be the father, than the maternal body is the real body of the actual mother. Just as that undifferentiated comfort and satisfaction which is the maternal body may be provided by an actual male body as much as by a female one, so too is the role of the paternal voice one which is effected as easily by a woman as a man. The point is not that the child sees a woman's care interrupted by a man's demands, but that the child sees the non-satisfaction of its demands as the result of interruption from elsewhere: there is always an elsewhere, of which the child is at least at first profoundly unaware, but on which it depends. A child brought up in the company of one sex (whether in same-sex parenting, or by the mother and grandmother) is just as much caught up in this symbolic sexual difference, between maternal body and paternal voice. The paternal voice is the shorthand for the child's attribution of the differentiation that has already come to divide the maternal body, and by which the maternal body is experienced only as something lost or to be regained, as past or future but never simply as present. Moreover, should we not also say that this maternal body is not experienced just as sentimental nostalgia, but also, because it is indifferentiation itself, as a threat to the very separateness of the self? The flipside of the fantasy of the maternal body as primordial comfort is as incessant devourer. Once there is an *elsewhere*, there can be no going back. The paternal voice is a name summing up all those *elsewheres*.

Let us pause for a moment and take stock. There are two things to note about the two terms, the maternal body and the paternal voice. First, they are ways of describing what happens at that (impossible) moment of emergence of something like an infantile subject. They describe differentiation, and the complex way in which this is, in a sense, a differentiation that has always already happened. The infant subject is not created out of nothing: it arrives in a world that is already profoundly human, and where that undifferentiated maternal body is, on the stage which is foreshadowed by the paternal voice, already profoundly differentiated in ways quite inaccessible to this infant which is as yet still barely there. Second, to call these *maternal* body and *paternal* voice is to suggest that this process of differentiation is from the outset inseparably linked to the entire question of sexual difference. And yet, as we have just argued, we must not forget that this is not a biologism: the maternal body

Science ... draws your attention to the fact that portions of the male sexual apparatus also appear in women's bodies, though in an atrophied state, and vice versa in the alternative case. It regards their occurrence as indications of *bisexuality*, as though an individual is not a man or a woman but always both – merely a certain amount more the one than the other. You will then be asked to make yourselves familiar with the idea that the proportion in which masculine and feminine are mixed in an individual is subject to quite considerable fluctuations. Since, however, apart from the very rarest cases, only one kind of sexual product – ova or semen – is nevertheless present in one person, you are bound to have doubts as to the decisive significance of those elements and must conclude that what constitutes masculinity or femininity is an unknown characteristic which anatomy cannot lay hold of. (Lecture 33, 'Femininity', *New Introductory Lectures on Psychoanalysis* (1933a), p. 114)

does not necessarily describe what is biologically female, or the paternal voice what is necessarily male. Sexual difference in this sense is thus not a matter of the child's learning to distinguish properties which are already there – what makes a boy, and what makes a girl. • That will come later, and only in the very processes through which the subject itself is formed. Sexual difference is a matter of the very emergence of the subject.

Empty difference

Throughout Freud, we can see a certain drama of boys and girls, mothers and fathers, which is steeped in the ways in which it is possible to be a girl or a boy, a man or a woman, a mother or a father, in the middle classes of late nineteenth- and early twentieth-century Vienna (Decker, 1999). Reading Freud, we easily become aware of the many ways in which Freud's world is like but not quite the same as ours – that we are reading a quite specific, historical drama. Families are structured differently: the sheer width of class differences meant that servants carried out many of what we would think of as parental, and particularly maternal, functions; the still high mortality of women during childbirth meant that it was common to find families in which a middle-class widowed father had remarried a younger woman and begun a second tier of the family, in which generation and chronological age were no longer in step.[14] The characteristic and highly publicised hysterias of our own time are the eating disorders, anorexia and bulimia. We find these in Freud's case histories, to be sure, but they are outweighed by a catalogue of symptoms which seem far less familiar today: chronic dyspnoea (breathing difficulties), *tussis nervosa* (compulsive coughing), aphonia (loss of voice), anaesthesia, pains or paralysis in the limbs or other areas of the body, paraphasia (an unawareness of the language in which one is speaking), loss of the sense of smell or taste – the people of Freud's day even seem to get *ill* in unfamiliar ways.

The differences are perhaps most obvious where sex is concerned. We see this everywhere in Freud, who may on various occasions – and sometimes on the same one – at once propose radically novel views of sexuality and yet seem to endorse many of what we have come to see as the commonplaces and prejudices of the late nineteenth-century European middle classes. It is not at all surprising that Freud most easily arouses outrage in his statements about women and female sexuality.•

But Freud's argument is only in part an argument about what the specific *content* of sexual difference might be – that is, about *what men are* and *what women are*, as if those terms represented entities with a fixed and determinable set of properties, a norm from which we could determine aberrations and which individuals are not *truly* men or women. To argue

The effect of penis-envy has a share ... in the physical vanity of women, since they are bound to value their charms more highly as a late compensation for their original sexual inferiority. ...

I cannot help mentioning an impression that we are constantly receiving during analytic practice. A man of about thirty strikes us as a youthful, somewhat unformed individual, whom we expect to make powerful use of the possibilities for development opened up to him by analysis. A woman of the same age, however, often frightens us by her psychical rigidity and unchangeability. Her libido has taken up final positions and seems incapable of exchanging them for others. There are no paths open to further development; it is as though the whole process had already run its course and remains thenceforward insusceptible to influence – as though, indeed, the difficult development to femininity had exhausted the possibilities of the person concerned. As therapists we lament this state of things, even if we succeed in putting an end to our patient's ailment by doing away with her neurotic conflict. (Lecture 33, 'Femininity', *New Introductory Lectures on Psychoanalysis* (1933a), pp. 132, 134–35)

from positive, given properties, generally biological or anatomical in their basis, is the strategy of the nineteenth-century sexology from which the argument of the *Three Essays* seeks to break. It may be an argument that still has its pull on Freud: dismiss it as he does; it often returns all the stronger for the disavowal. But underneath this, and making it possible, is the pull of another drama, which we are trying to unravel here. This is the drama of the very *possibility* of differentiation, whatever the specific differences it may tend to have as its result in a particular culture, in a particular time and place. In a word, the sexual difference we are interested in here is an *empty* difference: the bare fact that *there is* sexual difference, and from which, in the course of the vicissitudes of a life history, the specific forms of an individual's sexuality can develop.

It is not at all difficult to criticise Freud for taking as universals what are actually the features of middle-class middle-European societies of his time. Sophocles' Oedipus kills his father and marries his mother, and Freud famously uses this as the figure of the jealousy the infant must negotiate and overcome in order to arrive at a mature set of sexual identifications and object-choices. What, we might object, could we possibly find of that in societies in which the care of the infant is shared out across a number of women in the family (by the grandmother's generation, say, when the mother's generation is necessarily engaged in work), or in which the dead are treated as still present and taken into account in daily observances? The Viennese middle-class child's experiences are not universal, and it would be dangerous and culturally blind to assert that they are. The drama of separation is not the same for all human beings, in all cultures. But what *is* universal is the sheer fact of that separation: every human being, in order to function within its social world, whatever that social world might be, must go through some process of separation from the maternal body, some form of arrival within the complex system of cultural differences, which always and already surrounds it, whatever the actual content of those differences. • While specific properties are always necessarily culturally and historically located, *empty* difference – the sheer fact that *there is* difference, that *differentiation is necessary*, is universal.

[The Oedipus complex] represents the peak of infantile sexuality, which, through its after-effects, exercises a decisive influence on the sexuality of adults. Every new arrival on this planet is faced by the task of mastering the Oedipus complex; anyone who fails to do so falls a victim to neurosis. With the progress of psychoanalytic studies the importance of the Oedipus complex has become more and more clearly evident; its recognition has become the shibboleth that distinguishes the adherents of psychoanalysis from its opponents. ('The Transformation of Puberty', *Three Essays on the Theory of Sexuality* (1905c), p. 226: fn added 1920)

It is in this sense that sexual difference may run deep in the world – may even be inseparable from our very sense of there being a world.

Oedipus

A subject does not suddenly appear in the world. It develops, with that paradoxical temporality by which it is already in a sense there, or by which what it is, is also a matter of what it is not yet. A subject does not simply occupy a moving moment of present time; it is an anachrony, traversed at every moment by what it is not yet, or has already been. Its progress out of infancy is the drama of shifting love objects and identifications that make up the Oedipus complex and its dissolution.

As we have said, for Freud, Oedipus is the basic drama of separation and identification, above and beyond the obvious cultural variations in the constitution of the family. It is the name he gives to the negotiations involved in the basic process of differentiation at the heart of any sense of self-whatever. For the boy – and the boy is the model for Freud's description – the Oedipal situation is a first reaction to the differentiation we have called, for short, the *paternal voice*. The child wants to retain as its love object its original, infantile object, the mother, and so the only room left for the father in this scenario is as the hated rival for the mother's affection. This generally reaches its peak when the child is somewhere between three and five-years-old; with puberty, it stands to be dissolved as the boy begins to make his first adult identifications and choices of love objects.

At first, and for a long time, Freud sees the Oedipal drama as being essentially the same for both sexes.•   Around

As you see, I have only described the relation of a boy to his father and mother. *Things happen in just the same way with little girls, with the necessary changes ...* (Lecture 21, 'The Development of the Libido and the Sexual Organisations', *Introductory Lectures on Psychoanalysis* (1916–17), p. 333; emphasis added)

...the dissolution of the Oedipus complex would consolidate the masculinity in a boy's character. *In a precisely*

1924, though, Freud begins to suspect that this is not the case at all, and that the process may in fact be quite different for each sex.●

analogous way, the outcome of the Oedipus attitude in a little girl may be an intensification of the identification with her mother (or the setting up of such an identification for the first time) – a result which will fix the child's feminine character. (*The Ego and the Id* (1923), p. 32 emphasis added)

Let us begin with the normative heterosexuality Freud considers. For the boy, heterosex-

The female sex, too, develops an Oedipus complex, a superego and a latency period. May we also attribute a phallic organisation and a castration complex to it? The answer is in the affirmative; *but these things cannot be the same as they are in boys*. ('The Dissolution of the Oedipus Complex' (1924c), pp. 177–78; emphasis added)

ual development is a matter of separating from the other- sex parent (whose sex will nevertheless remain the object of sexual interest in adult life), and identifying with (and thus rivalling) the same-sex parent. For the girl, such a development involves separation from the *same*-sex parent (whose sex nevertheless remains the point of identification and rivalry), and taking the sex of the *other* parent as sexual object. We can see the asymmetry straight away if we diagram it out, as in Figures 2.2 and 2.3.

Even in this apparently simplest case of a normatively heterosexual family, one that seeks to offer itself as the most obvious and straightforward, the relationship between the sexes is far from binary. What upsets the binary symmetry is the point that no matter what sex you are, or your objects of desire and identifications, your first love was always a woman.

	Infantile love object (mother)	Mature identification with	Mature love object
Boy	other sex F	same sex M	other sex F
Girl	same sex F	same sex F	other sex M

Figure 2.2

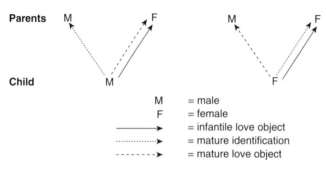

Parents   M   F   M   F

Child   M   F

M = male
F = female
———→ = infantile love object
·········→ = mature identification
------→ = mature love object

Figure 2.3

We have an impression here that what we have said about the Oedipus complex applies with complete strictness to the male child only, and that we are right in rejecting the term 'Electra complex' which seeks to emphasise the analogy between the attitude of the two sexes. It is only in the male child that we find the fateful combination of love for the one parent and simultaneous hatred for the other as a rival. ('Female Sexuality' (1931), pp. 228–29)

It is because of this asymmetry that Freud rejects Jung's suggestion of an 'Electra complex.' • Oedipus is not the same for girls and boys. The conclusion may seem obvious, but Freud did not formulate it for almost two decades after the ground-breaking *Three Essays on Sexuality*, and a decade and a half after he first gave it the name 'Oedipus complex'. No doubt this is an index of some sort of blindness: but given the general acuity of Freud's observations, and the radical and ingenious nature of the hypotheses they lead him to propose, it is, at very least, a quite remarkable blindness. Is it an accident that Oedipus himself was blind – that he blinded himself? Is blindness of one sort or another somehow connected with sexual difference? Henceforth, Freud will often speak of femininity as a mystery to which he has no key. The implications of this are far-reaching.•

Throughout history people have knocked their heads against the riddle of the nature of femininity ... Nor will *you* have escaped worrying over this problem – those of you who are men; to those of you who are women this will not apply – you are yourselves the problem. (Lecture 33, 'Femininity', *New Introductory Lectures on Psychoanalysis* (1933), p. 113)

The great question that has never been answered and which I have not been able to answer, despite my thirty years of research into the feminine soul, is 'What does a woman want?' (Letter to Marie Bonaparte, cited in Jones, 1964, p. 474)

Castration

One's sex is not just a given; Oedipus is something to be negotiated. The way through it – from infantile associations to mature object choices – is a matter of the famous **castration complex**. This is one of the famous sticking points of Freudian theory, based as it seems to be on an obvious phallocentrism, and thus easily and often dismissed or excused as one of those moments in which Freud is revealed to be, in the phrase which is used just as readily for excuse, dismissal or amelioration, 'of his time'. Let us unravel the story with an eye for the sorts of logic we have been examining so far.

In this we will need to keep firmly in mind that what Freud is calling castration is first of all an example of what he terms the sexual theories of children.[15] That is, before castration is a theory psychoanalysis has, it is, like the paternal voice, *the shorthand for the theorising the child does* – a fantasy intended to make sense of that enigmatic but unavoidable fact of sexual difference. Freud's theory of the castration complex is a theory of how the child makes sense of a world which is still largely inexplicable to it, and of how it comes to enter onto that *other stage* of difference.

It begins with the observation – and the puzzle – that some people possess a penis while others do not. • Why should this be so? Is it possible to *lose* the penis? Is it possi-ble that those who do not have it might have lost it some time in the past? Conversely, is there the risk that those who do have it might lose it some time in the future?

> ... the existence of two sexes does not to begin with arouse any difficulties or doubts in children. It is self-evident to a male child that a genital like his own is to be attributed to everyone he knows, and that he cannot make its absence tally with his picture of these other people. ...
>
> This conviction is energetically maintained by boys, is obstinately defended against the contradictions which soon result from observation, and is only abandoned after severe internal struggles (the castration complex).
> ('Infantile Sexuality', *Three Essays on the Theory of Sexuality* (1905c), p. 195)

That is, castration introduces a temporal dimension into sexual difference. For the boy, it is a threat of something that *might* occur, in the future, perhaps as a pun-ishment that might be averted by the right behaviour. For the girl, it has *already* occurred, in the past, for which it might perhaps be possible to compensate or find a substitute (a baby of her own).• For neither of them is this loss something happening on the timeline of direct experience or mem-ory, as a real event; it is always what has *not yet* or *already* happened.

This means that castration is an *absolute* loss, in the same sense in which the primal scene takes place in an absolute past that has never been pre-sent and remains

> There is an interesting contrast between the behaviour of the two sexes. ... when a little boy first catches sight of a girl's genital region, he begins by showing irresolution and lack of interest; he sees nothing or disavows what he has seen, he softens it down or looks about for expedi-ents for bringing it into line with his expectations. It is not until later, when some threat of castration has obtained a hold upon him, that the observation becomes important to him: if he then recollects or repeats it, it arouses a terrible storm of emotion in him and forces him to believe in the reality of the threat which he has hith-erto laughed at. ...
>
> A little girl behaves differently. She makes her judgement and her decision in a flash. She has seen it and knows that she is without it and wants to have it.
> ('Some Psychical Consequences of the Anatomical Distinction between the Sexes' (1925b), p. 252)

outside of any timeline. And like the primal scene, castration – even the mere threat of castration – need never have actually occurred, to the extent that any actual occurrence of any such threat is even quite superfluous and unnecessary to the whole logic. Castration is a *primal fantasy*. What's more, it is a primal fantasy *about loss*, about a loss that is so absolute as to be irretrievable: having never occurred in any present, it is a loss for which no present will ever be able to make reparation. It is thus not the loss, or even the threatened loss, of something one actually possesses or once possessed. It is a far more paradoxical thing: the loss of something one *never* actually possessed – an absolute unity with the mother – but which now acts as a yardstick for all those things one does possess, and makes them seem lacking.[16]

We should be clear about the twist that has occurred quite quickly here. If we began with a simple binary of *having* and *not having*, once castration enters the picture we are dealing with two quite different relationships to loss which are, surprisingly, no longer binary. Binarity, remember, is a relationship set up between two terms by a third, which is present in one and absent in the other. With castration, though, each sex is seen as having a different relationship to *loss*, an absence in the first place. What's more, this is not even any longer a sort of negative binary where one sex would *have* loss and the other would *lack* it. Loss has a quite different relation to each sex: absolute and irreparable for both, it is in the absolute past for one and the absolute future for the other. One sex is not the complement of the other, supplying whatever it lacks: each sex lacks, but in different ways, and as this is an absolute lack there is no possibility of its ever being filled. Far from being binary, then, castration is what leads us *out* of binarity, and into a radical *asymmetry* of the sexes.

Despite the baggage of connotation the term 'castration' carries with it, we should keep in mind that it is one of the sexual theories of children, a way of explaining the enigma of sexual difference. Castration is a name for the inevitable and, surely, profoundly *desirable* separation from the maternal body, and for the differentiation by which there is such a thing as a human subject. That is, castration is paradoxically the name not for the *loss* of pleasure, but for the very *possibility* of pleasure (and with that, of the consequent inbuilt cost and limit of all pleasures, that they never seem complete or enough). To refuse castration would thus be a potentially dangerous thing, with implications for the entire economy of the psyche. The fetishist, for example, carries out a complex manoeuvre Freud will later call *disavowal*, whose formula could be put succinctly as *I knew that this is the case, but I act as if it were not.*• The fetishist knows full well that women do not have a penis, but appoints a substitute to take its place – the fetish object. Fetishism is an incomplete denial: other more radical forms of disavowal are found at work in the psychoses, whose foreclosure may be so thoroughgoing as to disintegrate the psychotic's very sense of a world.

[The boy refuses] to take cognizance of the fact of his having perceived that a woman does not possess a penis. No, that could not be true: for if a woman had been castrated, then his own possession of a penis was in danger; and against that there rose in rebellion the portion of his narcissism which Nature has, as a precaution, attached to that particular organ. ... It is not true that, after the child has made his observation of the woman, he has preserved, unaltered, his belief that women have a phallus. He has retained that belief, but he has also given it up. ... Yes, in his mind the woman has got a penis, in spite of everything; but this penis is no longer the same as it was before. Something else has taken its place, has been appointed its substitute, as it were, and now inherits the interest which was formerly directed to its predecessor. ('Fetishism' (1927a), pp. 153–54)

And castration leads us to a quite different story for boys and for girls. For the boy, castration heralds the dissolution of Oedipus. Under its pressure, the boy gives over the incestuous desire for his mother and rivalry with his father. For the girl, though, any fantasy of castration is experienced as having already happened, not as a future threat. It leads her to attempts at compensation, as she transfers her attention from the parent without the penis to the one with. For the girl, castration comes *before* Oedipus. While castration leads the boy out of Oedipus, it leads the girl into it. The dissolution of the Oedipus complex is thus considerably more difficult for her, a gradual realisation that the compensation she was after, will remain unfulfilled. It is consequently, Freud argues, much easier for the girl to remain within the Oedipal stage, either wholly or through repression and dis-avowal.• Whichever way, there is an entire extra step in Oedipus for the girl: the passage from infantile to common heterosexual attach-ments of maturity involves a change of

> In girls the motive for the demolition of the Oedipus com-plex is lacking. Castration has already had its effect, which was to force the child into the situation of the Oedipus complex. Thus the Oedipus complex escapes the fate which it meets with in boys: it may be slowly aban-doned or dealt with by repression, or its effects may per-sist far into women's normal life. ('Some Psychical Consequences of the Anatomical Distinction between the Sexes' (1925b), p. 257)

sex of the object. Somewhere a reversal has had to take place, and there is nothing in the boy's negotiation of Oedipus to correspond to this. The asymmetry is spreading.

It is important to keep sight of this asymmetry. As we suggested above, it is something whose consequences dawned on Freud only in the mid-1920s. We should not be too hasty to dismiss those assertions of the riddle of femininity as being no more than the familiar and patronising tropes of patriarchy. Like Freud's earlier use of the nineteenth-century vocabulary of perversion in the *Three Essays on Sexuality*, they tend, for modern eyes, to hide the discovery they make. These assertions of enigma do not occur before that argument of the dif-ferent passages each sex makes through Oedipus and castration. Feminine sex-uality becomes a mystery in Freud's writing once it is no longer the symmetric complement of masculine sexuality. Once it is no longer possible to say that things happen in just the same way for girls as they do for boys – with, of course, all the necessary changes• – there is no longer any measure for it._If at this time Freud often distin-guishes himself from the feminism of his day, and refuses to treat the two sexes as equal, we can see some-

> As you see, I have only described the relation of a boy to his father and mother. Things happen in just the same way with little girls, with the necessary changes ... (Lecture 21, 'The Development of the Libido and the Sexual Organizations', *Introductory Lectures on Psychoanalysis* (1916–17), vol. 16, p.333)

thing more at work here than a recidivist insistence on woman's inferiority to man. This is also (and we know that contradictory ideas often inhabit the same space) a statement of a radical *in*commensurability of the sexes and the extent to which they simply lack common measure.• Once this possibility enters the field, we can no longer be sure what 'pure mas-culinity and femi-ninity' might be. Not only is this a

> We must not allow ourselves to be deflected from such conclusions by the denials of the feminists, who are anx-ious to force us to regard the two sexes as completely equal in position and worth; but we shall, of course, will-ingly agree that ... all human individuals, as a result of their bisexual disposition and of cross-inheritance, combine in themselves both masculine and feminine

characteristics, so that pure masculinity and femininity remain theoretical constructions of uncertain content. ('Some Psychical Consequences of the Anatomical Distinction between the Sexes' (1925b), p. 258)

consequence of the logic of castration, it is also, and perhaps unexpectedly, a move that opens up some of the very issues of difference which have informed many western feminisms since the 1980s.

In this asymmetry, sexual difference is not just a matter of bodily shape and function. It is a difference within the very psyche itself: men and women do not quite know each other, or desire in the same way. There are men and women, there are human beings, but there is no generic 'human being'. Sexual difference is that ineradicable and irreducible difference which is constitutive of the human, and yet which at the same time prevents 'the human' from having any sort of totality.• This is what Lacan means in that notorious and easily misread dictum that

One gets the impression that a man's love and a woman's are a phase apart psychologically. (Lecture 33, 'Femininity', *New Introductory Lectures on Psychoanalysis* (1933a), p. 134)

There is no sexual relationship. It is not, of course, that men and women do not have sexual relationships with each other (or even, for that matter, that those relations cannot be highly successful and long-lasting), but that there is no totality to the idea of the human, within which masculine and feminine could be given and complementary roles. There are no rules for a successful sexual relationship: if it is to occur, it is always to be invented anew each time.[17]

With castration, the *presence or absence* of the penis is not really the point after all, because what has been lost is not the actual penis but a phantasmatic organ which has never belonged to either sex, male or female. Castration is an experience of *loss*, whether one has an actual penis or not. Here, Lacan's term *phallus* is particularly useful, to distinguish between the real organ and that phantasmatic organ which, because it is the embodiment of loss for both sexes, comes to stand for pure empty sexual difference itself.[18] We have seen that loss tends to have a different temporality for each sex, irretrievable because it lies either in an absolute past or in an absolute future: on the one hand, the maternal body in its indifferentiation is an origin to which there can be no return, and on the other, nothing will ever be an adequate compensation or substitute for this primal loss.

Contingency

As we saw in various ways with the logic of the dream's 'residues of the day', and the formation of the symptom and the vicissitudes of the drive, from the very outset the subject is something which comes about only within the unrepeatable web of contingencies and singularities of a history. While we can work back and reconstruct the course of events and their causalities once it has all happened, we cannot do it the other way round, beginning with the initial conditions, and predicting the results from them. There are too many imponderables, too many things which are inseparably bound up in the result yet which need not have happened. At the heart of being human, what we share is the irreducible contingency of this process. This is why *the human* has no totality: subjects are always formed in and by that contingency, and have no essence other than their necessary openness to it.

Because of this, what Freud is suggesting here is not a form of biological determinism. It begins, as it must, with infants who are *already* male or female in two senses: they are *born with* one set of genitals or the other, and *born into* a world in which that is already a series of complex assignations. But these are only initial conditions: they guarantee no particular *ways of being* a woman or a man. As Freud argued in the case of the aims and objects of the drive, though certain outcomes tend to be more frequent than others, this is not because they are naturally hardwired into the infant psyche (which is on the contrary polymorphously perverse), but simply because they are more likely: the world tends to support some paths over others, as materially easier to realise.[19] Things can and do work out in all sorts of ways. • What Freud describes are typical rather than neces-

> I have no doubt that the chronological and causal relations described here between the Oedipus complex, sexual intimidation (the threat of castration), the formation of the super-ego and the beginning of the latency period are of a typical kind; but I do not wish to assert that this type is the only possible one. Variations in the chronological order and in the linking-up of these events are bound to have a very important bearing on the development of the individual. ('The Dissolution of the Oedipus Complex' (1924c), p. 179)

sary paths. Hence the frequent branching shape of his argument, especially in the metapsychological papers: *this* can happen, or *this*, or *this* ...•

To describe the possibilities of these vicissitudes, Freud makes a series of distinctions which are never quite consistent, but whose aim is always to separate the question of sex from biology. In a 1915 footnote to the 1905 *Three Essays on Sexuality*, for example, he distinguishs three uses of the terms 'masculine' and 'feminine'. The one he declares of most use to psychoanalysis is the *psychological* distinction between *active* and *passive*; the second is purely *biological*, as determined by

> What I have said so far by way of indication may be concluded by a short summary of the paths leading to the choice of an object.
>
> A person may love:
> (1) According to the narcissistic type:
>   (a)   what he himself is (i.e. himself),
>   (b)   what he himself was,
>   (c)   what he himself would like to be,
>   (d)   someone who was once part of himself.
> (2) According to the anaclitic (attachment) type:
>   (a) the woman who feeds him,
>   (b) the man who protects him. ...
> ('On Narcissism: An Introduction' (1914a), p. 90)

> Observation shows us that an instinct may undergo the following vicissitudes:
>   Reversal into its opposite.
>   Turning round upon the subject's own self.
>   Repression.
>   Sublimation. ...
>   Reversal of an instinct into its opposite resolves on closer examination into two different processes: a

change from *activity* to *passivity*, and a *reversal of its content*. The two processes, being different in their nature, must be treated separately. ('Instincts and Their Vicissitudes' (1915b), pp. 126–27)

calls the *sociological*, shows us, from an observation of actual individuals, that no one is in fact purely masculine or feminine in either of the other two senses, but has a mixture of traits (pp. 219–20). Yet in the same year as this addition to the earlier essay, in 'Instincts and Their Vicissitudes' he describes what he calls the three great polarities that dominate mental life, the first of which, activity–passivity, falls under what he calls the *biological* (p. 140). In *Civilization and its Discontents* from 1930 – and again in a footnote – he will restate the difficulty of connecting the biological and psychological meanings of masculinity and femininity, pointing out how psychology all too quickly elides them with the question of activity and passivity (pp. 105–07).

The 1933 lecture on 'Femininity' from the *New Introductory Lectures on Psychoanalysis* gets under way by raising objections to all such distinctions. The biological distinction is inadequate, as what we might ordinarily call masculine or feminine behaviour quite commonly bears little relationship to the genital morphology of the person who exhibits it. In cases like that, 'masculine' and 'feminine' are nearly always used to mean 'active' and 'passive', a distinction Freud now dismisses as of little use, and barely more than a rephrasing of the original problem.• Besides, all drives are by their very nature active, whether they are a man's or a woman's. Could we save the hypothesis by saying that psychological femininity is a matter of giving preference to passive *aims* (the achievement of which may in turn involve a great deal of active behaviour)? Freud sees the suppression of

Even in the sphere of human sexual life you soon see how inadequate it is to make masculine behaviour coincide with activity and feminine with passivity. ... Women can display great activity in various directions, men are not able to live in company with their own kind unless they develop a large amount of passive adaptability. If you now tell me that these facts go to prove precisely that both men and women are bisexual in the psychological sense, I shall conclude that you have decided in your own minds to make 'active' coincide with 'masculine' and 'passive' with 'feminine'. But I advise you against it. It seems to me to serve no useful purpose and adds nothing to our knowledge. (Lecture 33, 'Femininity', *New Introductory Lectures on Psychoanalysis* (1933a), p. 115)

aggressiveness in women as an example, and the way in which it tends to a characteristically feminine masochism. But then, what recourse would we have for describing male masochism except to call it a feminine trait? The argument seems all too easily to go around in circles.

Freud's answer to these increasing knots, at least in the lecture on femininity, is to see the question itself as faulty, or at very least as premature. Instead of asking *What are the characteristic qualities of femininity and masculinity?*, he reaffirms the question psychoanalysis has asked all along, the question of contingency: *How do people come to be men or women, in all the variety of ways of being either?●* Genital difference gives rise to a proliferating, centrifugal series of other differentiations no longer governed by biological fact. We have some-

And now you are already prepared to hear that psychology too is unable to solve the riddle of femininity. ... In conformity with its peculiar nature, psychoanalysis does not try to describe what a woman is – that would be a task it could scarcely perform – but sets about inquiring how she comes into being, how a woman develops out of a child with a bisexual disposition. (Lecture 33, Femininity, *New Introductory Lectures on Psychoanalysis* (1933a), p. 116)

thing similar to the relationship between *drive* and purely animal *instinct*. Sexuality is always deflected from genital, biological sex; masculinity and femininity are different ways of sustaining that loss of what was never possessed in the first place, for which the Freudian shorthand is castration.

Prohibition and impossibility

Almost 15 years after he had given the Oedipus complex its name, and a good decade after those footnotes complicating that opposition of active and passive had started appearing in later editions of the *Three Essays*, Freud would describe the boy's negotiation of Oedipus in terms of that very opposition.● If we had not already seen the complications of those terms, we might expect that the active choice would be the masculine one, the one the boy should decide to take, and the passive choice would be the feminine one that he should reject. Things are of course not quite so simple. Both active and passive ways are open to the boy's (active) choice, *but only because both of them are already foreclosed*: whichever way the boy chooses, that

The Oedipus complex offered the child two possibilities of satisfaction, an active and a passive one. He could put himself in his father's place in a masculine fashion and have intercourse with his mother as his father did, in which case he would soon have felt the latter as a hindrance; or he might want to take the place of his mother and be loved by his father, in which case his mother would become superfluous. The child may have had only very vague notions as to what constitutes a satisfying erotic intercourse; but certainly the penis must play a part in it, for the sensations in his own organ were evidence of that. So far he had had no occasion to doubt that women possessed a penis. But now his acceptance of the possibility of castration, his recognition that women were castrated, made an end of both possible ways of obtaining satisfaction from the Oedipus complex. For both of them entailed the loss of his penis – the masculine one as a resulting punishment and the feminine one as a precondition. If the satisfaction of love in the field of the Oedipus complex is to cost the child his penis, a conflict is bound to arise between his narcissistic interest in that part of his body and the libidinal cathexis of his parental objects. In this conflict the first of these forces normally triumphs: the child's ego turns away from the Oedipus complex. ('The Dissolution of the Oedipus Complex' (1924c), p. 176)

fantasised Oedipal satisfaction is simply not available. This is not because the four- or five-year-old child is obviously incapable of having intercourse with the mother; the point is more that *even if he were, it would not give him what the fantasy promises*. Both options, passive or active, would involve a refusal of difference, and a retreat to a state of undifferentiation, which is to say non-being: in effect, his own death as an individual being. The boy realises that Oedipal attachments offer only a choice of no-win situations, and that the only thing to do is go elsewhere.

Something odd and very interesting is happening here. While the Oedipal scenario claims to be forbidden (under threat of castration), it is actually impossible. *There is no need for that threat of castration, when the Oedipal relation is actually in principle, and from the beginning, impossible.* The threat of castration is thus not only not a real threat, something that does not actually have to take place: it is part of the fantasy, part of the child's way of explaining that mysterious brute fact of sexual difference. The child's fantasy is that the Oedipal relation is, after all, obtainable, or at least would be if it were not under a prohibition. The prohibition thus actually sustains the very relation it bars.

(We have been here before. This was the mechanism behind the fantasy of the paternal voice and the way it served to disguise an impossibility and turn the non-fulfilment of desire from a necessity into a contingency: *if it were not for the demands of others, my desires would be satisfied.* Here, that disguise is strengthened into prohibition, but the Oedipal drama was already implicit in the earlier version.)

We need to be quite clear about this: the fantasy is that *the only thing standing between me and my desires is that someone has forbidden them to me.* Such a desire, the fantasy promises, is not only possible to achieve but, because it is held in check only by the counterforce of prohibition, must also be a deeply transgressive force. Fantasy sees itself, *and as part of the fantasy*, as going where the strictures of the Law will not allow, and in doing that as threatening the Law with dissolution. This is an important point, and we shall return to it in the next chapter. What it implies is that *we should be wary of any model which suggests that the social and cultural are essentially a series of prohibitions on an otherwise free set of desires.* Such a view is precisely fantasy, a *social* fantasy in its purest form: that is, a fantasy *about* the social world and the way it works, and a fantasy that circulates *within* the social world. It imagines that all that stands between me and the attainment of my desires is the social world's refusal to countenance them.

Far from being what disrupts or even threatens to disrupt the Law, then, we should insist that this fantasy is *the precise point at which the Law is installed.* The dissolution of the Oedipus complex – that moment at which the child will at last have rejected the desire to return to the indifferentiation of the maternal body and affirmed its own differentiation within the world – is, after all, also the moment when the child takes its place on that other stage where it has been all along, within the symbolic networks of the cultural and social. In a word, the end of Oedipus marks the moment of installation of the superego.●

And if the passage through

The broad general outcome of the sexual phase dominated by the Oedipus complex may, therefore, be taken to be the forming of a precipitate in the ego, consisting of [mother- and father-] identifications in some way united with each other. This modification of the ego retains its special position; it confronts the other contents of the ego as an ego-ideal or super-ego. (The Ego and the Id (1923), p. 341: emphasis in original)

In boys ... the complex is not simply repressed, it is literally smashed to pieces by the shock of threatened castration. Its libidinal cathexes are abandoned, desexualised and in part sublimated; its objects are incorporated

Oedipus is quite different for each sex, does that not also imply that each sex tends also to have a quite different relation to the superego which results from this passage? This is indeed what we find in Freud's arguments. It may jostle shoulders with what often strikes the modern reader as misogyny, for here Freud often expresses the difference between the sexes as a matter of women's failure to be masculine.• But what if we insist on the very implication of Freud's own argument that he overlooks in such cases – that the relationship of the sexes is here, as elsewhere, not complementary but incommensurable and asymmetric? The super-ego is not the property of one sex, but of *neither*. The point is not that men live up to it but women do not. It is that *neither sex* can possibly live up to it, because the demands that the superego makes are strictly impossible: as we saw in the first chapter, they are double binds. (It is hardly surprising that two of the most frequent words Freud uses to describe the superego should be *cruel* and *severe*.) As with castration – the symbolic drama of separation and individuation out of which the superego is formed – each sex tends to have a quite different relationship to that impossibility.

into the ego, where they form the nucleus of the super-ego and give that new structure its characteristic qualities. In normal, or, it is better to say, in ideal cases, the Oedipus complex exists no longer, even in the unconscious; the super-ego has become its heir. ('Some Psychical Consequences of the Anatomical Distinction between the Sexes' (1925b), p. 257)

I cannot evade the notion (though I hesitate to give it expression) that for women the level of what is ethically normal is different from what it is in men. Their super-ego is never so inexorable, so impersonal, so independent of its emotional origins as we require it to be in men. Character-traits which critics of every epoch have brought up against women – that they show less sense of justice than men, that they are less ready to submit to the great exigencies of life, that they are more often influenced in their judgements by feelings of affection or hostility – all these would be amply accounted for by the modification in the formation of their super-ego which we have inferred above. We must not allow ourselves to be deflected from such conclusions by the denials of the feminists …, who are anxious to force us to regard the two sexes as completely equal in position and worth; but we shall also, of course, willingly agree that the majority of men are also far behind the masculine ideal and that all human individuals, as a result of their bisexual disposition and of cross-inheritance, combine in themselves both masculine and feminine characteristics, so that pure masculinity and femininity remain theoretical constructions of uncertain content. ('Some Psychical Consequences of the Anatomical Distinction between the Sexes' (1925b), pp. 257–58)

In the impossibility and contradictions of its demands, the superego is without unity or totality. From the outset, Freud had seen the superego as the moment of common cultural binding. • But what happens in this commonality if the superego is divided

The ego ideal [superego] opens up an important avenue for the understanding of group psychology. In addition to its individual side, this ideal has a social side; it is also the common ideal of a family, a class or a nation. ... The want of satisfaction which arises from the non-fulfilment of this ideal liberates homosexual libido, and this is transformed into a sense of guilt (social anxiety). Originally this sense of guilt was a fear of punishment by the parents, or, more correctly, the fear of losing their love; later the parents are replaced by an indefinite number of fellow-men. ('On Narcissism: An Introduction' (1914a), pp. 101–02) against itself? What if the cultural sphere, the lived relation to the social, is thus also necessarily split? It is to that question we shall now turn.

Sexual Difference:
'The Dissolution of the Oedipus Complex' (1924c), 'Some Psychical Consequences of the Anatomical Distinction between the Sexes' (1925b) and 'Female Sexuality' (1931)

Though the figure of Oedipus is invoked at least as early as *The Interpretation of Dreams* in 1900, it is not until the 1910 paper on 'A Special Type of Object Choice Made by Men' that Freud uses the term 'Oedipus complex'.[20] The idea of a castration complex dates from about this time too: Freud speaks of it in his 1908 article 'On the Sexual Theories of Children', and it has an important role to play in the 'Little Hans' case history of the following year ('Analysis of a Phobia in a Five-Year-Old Boy'). For almost the next decade and a half, though, Freud spoke of the passage through the Oedipus complex as essentially the same for boys and girls. It is only with the 1924 paper, on the dissolution of the complex, and its elaboration in the 1925 paper, that he would see the course of development as different for each sex, due to the necessarily different relationship each has to castration.

These proposals get restated in the 1931 paper on 'Female Sexuality', which concludes with a brief review and in many cases rebuttal of some of the psychoanalytic literature sparked by the 1925 paper. Two years later, the well-known lecture on 'Femininity' in the *New Introductory Lectures on Psychoanalysis* would repeat much of this material for a lay audience, with some further speculation on the consequences for the differences in psychology between the adult man and woman. In particular, since the dissolution of the Oedipus complex is also the time of the installation of the superego, and as each sex undergoes that in a quite different way, Freud argues that men and women tend to have very different relationships to the superego, and thus to the morality it represents.

Notes to Chapter 2

[1]This passage follows directly from the passage we earlier cited on the necessity of beginning a truly scientific investigation with a rather vague set of concepts which data and observation can then make more precise. In a word, the particular concept Freud had in mind here was the drive.

[2]See also the account Freud gives of sucking and breast-feeding in Lecture 20, 'The Sexual Life of Human Beings', *Introductory Lectures on Psychoanalysis* (1916–17), vol. 16, pp. 314–150.

[3]Freud's German has a simple term for this attachment and divergence, *Anlehnung* – literally a leaning-on, and figuratively (and in everyday German), the taking as a model, or following the example of something. The English translation of the Standard Edition unfortunately obscures this: sometimes it uses the coined word *anaclisis* (from Greek words meaning much the same thing as *Anlehnung*), and sometimes it just paraphrases it in other terms altogether, so that the sense of a single consistent term is quite lost.

[4]Slavoj Žižek points out how precisely the old Coca-Cola slogan 'Coke is it' describes the object-cause of desire (Žižek, 1989, p. 96). Coke is *what*? The object of the drive, the thing one wants. This desire is not satisfied in the way that thirst might be. Coke remains *it*, the object of desire, after the thirst has gone, and even if the actual bottle of Coke one drinks happens to be warm, flat, and faintly disgusting in the mouth. This is not felt as a failure of the drink itself, evidence that Coke *is not* it, because the Coke that is the object of this desire never was a particular bottle of the product anyway, but always an impossible phantasmatic Coke. By the same logic, the more intensely I want something, the more likely I am to find that the actual object is disappointing once obtained, just another object among others, and one which has in no way met my desire.

[5]See also Lecture 20, 'The Sexual Life of Human Beings', *Introductory Lectures on Psychoanalysis* (1916–17), vol. 16, pp. 315–17, and *The Question of Lay Analysis* (1926b), pp. 207–17.

[6]This narcissistic object-choice will also become a cornerstone of Freud's theories of male homosexuality. We can trace the development of his thought in a single footnote which Freud added to the *Three Essays on the Theory of Sexuality* in 1910, and expanded on in 1915 and 1920: pp. 144–47, fn 1.

[7]Jean Laplanche's objection to this object-less interpretation of primary narcissism is that it postulates 'an initial state in which the organism would form a closed unit in relation to its surroundings' (Laplanche, 1976, p. 70; also Laplanche, 1989; Laplanche and Pontalis, 1972, pp. 337–38). It seems to me that the answer to this is simple: this primary narcissism is object-less not because it forms any sort of whole or closure, but because it is undifferentiated. Among other things, it simply does not make that distinction between inside and outside which the complaint attributes to it.

[8]See in particular the *Three Essays on the Theory of Sexuality* (1905c), pp. 181–83.

[9]'Instincts and Their Vicissitudes' (1915b), p. 119.

[10]Not surprisingly, given the structure of middle-class European households in the late-nineteenth and early-twentieth centuries, the figure of the nursemaid, or wet-nurse, often plays an important part in the family dramas Freud's patients tell him. One way of responding to this is that it marks off one of those moments in which Freud's world so obviously differs from our own, and in which we can feel we are reading social anthropology rather than accounts of our contemporaries. A footnote from *The Interpretation of Dreams* shows this well. In the discussion of a dream in which the breasts of the dreamer's wet-nurse figure significantly, Freud informs us in a footnote that, 'The imaginary nature of the situation relating to the dreamer's wet-nurse was proved by the objectively established fact that in his case the wet-nurse had been his mother' (1900, vol. 4, p. 289, fn 1). That the wet-nurse was also the mother is, for Freud, not at all to be taken for granted. It even appears to be slightly unusual, enough to require objectively establishable evidence and a punctilious footnote. At moments like this, Freud can seem quite alien to us, a voice from another culture altogether.

But to leave it at that would be a good example of moving too fast, and thus missing what is truly illuminating about the example. What it also shows is what we have suggested previously: that the maternal body is never simply the literal body of the mother, even if, in the limit case, the mother should be the only one to provide the child's nourishment and comfort.

[11]The formulation is Louis Althusser's (1994, p. 130).

[12]See Laplanche's suggestion of a *primal seduction* (Laplanche, 1989, pp. 126–30; Laplanche, 1999, pp. 126–29).

[13]Here, I am drawing on Lacan's shorthand for this *elsewhere*, collapsing all those calls and gazes and demands onto the one symbolic personage, as *the name of the father* ('It is in the *name of the father* that we must recognise the support of the symbolic function which, from the dawn of history, has identified his person with the figure of the law' (Lacan, 1977a, p. 67)).

[14]This is precisely the situation in Freud's own family. Freud's mother, Amalie Nathanson, was three years younger than Emanuel, one of her stepsons from Jakob Freud's first marriage, and only a year older than Philipp, the other. The household in which Freud spent his childhood included Emanuel and his wife Maria, and their two children, John and Pauline, both of them about the age of the young Sigmund, their playmate and uncle. It was a family with two mothers, each of them of the same generation as the older brothers. The only woman of Jakob's age in the family, at least in the early years, was a nurse who, childless herself, also played the maternal role for the three children. The family situation from which the discoverer of the Oedipus complex came was hardly uncommon at the time (Appignanesi and Forrester, 2000, pp. 14–16).

[15]Although the second of the 1905 *Three Essays on Sexuality* deals briefly with the castration complex in a section on 'The Sexual Researches of Childhood' (pp. 194–97), this was not added until 1915. The idea of a castration complex was first developed in a 1908 article, 'On the Sexual Theories of Children' (p. 205). This contains a much fuller argument, which will be developed and repeated in much of Freud's later writing on the topic.

[16]Slavoj Žižek asks us to imagine a series of pleasurable experiences at which one aims; then castration 'does not consist in depriving [the subject] of any of these experiences, but adds to the series a purely potential non-existent X, with respect to which the actually accessible experiences appear all of a sudden as lacking, not wholly satisfying' (Žižek, 1997, p. 15)

[17]There is no sexual relationship in the sense that nothing binds the sexes together as two halves of a unity. Or, to complicate that by turning it inside-out, what they have in common is *nothing at all*: a lack, a common absolute loss of the indifferentiation of the maternal body, towards which it is possible to adopt two quite different stances. Lacan represents these stances in his mathemes of *sexuation* (Lacan, 1998, pp. 78–89). These stances are not subjective so much as logical possibilities of any system inasmuch as it is logically incomplete. Neither are they a biologism, for they do not describe something following inexorably from the genital configuration of any individual. They represent instead the way in which the symbolic order is radically, necessarily and constitutively incomplete: because it is a process of pure differentiation, it can have no totality. If it has no totality, there are necessarily always at least two different and mutually incompatible ways of inhabiting it: for Lacan, these correspond to sexual difference and the ways in which the social, the cultural, the Law, provide certain defaults for sexed human beings. See, for example, Lacan, 1998, pp. 12, 34–35; and the fable of the two children in the railway carriage in Lacan, 1977a, p. 152.

[18]The distinction is a common one since Lacan, though it is not one Freud makes: he uses the term only infrequently, and then as a synonym for *penis*. See in particular Lacan, 1977a, pp. 281–91; and Lacan, 1998, pp. 64–89.

[19]Pierre Bourdieu speaks of this as *habitus*, his term for the ways in which subjects incorporate the objective realities of their world (Bourdieu, 1990).

[20]The particular object choice referred to in the title is of a woman who is either already committed to a relationship or is of 'bad repute sexually' (p. 166); the role of the man who chooses her as his love object is to 'rescue' her (p. 168). It is not at all difficult to read that in Oedipal terms.

THREE SOCIAL

Siren

I am driving along a freeway or a stretch of open road in my car when I hear a siren.

Immediately I glance at my speedometer. The reaction is almost instantaneous, and so completely automatic as to give the impression of bypassing any conscious thought altogether. By the time I become aware of what I am doing, I am already looking at the speedometer. In the sheer unthinking rapidity of the reaction, and mild though if is, it seems closer to one of those sheerly bodily reactions of panic, like the sensation of falling. My heart rate has increased ever so slightly.

Now that awareness has caught up, I can feel slightly foolish for that reaction. I had, after all, glanced at the speedometer just a moment or so ago, and then as now was travelling comfortably within the speed limit. I am not in the habit of speeding, but (and here I am already talking to the imaginary police officer who I've just confirmed would have had no reason at all for pulling me over) sometimes, on an open road like this one, or down a slight hill, your speed just creeps up without your knowing it. Staying within the speed limit is a constant process of checking and making adjustments as you go, depending on the nature of the road, the weather, the other traffic. Sometimes you look at the dial and find that you're just over, and pull back: what bad luck it would be for a radar gun to be fired at you at just that time, and how unfair an image that would be of your actual driving habits. Who, I wonder, am I rehearsing all this for? The slightly disconcerting thing about it is that even though I was not guilty of anything, I reacted automatically as if I were. I suspect that no matter how good my record as a driver might be, I might well still react in such a fashion: just for a fraction of a second and then dismissed, but as unstoppable as a blink when something approaches the eye. There is something insatiable about the implicit demand I reacted to: nothing would be good enough for it. Perhaps, I suspect, what it really wants (what who wants?) is precisely that pre-emptive knee-jerk reaction of an assumed guilt.

I know also that the siren was not meant for me personally – it's already receding, heading in another direction altogether – but even as that knowledge registers I have already carried out a quick mental check, no more than an instant's worth, just to be sure (lights, tyres, registration sticker …). In that, it has had exactly the same effect it would have had if it had been meant for me. Which means that it does not have to be aimed at me personally for it to work. It works on me because at the moment of my hearing it, there is a quite involuntary moment in which I try it on for size, as it were – treat it as if it were addressed to me. Most of the time, of course, after that tiniest of initial starts, I then drop it with ease, knowing quite well that it's not for me, and perhaps even feeling slightly foolish for ever having entertained the idea that it would have been. But it is that initial involuntary moment which is interesting. I will do it all over again the next time I hear a siren while I'm driving. It is not a matter of choice.

To some extent the involuntary nature of this is built into the very process of making and exchanging meaning. To be surrounded by others is to be doing constant low-level filtering of the hubbub around you, to determine just what of it concerns you and what doesn't. I'm walking along the street and I hear somebody say my name, so I turn to see if it's really meant for me. Better still, I'm walking along the street and simply hear someone calling out 'Hey!', no name at all. Most of the people in earshot try the *call on: momentary pauses, turning to see, then moving on.[1] Even to get started on the usual process of making sense of an utterance involves determining just what, out of the hubbub of sounds around us, has some bearing on us and what can be safely ignored. But that alone does not seem to account for the reaction the siren induces, that start of something like an involuntary assumption of guilt. Neither, in the case of that call in the street, does it even quite account for my prior sense of answerability: a call comes out of nowhere, and before I even know what it is about, I react with a deep, immediate, almost bodily knowledge (my body stops and begins to turn before I've consciously made any decision) that in some sense I am answerable to or before this call.*

In this reaction which kicks in before I am even aware of it, I treat the siren as if it were indeed addressed to me. But who or what could then be addressing it to me? It is certainly not the police officer in the car to which the siren is attached, the person who flicked the switch on the dashboard to start it. That person has not the faintest inkling of or interest in my existence (and somewhere in the distance, the sound has stopped now); neither do I have the faintest idea who they might be. Indeed, it would be quite paranoid of me to assume that somehow this is a personal communication, meant for me alone: someone has seen me travelling along this road and decided to give me a start and then cover their tracks by heading off in a different direction. If it has addressed me, it is in the same sense that it has addressed everyone who has heard it. This is a quite impersonal address, like that of radio or television: it doesn't address me personally, but an entire demographic, with the invitation to anyone who might be listening to consider themselves addressed (If you've just tuned in, welcome to the show ...). We usually find it quite easy to distinguish this impersonal address from a personal address: it would be extremely disconcerting, at very least, if the radio addressed us personally, by name ...

In the case of radio or television, it is not hard to say where we're addressed from, who or what is doing the addressing, even though that address may be complex and multiple (from the host who looks out of the screen at us, to the show itself, through to advertisers, the network, and so on). Who or what might that effective address be coming from in the case of the siren? It does not depend on the person operating the siren, or on their intentions. For me to feel as I did does not even depend on that person's being a police officer: it would work in just the same way if the siren had been triggered off by a fault in the police car's wiring, or didn't even belong to a police car at all.[2]

What addresses me in this way, and before which I react with all the signs of guilt, even if quite momentary, is more like Law itself: Law, with a capital, in the abstract rather than any particular law. What the siren makes me rudely aware of is not any particular guilt (I didn't have any before I heard it, and haven't infringed any laws), but a quite unspecified, completely general, empty – and thus completely endless – capacity for guilt in the eyes of this Law. I am always capable of being guilty of something, even if I should go through my life without infringing a single law. I may be innocent until proven guilty, but underlying that as its very possibility is my subjection to the law in the first place: that empty potential for culpability is ineradicable, and does not yield for a single instant. It rests on me as an obligation to the Law, a responsibility in that most basic sense of the word: I am obliged to respond. In this siren call, I am in effect called on by the Law – or rather reminded that as subject to the Law I am one who can be called on by it at any time. It calls on me with an obligation to respond. There is no particular content needed to this response – and indeed, no response will be fully adequate, in that it will not discharge that obligation. All it is asking of me is response, empty response: that involuntary moment of awareness of being a subject in this mode of being-subject-to.

And with that, perhaps we need to revise our earlier suggestion. If the very process of engaging with the hubbub of meanings around us is a sort of filtering process, of making decisions on what does and does not concern us, do we not even there begin with something like an obligation? I respond to hearing my name called because I have some sort of obligation to those who know it and are likely to call me in this way. I respond because I am in a sense already called on, before this particular occasion in the street. I am already and in general called on to answer the call of a friend, or of family, or perhaps just of those who know me. I am already called on, as I have been from those times I cannot even remember. To be called on would seem to be an ineradicable dimension of my being a person.

Foreign territory

The unconscious inhabits us as something that is not subject to our control or knowledge. It is the name for what there is in us that acts behind our backs, within and between our very words and actions. It is not a consciousness at one remove, a more authentic self to which we should be true or with which we have to make our peace, but rather the gaps in consciousness. Though it is already 'internal foreign territory', it is not a particular location within ourselves, even a secret one. It is more like a fold, bringing the outside within. It is not even mine; even though it inhabits me. What connections can there be between this internal foreign territory and that more obvious foreign territory which lies outside and beyond the subject, the world in which he or she lives?

Questions of culture and society engage Freud in many of his writings, from the 1908 paper on '"Civilized" Sexual Morality and Modern Nervous Illness'[3] through to the last work he would publish in his lifetime, *Moses and Monotheism* (1939). In the quarter-century from one war to the next, it forms an increasingly important theme of his writing. In it, most of the dominant concerns of his clinical and theoretical work will appear, refracted and in a new guise: the early paper on '"Civilized" Sexual Morality' draws on the concept of the drive outlined in the *Three Essays on the Theory of Sexuality* from three years before; *Totem and Taboo* will translate the Oedipus complex which had received its name some two years before; aspects of this will also be developed further in *Group Psychology and the Analysis of the Ego* (1921) and *Moses and Monotheism* (1939); the death drive which first makes its appearance in 1920 in *Beyond the Pleasure Principle* informs much of the work of the 1930s, including *Civilization and its Discontents*, the open letter 'Why War?' to Albert Einstein, and, again, *Moses and Monotheism*.

Freud reminds us that utterances are never just representations, but are always also acts within a situation: repetitions, actings-out and, moves in a game whose entirety is in principle not accessible to the one immersed in it. His own writings on culture and the social are themselves furrowed by the obvious larger urgencies of the world out of which they arise, from the 1915 'Thoughts for the Times on War and Death' to the ways in which the persecution of the Jews returns as a dark refrain throughout *Moses and Monotheism*, written in the years after Hitler's rise to power (its third section would receive its first public airing at the Paris Congress several months after Germany had annexed Austria in the 1938 *Anschluss*, and would be published only after the old and by now desperately ill Freud had fled Vienna for England).

They are furrowed also by other smaller-scale but nevertheless pressing anxieties as well. Almost from the moment of its founding at the Second Psychoanalytic Congress in Nuremburg in 1910, the International Psychoanalytic Association had been a divided and unstable body. Freud's indirect announcement, through Sandor Ferenczi, that Jung would be appointed president of the new organization infuriated many of his own followers – Jung so obviously the favoured son though a relative newcomer, Swiss rather than Austrian, gentile rather than Jew, and from the outset far from in agreement with Freud on major issues. By the time of the Third Congress, at Weimar in 1911, Alfred Adler would have resigned his own presidency of the Vienna Society, and then his membership and the editorship of the *Zentralblatt für Psychoanalyse*, taking with him his co-editor and vice-president Wilhelm Stekel and nine supporters. In the middle of 1912, Ernest Jones suggested to Freud the possibility of a secret steering committee, one of whose clear but unstated aims would be to keep watch over the unorthodox Jung. Freud agreed enthusiastically, and the following year presented intaglios, subsequently made into rings, to each of the six chosen sons (Jones, Ferenczi, Rank, Abraham, Eitingon, and Sachs). It is hard not to see this emerging directly in *Totem and Taboo*, on which Freud was working between 1910 and 1913, with its Oedipal myth of the founding of the social bond as the sons' overthrowing of the primal father, or in the later view of the social bond in *Group Psychology and the Analysis of the Ego*. Jung would resign his own presidency and his editorship of the *Jahrbuch für Psychoanalytische Forschungen* (*Yearbook of Psychoanalytic Research*) in 1914, and the committee itself would be split with dissension in the 1920s as both Rank and then Ferenczi became estranged; Freud's daughter Anna would replace Rank on the committee in 1926 (Grosskurth, 1991).

Freud's writings on society and culture offer themselves as the public utterance of a public intellectual, speaking from the perspective of his own professional, disciplinary knowledge in the hope that it may contribute to the understanding of an issue of general concern. They are aware of the task they have set themselves, of their own inadequacies and shortcomings, and of the ways in which the expertise that is their very claim to be heard goes hand in hand with an ignorance.● Going beyond the strict brief

I am fully conscious of the deficiencies of these studies. I need not mention those which are necessarily characteristic of pioneering work; but others require a word of explanation. The four essays collected in these pages ... seek to bridge the gap between students of such subjects as social anthropology, philology and folklore on the one hand, and psychoanalysts on the other. Yet they cannot offer to either side what each lacks – to the former an adequate initiation into the new psychological technique or to the latter a sufficient grasp of the material that awaits treatment. ('Preface', *Totem and Taboo* (1913), p. xiii)

of psychoanalysis, they defer to other expertises, whose voices are sometimes allowed to flood the text: *Totem and Taboo*, in particular, is at times a tissue of quotations and paraphrases from social anthropology, only after which Freud draws the psychoanalytic conclusion.

But this deference is also the flip side of an implicit claim that *this territory too belongs to psychoanalysis*. Psychoanalysis has no clear boundaries; it spreads into all sorts of areas that have not previously been thought of in its terms.• In claiming their right to its attention, psychoanalysis finds it must then distinguish itself from whatever disciplines might already claim them as its own. Fully aware of the interest and implications of his work for philosophy, for example, Freud also distinguished it from philosophy, and insisted instead on its scientificity.• This is the concern any new discipline must have, as it argues for its own necessity: *No other discipline*, psycho-

The relations of an individual to his parents and to his brothers and sisters, to the object of his love, and to his physician – in fact all the relations which have hitherto been the chief subject of psychoanalytic research – may claim to be considered as social phenomena; and in this respect they may be contrasted with certain other processes, described by us as 'narcissistic', in which the satisfaction of the instincts is partially or totally withdrawn from the influence of other people. The contrast between social and narcissistic ... mental acts therefore falls wholly within the domain of individual psychology, and is not well calculated to differentiate it from a social or group psychology. (*Group Psychology and the Analysis of the Ego* (1921), p. 69)

Neither speculative philosophy, nor descriptive psychology, nor what is called experimental psychology (which is closely allied to the physiology of the sense-organs), as they are taught in the Universities, are in a position to tell you anything serviceable of the relation between body and mind or to provide you with a key to an understanding of possible disturbances of the mental functions. (Lecture 1, 'Introduction', *Introductory Lectures on Psychoanalysis* (1916–17), vol. 15, p. 20)

analysis must say, *no other practitioners in neighbouring areas – doctors of medicine, psychologists or psychiatrists, philosophers, sociologists or anthropologists – can do what we do.* Such marking and remarking of disciplinary boundaries is a necessarily acute concern for psychoanalysis, hemmed in as it is by a large, powerful and not necessarily sympathetic medical establishment from which it needs both recognition and autonomy.[4] Boundaries are made and dissolved, transgressed and pushed into other shapes, made ambiguous and no longer easy to distinguish.

In Freud, then, the question of the social is never less than anxious – and often urgent, under the pressure of the social itself. With its conflicting demands, incompatibilities and double binds, and the constant need to negotiate a workable path through them, the social is precisely that 'other stage' on which all of the dramas psychoanalysis has taken as its object have been played out. This is why the question of the relations of psychoanalysis to social and cultural theory is such a complex one.

Sometimes that relationship appears to take the shape of an 'applied psychoanalysis,' in which psychoanalysis is a template placed over some other field in order to draw a loose analogy. *Totem and Taboo*, for example, starts off from a series of extended parallels between what psychoanalysis suggests about the development of a child from infancy to maturity, and human history itself; between an individual's maturity and the Western culture Freud knows; between infancy and prehistoric cultures; between those cultures and various contemporary non-Western cultures; and between all of those 'primitive' cultures and the behaviour of the neurotic.•

Group Psychology and the Analysis of the Ego draws a parallel between the periodic excesses of carnival, in which all sorts of social prohibitions are infringed, and the cyclic alternations between depression and manic activity in individuals (p. 131–33).[5]

> [I]n a certain sense, [prehistoric man] is still our contemporary. There are men still living who, as we believe, stand very near to primitive man, far nearer than we do, and whom we therefore regard as his direct heirs and representatives. Such is our view of those we describe as savages or half-savages; and their mental life must have a peculiar interest for us if we are right in seeing in it a well-preserved picture of an early stage of our own development.
>
> If that supposition is correct, a comparison between the psychology of primitive peoples, as it is taught by social anthropology, and the psychology of neurotics, as it has been revealed by psychoanalysis, will be bound to show numerous points of agreement and will throw new light upon familiar facts in both sciences. ('I. The Horror of Incest', *Totem and Taboo* (1912–13), p. 1)

But if that were all there is to it, would this analogy-making not run the risk of being profoundly *un*psychoanalytic, in the sense we have seen before, and which Freud stated quite clearly at the very outset of the entire psychoanalytic project? Psychoanalysis must, after all, distinguish itself from the dream book which knows in advance just what every possible dream can mean, and immerse itself in the unrepeatable and unforeseeable singularity of an individual life history: the 'science of biography'. There are moments in all of these studies when what we find is not just what we already knew (and now in a new place), but what we didn't; when we find not only what psychoanalysis might have to teach us about culture and the social, but at the same time what a consideration of the social does to the very idea of psychoanalysis. Instead of finding psychoanalysis at the heart of any knowledge of the social, the key that can explain it even where its own sciences have failed, we find that questions of the social and the cultural are oddly already at the heart of psychoanalysis, and have been all along. To *apply* psychoanalysis is to find, as if it were new, within it, another internal foreign territory.

Myth

Totem and Taboo (1912–13)

This book of four essays is Freud's first sustained attempt at writing on socio-cultural and anthropological matters from a psychoanalytical perspective. It shows a wide range of reading and documentation: each essay gives a good deal of care to assembling and citing or paraphrasing cases from the literature. The initiating hypothesis is a common one in nineteenth-century anthropology: still-surviving, so-called 'savage', cultures represent a window back into the past of 'our own' Western culture, to which they compare as infant to adult. To this, Freud adds a particularly psychoanalytic layer: if the contemporary Western neurotic is also caught in a sort of infantilism, then psychoanalysis and social anthropology may throw light on each other. The subtitle says it clearly: 'Some Points of Agreement between the Mental Lives of Savages and Neurotics'.

The first essay is on 'The Horror of Incest', which it places in the wider context of exogamy: totemic clan relationships forbid sexual relations and intermarriage between members of the same totemic group, even though those members may not be of related families. Most of the essay is a compendium of examples. It concludes with a brief argument that this agrees strikingly with what psychoanalysis has shown us about the mental life of neurotics, who have not managed to negotiate the incestuous Oedipal fixations that still continue to play a major part in their mental life.

The second essay, 'Taboo and Emotional Ambivalence', compares taboo to the elaborate rituals for avoidance and reparation involved in the obsessional neuroses. In both cases, there is an ambivalence towards the object of the taboo (which may be taboo because it is defiled as easily as because it is sacred), which suggests a contradictory mixture of desires, through which the prohibition attempts to steer a path. The third, on 'Animism, Magic and the Omnipotence of Thoughts', runs a parallel between the obsessional neurotic's insistence on a causality behind events with superstition and a belief in magic.

The final essay, 'The Return of Totemism in Childhood', brings us back to the question of exogamy, and is best known for its hypothesis – quite late in the piece – of the primal horde, which links the beginnings of religion, morals and indeed society itself with the Oedipus complex. This is Freud's myth of the earliest stages of humanity (he freely admits that such a society has never actually been observed (p. 141)). The proto-social grouping is ruled by the primal father, who owns all the women of the group and drives out all his sons as they grow up, who then become potential rivals. The sons eventually band together and kill the father, eating him to complete their identification with him. The violence of their ambivalence towards the father, who is both loved and hated, produces an immense and insatiable guilt, whose displacement results in the two aspects of the totemic (Oedipal) taboos: prohibitions on killing the (father's) totemic animal and on sexual intercourse with women of the same totem. From this come all the cultures we know.

I: Fantasies of the social

Primal fantasy

With the dissolution of the Oedipus complex, the child comes to free itself from its incestuous attachments to its parents. In this, the child also provides for itself some sort of solution to the dilemma of differentiation and individuation that Freud sums up as *castration*. Any such solution is bound to be less than perfect, because the loss for which castration is the shorthand is an absolute one; it will be an *ad hoc* solution, pieced together, as so much in the child's subsequent life will also be, out of what is available at hand in the singularities of that life; it will be provisional, as a life is always open to the unforeseeabilities of a future; and it will be sexed, for Oedipus is negotiated differently by each sex. Castration, we remember, is essentially a *primal fantasy*: it has its roots in the sexual theories by which the child tries to figure out for itself the enigmas of difference and differentiation. As a fantasy, it is not a description of an actual event or threat, but a summation of and way of coming to terms with that irreparable loss of undifferentiation at the heart of the very possibility of a self.

And the dissolution of Oedipus is not a private drama, for it is also the drama of the child's taking some sort of place in a world. As we have seen, the arrival of subjectivity is complex and retrospective. That sense of infant self-awareness does not happen in an instant – one moment there is no subjectivity, the next there is – but as a *having already been there*. From its very earliest moments of awareness – indeed, from well before that – the infant already has a history, a series of places prepared for it, dramas in which it is already an actor, desires it already answers or refuses or profoundly alters, all of them taking place on that 'other stage' of which the child will only gradually become aware.

We have used the term *paternal voice* as a shorthand for everything that intrudes on the profound indifferentiation of the maternal body. At first the merest sliver of difference, the paternal voice will unfold into an entire world, and one that reveals itself as having always and already been there. Where does this difference, this *world*, come from? This is the enigma facing the child.[6] Along with that 'I', with its strange, elusive temporality of always having been there already, comes a world with the same temporality. If castration is a primal fantasy of what difference is and how it comes about on the level of that 'I', one would expect there to be a corresponding fantasy, a version of the same one, of what happens on that 'other stage' of the world. *Where does the paternal voice come from?*

The primal horde

This is the question addressed by the famous myth of the **primal horde**, which first appears in 1913 in *Totem and Taboo*, and plays a role in all of Freud's major writings on culture from that point on.

The story comes from Charles Darwin's suggestion in *The Descent of Man* (1875) that the very earliest recognisably human societies may have resembled the social groupings of the great apes, in which a dominant male has exclusive sexual rights to all females, and defends this against all the other males of the group.

Freud adds his own twist, though.• In the social groupings

[In the primal horde we find] a violent and jealous father who keeps all the females for himself and drives away his sons as they grow up. This earliest state of society has never been an object of observation. ... One day the

> brothers who had been driven out came together, killed and devoured their father and so made an end of the patriarchal horde. United, they had the courage to do and succeeded in doing what would have been impossible for them individually. (Some cultural advance, perhaps, command over some new weapon, had given them a sense of superior strength.) Cannibal savages as they were, it goes without saying that they devoured their victim as well as killing him. The violent primal father had doubtless been the feared and envied model of each one of the company of brothers: and in the act of devouring him they accomplished their identification with him, and each one of them acquired a portion of his strength. The totem meal, which is perhaps mankind's earliest festival, would thus be a repetition and a commemoration of this memorable and criminal deed, which was the beginning of so many things – of social organisation, of moral restrictions and of religion. ('IV. The Return of Totemism in Childhood', *Totem and Taboo* (1912–13), pp. 141–42)

of apes, one dominant male is replaced by another: with the inevitabilities of age, sooner or later the currently dominant male is bound to be overthrown by a stronger and younger challenger (who may of course be – and is even likely to be – one of his own sons). In Freud's version, the primal father is overthrown not by an individual challenger but by a union of the sons against him: the role of primal father does *not* pass to any of the sons, but now remains permanently empty – and *this emptiness* comes to define specifically human society. Culture begins not with the addition of something new to the purely animal or pre-human level, but with *a subtraction*. What results is a peculiar sort of structure around a central and essential absence, whose consequences we shall follow. It is in this, rather than in that loose parallel between the infancy of an individual and the 'infancy' of human society (which is always to infantilise some other, inevitably non-Western, society), that psychoanalysis finds its purchase as a way of theorising culture: psychoanalysis is the most thorough unravelling of the logic of such absence.

Freud is clear that the primal horde is a *hypothesis*: the earliest stages of human society are, after all, forever beyond direct observation. As with our other fantasies of primality – the primal scene, castration – it functions in the mode of *as if*. Its claim must be the limited and paradoxical one of the primal scene: it need not ever have occurred on a timeline, but everything happens as if it had. Just as analysis does not do that impossible thing, dig up and reveal the unconscious itself, but instead constructs a conscious chain of causality that would have exactly the same effect, so too with the story of the primal horde. It stands in place of what is in principle unreachable, that very emergence of culture and the social. It is not that moment itself, and cannot be. Freud calls it the beginning of social organisation, but in the story he tells, such an organisation is already clearly there, before this beginning. The brothers who can even conceive of the idea of banding together against the father are already social, through and through, in a sense to which their actual banding together will add nothing except confirmation. They already have what can only be described as a social bond with each other: a sense of solidarity in a common situation, shared emotional investments, a common language, an ethics which goes beyond self-interest into a calculation of the interests of others and a realisation of their inseparability from one's own, and the concepts of mutuality, obligation, and responsibility. The reality principle – the deferral of immediate pleasure – is given a twist that reveals what has all along been its social dimension: speculation on a future pleasure comes about only in a circuit which is from the outset necessarily social, involving not only others but the very nature of the bond amongst them and the prior structure of the world into which they are born. This social dimension is installed, with the reality principle, at the very heart of the pleasure principle.

The father's death turns a deprivation into a prohibition, the double taboo of totemism: on the one hand, it is forbidden to kill the totemic animal, which Freud suggests has come to stand for the father, and on the other hand, it is forbidden to have sexual relations within the same totemic clan. But if in the logic of primal fantasy prohibition hides impossibility, may we not then suspect that the initial deprivation was itself also hiding a double impossibility, even during the father's lifetime? The fable of the horde is meant to describe a situation before the installation of the taboos against endogamy, in order to explain how they came about. There cannot yet be any taboo against incest in the primal horde: there is only an all-or-nothing division between the father who has access to all women without exception, including his own mother and daughters, and the sons who have no access to any of the women, whatever their relation. The father is the singular exception to the rule of deprivation on which the group is constructed, the one who claims a pleasure available to him alone. The primal father is the ultimate Oedipal son, who has defeated all competition for the exclusive comfort of the maternal body. But as we have seen, there never has been a time in which the child's claiming of the actual mother could really be a return to that indifferentiation of the maternal body: the maternal body is not the body of any actual person, and to return to an indifferentiation is not a satisfaction so much as the loss of the very subject who seeks satisfaction. Return is not an option: it is the fantasy of the Oedipal infant boy. The primal father is thus not only the exception; he is a completely impossible exception, the very embodiment of an impossible satisfaction, foreclosed not only to the sons, but as the very condition of subjectivity.

In the same way, there never has been a time when killing the father could be an abolition of the paternal voice, that sliver of difference which arises within the indifferentiation of the maternal body. The paternal voice has never belonged to any real, mortal father, but is at best lent, just as the law is independent of its bearers. The father has after all presumably gained his own position and power by the deposition of the previous incumbent, just as in the ape hordes Darwin describes; he is there through the murder of his own father, and in the normal course of things would in turn be deposed by one of his sons (rather than all of them in concerted action). Incumbents come and go, but that paternal voice which demands obedience and backs it up by threat remains constant through all the various depositions and accessions. The very presence of the actual figure of the father simply serves to hide the fact that one cannot kill that paternal voice, which, as differentiation itself and the fantasised source of prohibition, is what the Oedipal son really aims at in the return to the maternal body. The brutality of the father's force and the fear this invokes let the sons imagine that this sheer force is all that keeps them from the satisfaction of their desires, and thus hides and keeps alive the fundamental impossibility of those desires.

Groups:
Group Psychology and the Analysis of the Ego (1921)

Published the year after *Beyond the Pleasure Principle*, *Group Psychology* has not yet taken on board the implications of the concept of the death drive, though Freud refers to the binding forces of libido as *Eros*.

This extended essay is concerned with 'the individual man as a member of a race, of a nation, of a caste, of a profession, of an institution, or as a component part of a crowd of people who have been organised into a group at some particular time for some definite purpose' (p. 70). That is, its starting point is the individual, and the problem it sets itself is the ways in which individuals combine into the unity of a group. How do groups cohere, from the least ordered group which may emerge spontaneously and then vanish again just as quickly – the crowd – to the most ordered and enduring groupings such as the Army or the Church? The problem is phrased in terms of what is essentially a social contract theory, though there is (not surprisingly) much in the essay which works against such a framework.

Freud begins by reviewing some of the extensive previous literature on the topic: Le Bon's description of the 'group mind', in which individual characteristics are dissolved to have their places taken by collective and more worrying properties, such as irrationality, contagion, suggestibility and a feeling of invincibility; and McDougall's description of ways in which a group achieves a greater rationality (by having a more definite structure, and continuities such as traditions and customs). In place of the rather vague term 'suggestion' (or, even more abstractly, 'suggestibility') which is often offered as an explanation for group behaviour, Freud argues that *libido* is the basic binding force of a group. In organised groups such as the Church and the Army, this works in two directions: there are libidinal ties to the leader, and libidinal ties of another sort to all of one's fellows under that same leader. More specifically, in groups of this sort, the leader has been placed in the position of the ego-ideal (superego) for each of the other members of the group, and that allows those members to identify with each other as having a common libidinal object. Remove the leader, or at least the structure of leadership, and the binding force of the group disintegrates.

This is where Freud differs significantly from Trotter's earlier hypothesis of a 'herd instinct' by which individual organisms would tend to aggregate. For Freud, that is quite insufficient to explain the dynamics of a hierarchy, or why there are any leaders at all. For him, the human being is not so much a herd animal as a *horde animal* – and here we return to the myth introduced at the very end of *Totem and Taboo*. This, Freud argues, explains some of the uncanny aspects of the coerciveness and suggestibility of groups: the unconscious of every group is still always the configuration represented by the primal horde, and the leader, that shared ego-ideal, is always in part the primal father. From this, Freud is able to offer a concise definition of suggestion in psychoanalytic terms: 'a conviction which is not based on perception and reasoning but upon an erotic tie' (p. 128).

II: The social superego

Disobey this edict

What holds this horde together is already something other than the strongest individual in the group, who is always open to deposition anyway. From the outset, something is always already there, preceding the individual, no matter how far back we go: some sort of frame into which the individual arrives. This minimal *something else* is the dimension of the cultural and the social. Because it is there before any individual, it is not something one derives additively from the properties of the individual human being – as, for example, in social contract theories of society, where individuals agree to band together for their common good. On the contrary, as the story of the overthrow of the primal father shows, it is subtractive: it comes about by an omission, a gap, a place that structurally has to remain empty. It is the death of the father, not his possession of some greater vitality, that is the beginning of social organisation, of moral institutions and of religion.• The primal father is in effect already overthrown, already as good as dead, from the outset, because his power comes from elsewhere and is independent of its holder. The essence of the primal father is that he be dead. Even during his own lifetime, his power is nothing more than an advance drawing on his own death.[7]

The inverse counterpart to this is that this power and its succession

In order that these latter consequences may seem plausible, leaving their premises on one side, we need only suppose that the tumultuous mob of brothers were filled with the same contradictory feelings which we can see at work in the ambivalent father-complexes of our children and of our neurotic patients. They hated their father, who presented such a formidable obstacle to their craving for power and their sexual desires; but they loved and admired him too. After they had got rid of him, had satisfied their hatred and had put into effect their wish to identify themselves with him, the affection which had all this time been pushed under was bound to make itself felt. It did so in the form of remorse. A sense of guilt made its appearance, which in this instance coincided with the remorse felt by the whole group. The dead father became stronger than the living one had been – for events took the course we so often see them follow in human affairs to this day. What had up to then been prevented by his actual existence was thenceforth prohibited by the sons themselves, in accordance with the psychological procedure so familiar to us in psychoanalyses under the name of 'deferred obedience'. They revoked their deed by forbidding the killing of the totem, the substitute for their father; and they renounced its fruits by resigning their claim to the women who had now been set free. They thus created out of their filial sense of guilt the two fundamental taboos of totemism [against killing the totemic animal, and against marriage and sexual relations with a member of the same totemic clan], which for that very reason inevitably correspond to the two repressed wishes of the Oedipus complex. Whoever contravened these taboos became guilty of the only two crimes with which primitive society concerned itself. ('IV. The Return of Totemism in Childhood', *Totem and Taboo* (1912–13), p. 143)

work, oddly, by breaching their own conditions. The primal father is the exception to his own rules, of course: he is the one who has all the women denied to the other men of the horde, and the one who has done what none of the others could in deposing his predecessor. His exceptionality is at the heart of the entire structure of his power, the thing that makes it work. His command amounts to a *Do not be like me! Do not occupy my place! You shall not replace me!*

But something very odd follows from this. In their concerted deposition of the father, are the sons not *obeying* that command, *You shall not replace me!*, by taking it through one further turn? They do not replace him: they even take steps to ensure that the position he occupied is left permanently vacant, preserved forever from usurpation. In their very overthrow of him, then, are they not even behaving *more* faithfully than when he was alive? The father's edict is now invulnerable to transgression because it incorporates its own transgression: to transgress it is to preserve it. If that transgression is what it takes to make the command invulnerable and ensure that the father will never be replaced, does not the command, then, necessarily even *demand* its own transgression? Once it folds its very contradiction back on itself in this way, there can no longer be any outside to this edict. The primal father's edict is simultaneously *Do this!* and *Do not do this!* While it demands obedience, it also, and completely paradoxically, demands that one disobey it: one obeys by disobeying and disobeys by obeying; to disobey is to obey, and to obey is to disobey. It is an edict with no outside.

This is not a description of some fantasy of totalitarian power where disobedience is impossible and one has no choice but to obey.[8] If it were, it would be of very little interest: every form of power breeds its own dissent, even if that should be severely circumscribed. The totalitarian fantasy does not take into account the utter paradoxicality of this bond: if disobedience is impossible, this is for exactly the same reasons and *in the very same instances* that *obedience* is impossible. At the very moment one obeys, one has no choice but to *disobey*. The social bond, the Law binding us, is not a bond of obedience, threatening us with punishment for disobedience. It is a much stranger thing, a bond of the impossibility of obedience *or* disobedience. Oddly enough, it is a bond all the stronger for its impossibility: a *possible* bond risks dissolution once its conditions are met, but an *impossible* bond can never be met, and so its obligations and ties can only multiply. At the heart of the social, then, we find again the very structure we found at the heart of the psyche: the double bind. And just as before, this double bind is there not as a pathology or dysfunctioning of what should otherwise be unparadoxical and non-contradictory, but as the condition of there being any sort of social bond whatsoever. There can be a social bond only because it is inherently and necessarily contradictory, paradoxical and impossible.

A double bind is quite independent of any or all of the individuals involved in the situation, as well. It is a logical knot belonging to the situation, not some sort of ability or inability of any of the players; on the contrary, a double bind means the *a priori* impossibility of any individual to negotiate it without contradiction. No one is adequate to the double bind: there may be better or worse things to do in a given double bind, but the double bind is itself profoundly not a matter of individual choice or making. The double bind makes one acutely and even uncomfortably aware of the gap between what one can do and what the situation demands. It confronts one with a dimension quite different from that of the individual or the personal.

Freud suggests that it is a matter of simple pragmatics for the sons to leave the father's place vacant: if none of the sons is strong enough to fill that place on his own, uncontested, then mutual self-interest suggests that leaving it vacant will minimise conflict.• But as we have seen, structurally that place is one that cannot be filled: it has to be left vacant as a condition of the very organisation of the social. This can be a decision only in the retrospective sense of an affirmation, like that of falling in love. I do not choose to fall in love (the very thought of it cannot help but appear comically naïve, or just a bit sinister, like stalking). Falling in love happens without our conscious will, as the very phrases we use say over and over: we fall, are swept away, unable to help ourselves, lost, not knowing what has come over us ... I always realise after the event that I *have* fallen and that I am now in love: everything is always just a little bit too late, as if I wasn't actually quite there when it happened. My will comes into it as an affirmation, in retrospect: now that I *am* in love, I affirm it as something I want, more than anything. I know that it has now become so much a part of my life that I can no longer even see myself without this love. Take it away and I do not go back to what I was before: I disintegrate.

> Sexual desires do not unite men but divide them. Though the brothers had banded together in order to overcome their father, they were all one another's rivals in regard to the women. Each of them would have wished, like his father, to have all the women to himself. The new organisation would have collapsed in a struggle of all against all, for none of them was of such over-mastering strength as to be able to take on his father's part with success. Thus the brothers had no alternative, if they were to live together, but – not, perhaps, until they had passed through many dangerous crises – to institute the law against incest, by which they all alike renounced the women whom they desired and who had been their chief motive for despatching their father. In this way they rescued the organisation which had made them strong .... ('IV. The Return of Totemism in Childhood', *Totem and Taboo* (1912–13), p. 144)

The same logic is at work in the decision to leave the position of the father vacant. It is a forced choice, one that cannot go any other way. Even if one of the sons were to take over the dominant role, deposition itself has already forever separated that role from the holder of it: the role itself is what remains, above and beyond any of its incumbents, essentially empty. What one does is affirm this, after the event, *as if* it were a free decision. The same is true of any 'social contract' theory, of which Freud's story is an example. There is no historic moment at which free individuals decide to band together for their common good; the only individuals there are, are those who are born into an already existing social world. Even dissent involves precisely that affirmation, which is the very structure of responsibility: *Even though I did not make the world this way and had no choice in the matter, I take responsibility for it, for doing something about it.*

The logic of affirmation is the flipside to the logic of prohibition: both of them hide an impossibility. What makes them forms of the social bond is not that, in the one case, we as individuals form our society according to our wills and desires or, in the other, that we as individuals are prevented from exercising our wills and desires by the regulations and prohibitions of society. Both of those options are too much and too little. On the one hand, they see the social as something quite exterior to the individual – as if the social were simply some sort of tool towards the realisation of an essentially individual project, or some sort of obstacle in the way of such a project (this is the logic of 'self-realisation'). On the other hand, they tend to collapse the social and the individual, as if they were both essentially the same thing – as if the social were just a collection of individuals (the logic made famous by Margaret Thatcher, the British prime minister between 1979 and 1990, whose 'There is no such thing as society' rationalized selling off public utilities to private enterprise), or as if the individual were just the determinable product of its social grouping. On the one hand, social and individual have nothing to do with each other except as sheer external envelope or obstacle; on the other the two become indistinguishable.

The trick is not to choose either of those options, external or indistinguishable, *or* to seek some sort of happy medium or compromise between them. It is to take *both at once*, in all the impossibility of any compromise. The social is indeed radically exterior to the individual, but only to exactly the same extent that not the slightest separation of the two is possible. We have seen this before: it is the logic of the unconscious as inner foreign territory. Affirmation and prohibition, as we have been outlining them here, are forms of the social bond because they set up a relation of impossibility between social and individual. That the bond is a double bind ensures not only that it is law-bound, but that what follows with necessity is also *never enough* to determine the link.

The nature of the bond

In *Group Psychology and the Analysis of the Ego* (1921), Freud asks what the nature of the group bond must be, and comes to the conclusion that it is doubled and indirect: there must be two sorts of bond at work, one of which is the consequence of the other.

First of all, there must be an object of interest common to all the members of the group, in what is essentially a libidinal relationship. The dynamic here is again very much like falling in love: the object of one's affection can be over-valued, immune from the sort of criticism the superego or ego- ideal usually offers of oneself, and even capable of over-riding the superego; the lover may do whatever the loved one desires or is perceived as desiring, even where that clashes with basic demands of morality. In other words, the desired object is effectively put in the place of the super-ego, and takes over its function.•

For the group, this object may be a beloved or admired leader, certainly, but it may be all sorts of other things as well, from God and Nation (the church and the army are two of Freud's major examples) to some far more modest common passion or activity (as in fan groups or hobby groups). What is important is that it be a shared object, common to a number of people all of whom put it in the place of the ego-ideal in the same fashion. That commonality is what provides the group bond, as a relationship of identification with those others: *I identify with X, Y and Z because we all love the same thing.* Freud diagrams this as in Figure 3.1.

> In connection with this question of being in love we have always been struck by the phenomenon of sexual overvaluation – the fact that the loved object enjoys a certain amount of freedom from criticism, and that all its characteristics are valued more highly than those of people who are not loved, or than its own were at the time when it itself was not loved. ... [The] illusion is produced that the object has come to be sensually loved on account of its spiritual merits...
>
> ... Contemporaneously with this 'devotion' of the ego to the object, which is no longer to be distinguished from a sublimated devotion to an abstract idea, the functions allotted to the ego-ideal entirely cease to operate. The criticism operated by that agency is silent; everything that the object does and asks for is right and blameless. Conscience has no application to anything that is done for the sake of the object; in the blindness of love remorselessness is carried to the pitch of crime. The whole situation can be completely summarised in a formula: *The object has been put in the place of the ego-ideal.* (*Group Psychology and the Analysis of the Ego* (1921), pp. 112, 113)

The group bond thus has two components, a *libidinal* relationship to an object, and the relationship of *identification* this leads to with others who share that libidinal attachment. For any one member of the group, the two sorts of relationship thus look like Figure 3.2.

When that shared object of affection is a leader, it is clear how close this is to the myth of the primal father from *Totem and Taboo*, which Freud will explicitly invokes again here. Like that relationship, *the social bond is based on an exception. The exception to the rules is the thing that holds it all together.* Just as the horde is bound together by the primal father who is not subject to its laws, so too is the bond of identification that ties the members of a group together based on an exceptional object.

At first sight, this object may be one of two things. It may be a member of the group, who is thus never just one member among many: we do not so much identify with the leader as put him or her in the place of the superego. But it may just as easily be something that is not a person at all, but has quite a different sort of existence (the passion for model trains which brings hobbyists

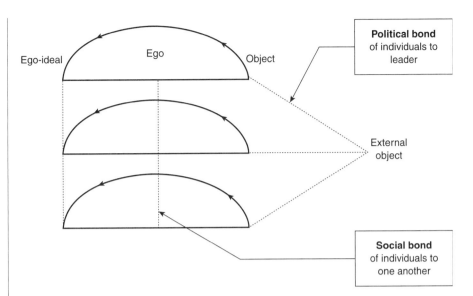

Figure 3.1 (adapted from *Group Psychology and the Analysis of the Ego* (1921), p. 116)

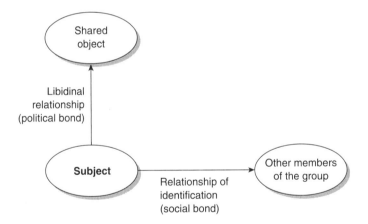

Figure 3.2

together, or the idea of Nation that sustains patriotism and is qualitatively quite different from any or even all of the actual members of that nation). But this second case points to what we already know from the primal horde: that the father is always already dead, and his place is essentially empty. Even when that shared object is a person, it is not that person as such who is the object of our desire. We recognise this when we use the word *charisma* for that force which attracts us to a certain person. Charisma – like charity, with which it shares an etymology, the Greek word χάρις, a gift or favour – is the name for what comes to its bearer from elsewhere, invested like a gift on the one who wears it, rather than owned; in this, *charisma* always exceeds any conceivable *talent* (which is what we *do* own – from the Latin *talentum*, inclination of mind). This is the logic of desire itself, after all. What I love in the loved one, that very thing which makes them so lovable, is always a strangely fantasmatic quality which recedes whenever I try to say just what it is. It need not even correspond to anything at all I can actually observe in that person. *You are cruel, you are thoughtless and self-ish, you play me along – but I still love you*: that object which is at the core of my desire is something with which my love invests the loved one. This is not the lover's narcissism or solipsism, a closed circuit of fantasy which returns to no one but the lover, as this impossible bestowed object makes an actual difference to, in and for the loved one. *Now that I am loved, I am no longer the same person.*

May we not say something similar of the political bond, the libidinal relationship that is at the heart of the group bond? It comes about not from the properties of the object in itself, but as an investiture. If in some alternative universe, they had never had any connection whatsoever with the British throne, but had lived out their lives as sheep farmers, paper merchants and middle management, would we possibly ever think of the Windsor family as charismatic? Such investiture may be all but tautological: we all know the celebrity phenomenon of being 'famous for being famous', of a charisma with no visible means of support.[9] Alternatively, does not such a separation suggest why in the political arena, *argumentum ad hominem* may often turn out to be such an ineffective strategy in contemporary liberal democracies? As the Reagan, Clinton, and Bush administrations have demonstrated in different ways, to point out the personal failings of an incumbent – intellectual abilities, literacy level, or sexual conduct – often has no effect on that incumbent's popularity, and may even increase it. What it draws attention to is precisely that gap between person and role, and the way in which that charisma is an investiture which works across and even depends on the gap. Far from threatening any political ideals, what such revelations may do, on the contrary, is confirm the powerful political fantasies which sustain the process: what they say may not be the intended *The president is an ignoramus*, but instead, *How much the president knows is either irrelevant (that's what staff are there for) or the very point of identification (the president is simply human)*.[10] *Forrest Gump* and before it the far more disconcerting *Being There* are not themselves fantasies about politics so much as canny films about political fantasy.

It is also clear that the group relationship as Freud conceives it here – on the one hand, a libidinal bond, on the other, a bond of identification – is a variation on the familial relationships of the Oedipus complex. Figure 3.3 shows Oedipus in its unresolved form, for both sexes: the mother is the desired object, and the father is the deadly rival because, just like me, he demands the mother's affection and thus threatens to supplant me. It is also very close to the standard resolved form in the case of male heterosexuality, where my libidinal objects are now female, and I identify with and rival other men in the light of that. We shall have to pay attention to features of both of these variations. The similarity of the two may mean that it is particularly easy for one to merge into the other – for the resolved form to mask aspects of the unresolved.

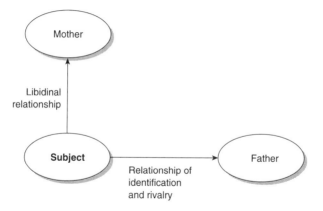

Figure 3.3

For now something interesting and unexpected has occurred. If we are indeed to take the group bond as a variation on Oedipus, the obvious correspondence of positions would appear to be oddly reversed. According to this diagram, the position of the leader is not, as one might think, that of the father, but that of the *mother*. Why should this be so?

One part of the answer is that Freud's original diagram implicitly describes a set of relationships among men. The person I identify with in the social bond is, in this diagram, a(nother) man. Indeed, the social bond is so often and so generally seen as a fraternity, a bond among brothers.[11] It is also thus a bond that is likely to flip over into rivalry. The men with whom I identify as my brothers in this fraternity are also my potential heterosexual rivals. Beyond this, though, identification itself is always close to a rivalry: the one who is like me is the one who can take my place. The social bond of such a fraternity is unstable: *I am like him* is always the flipside to *He must not be like me* (Borch-Jacobsen, 1988, pp. 26–27 *passim*). And the object of this rivalry in the unresolved complex is the maternal body. Oedipus is an attempt to explain how it is that this maternal body comes to be something other than the undifferentiated bliss that fantasy demands, and is instead already split against itself. The rivalry of brothers meets the Oedipal question, *Why do I not have my enjoyment?* with the answer, *My rival has stolen it from me.*[12] The social bond has within it the possibility of internecine warfare.

Civilization:
The Future of an Illusion (1927)

This is Freud's first major statement of the antagonism between culture and the individual. (Freud's term, *Kultur*, is generally translated as 'civilisation' in the Standard Edition.) As social bonding is essentially libidinal, every culture

Social

places a libidinal impost on its members; it demands work and a renunciation of many of the satisfactions of the drives. These demands are social prohibitions; they produce frustrations within the individuals, and privations in lived social life. The function of the superego is to internalise the oppositions these provoke, and by turning them into satisfactions reduce that culture's reliance on coercion. Two of the ways in which that can happen are through art and the essay's principal topic, religion.

For Freud, the source of the religious impulse is in the child's powerlessness and the protective figure of the father. It functions to reassure about what is not and cannot be known, and as such corresponds quite precisely to the psychoanalytic category of fantasy. This is where the term *illusion* of the title is important: an illusion is not an error but a *wish*, and as such is susceptible neither to proof nor disproof, both of which leave that aspect of wishing untouched. Religion functions in much the same way as obsessional neurosis, with its ritual observances for adverting misfortune, and is thus, like neuroses, something to be replaced by the rational decisions of the intellect.

Like *The Question of Lay Analysis* of the previous year, *The Future of an Illusion* is carried on for the most part as a dialogue with a critical opponent.

Civilization and its Discontents (1930)

The Future of an Illusion had set up an opposition between the drives' demands for satisfaction and the cultural restrictions placed on that satisfaction. But now another question arrives to complicate matters. What if the resistances to the sexual drives are not only cultural, but also somehow innate to the very concept of drive – if it is not just a matter of the social repression of a drive which could otherwise achieve its aim, but of 'something in the nature of the function itself which denies us full satisfaction and urges us along other paths' (p. 105)? That new factor is the death drive, whose resistances threaten not only the satisfactions of the sexual drives, but also, in their manifestations as aggression, the fabric of the cultural itself. The task of culture is thus not only to restrict the satisfactions of the sexual drives in order to use the libidinal energies for the purposes of social bonding; it is also to inhibit the aggressiveness which is the manifestation of the death drive, and which constantly threatens from within to undo that social bond.

This gives a new function to the superego. Where *The Future of an Illusion* saw it as the means of internalising the demands of the social and turning its restrictions into ideals, now Freud sees the superego as culture's way of obtaining 'mastery over the individual's dangerous desire for aggression by weakening and disarming it and by setting up an agency within him to watch over it, like a garrison in a conquered city' (p. 124). In particular, this is the function of *conscience* and its consequent guilt. As the superego is an internalisation of authority, even wishes cannot be hidden from it, and conscience turns out to be a far more severe, implacable and relentless judge than any external authority. Under such a regime, the guilt it produces may multiply: to renounce a satisfaction of the drives is not to lay that guilt to rest, but to keep it alive and even renew it, as the very renunciation becomes a proof that one was guilty in the first place. The superego does not so much neutralise the agressiveness of the death drive, as master it by turning it back against itself, and thus perpetuating it as a tension at the heart of both the social and the individual subject.

For *Civilization and its Discontents*, the social is irremediably split at its heart, and this split is the very engine of its working.

Moses and Monotheism:
Three Essays (1939)

Moses and Monotheism is the last book Freud published in his lifetime. It seems to have been drafted in much its present form and structure by late 1934. The delay in publication is due to a number of factors which include his continuing dissatisfaction with it (especially with the third of its three essays, the only one not published separately before the book), his worries about its reception in a dominantly Roman Catholic country, and the political situation in Austria. He seems to have made revisions intermittently until its publication in 1939.

The first essay, 'Moses an Egyptian', considers the legend of Moses' birth, abandonment to the Nile and rescue by Pharaoh's daughter as a variation on what an earlier article called 'Family Romances' (1909) – that is, on the child's fantasy that its parents are not really its own, and that the child is in fact a foundling from a noble family. The fantasy thus gives the child two families: in its usual form, the first of these (the child's origin) is fantasised, while the second is the child's real family. To read the Moses story as a family romance is thus to see Moses as an Egyptian who became a Jew, rather than a Jewish child adopted by Egyptian royalty: the word *mose*, child, is common on Egyptian monuments.

The second essay, 'If Moses was an Egyptian …' develops this argument. What then would have been the religion Moses gave to the Jews? It was clearly not the very different and intensely polytheistic Egyptian state religion, but it may, Freud suggests, have been an Egyptian religion. He proposes the monotheistic religion of the sun god Aten, which flourished very briefly in the Eighteenth Dynasty with the seventeen-year reign of Amenophis IV (Akhenaten) and his wife Nefertiti in the fourteenth century BC Aten was worshipped as the sole creator and source of all things, to the exclusion of all magic, sorcery and myths; like Judaism, the Aten religion had nothing to do with life after death or the next world. Freud speculates that Moses would have been a member of the royal house who, with the collapse of Akhenaten's reign, went into exile with his followers: the Exodus. In the course of these travels, they would have taken over the worship of another god, Yahweh, probably from the Midianites. Yahweh was a fierce bloodthirsty demon who walked by night, and the figure of the aristocratic Egyptian who led his people out of captivity became identified with the historically quite different figure of the founding priest of this religion. The Moses of the Bible is thus a composite figure in a complex fusion of different stories.

The third essay, 'Moses, His People and Monotheistic Religion', is the one which gave Freud most trouble; it is the longest (longer than the first two combined), the most tentative, and the most uneven in its structure, full of repetitions, doubts, and apologies. It is also the one in which psychoanalytic theory attempts its greatest purchase on the Moses story, drawing once again on the myth of the primal father from *Totem and Taboo*, the dynamics of groups from *Group Psychology and the Analysis of the Ego*, and continuing the arguments on the correspondences between religion and neurosis made in *The Future of an Illusion* and *Civilization and its Discontents*.

Neuroses have their etiology in traumas from earliest childhood, which characteristically may have long periods of latency. The equivalent of such a trauma in the (pre)history of the Jewish people is the murder, according to Sellin's theory, of Moses by his own people. At the foundation of Judaic monotheism we have once again a version of the story of the primal father, the remorse for whose killing is at the root of the fantasy of the Messiah who returns to lead his promised people to redemption and the promised land.

Freud clearly admits the difficulties involved in moving like this from categories of individual psychology towards some sort of 'group psychology'. Where, for instance, does the memory of such a group lie, for such a trauma to remain active over so many generations? Freud's answer is that just as with individuals, it lies in 'unconscious memory-traces' (p. 94). An individual's life is affected not only by what she has experienced herself, but also by an 'archaic heritage' of phylogenetic events (p. 98). Certain symbols, for example – and here Freud seems to be drawing surprisingly close to Jung, a quarter-century after their break – seem to be universal, as if the thought-connections they represent had become part and parcel of a general human heritage. Childhood neuroses can seem to have a multi-generational aetiology. Some experiences may be preserved in a way akin to animal instinct (and here is one of the rare occasions in which the word Freud uses is *Instinkt* rather than *Trieb*). It is in ways like this that humans have always in some sense known of the primal father and his killing. Only such an explanation, Freud argues, can come to grips with the ways in which such phenomena as religion can be so independent of and even resistant to logical thought.

The second part of the essay recapitulates the entire book so far, expanding and elaborating at times. It deals with the question of the people of Israel as the chosen people: the figure of Moses the leader borrows his authority from the relationship to the father, and this in turn lends itself to the relation to God. The Mosaic God is increasingly dematerialized and desensualized, in a renunciation of the drive which is also a birth of the ethical; the symbolic covenant of circumcision stands for the acceptance of castration which makes this possible. With Christianity, the coming of Christ and the restoration of the presence of God stand in relation to the killing of the primal father as the return of the repressed, guilt now turned by sacrifice into rapturous devotion.

III: The opening of history

Something does not follow

Group Psychology and the Analysis of the Ego starts from an elision of *the group* with *the social*: Freud uses the terms *group psychology* and *social psychology* as synonyms. •

The contrast between individual and social or group psychology, which at first glance may seem to be full of significance, loses a great deal of its sharpness when it is examined more closely. It is true that individual psychology is concerned with the individual man and explores the paths by which he seeks to find satisfaction for his instinctual impulses; but only rarely and under certain exceptional conditions is individual psychology in a position to disregard the relations of this individual to others. In the individual's mental life someone else is invariably involved, as a model, as an object, as a helper, as an opponent; and so from the very first individual psychology, in this extended but entirely justifiable sense of the words, is at the same time social psychology as well.

The relations of an individual to his parents and to his brothers and sisters, to the object of his love, and to his physician – in fact all the relations which hitherto have been the chief subject of psychoanalytic research – may claim to be considered as social phenomena; and in this respect they may be contrasted with certain other processes, described by us as 'narcissistic', in which the satisfaction of the instincts is partially or totally withdrawn from the influence of other people. The contrast between social and narcissistic ... mental acts therefore falls wholly within the domain of individual psychology, and is not well calculated to differentiate it from a social or group psychology. (*Group Psychology and the Analysis of the Ego* (1921), p. 69)

His argument is that because the individual is always formed in a set of relations with others, individual psychology is already, from the outset, a group psychology. The problem with group psychology as it has hitherto existed, he argues, is that it has ignored those smaller-scale group relations about which psychoanalysis already has a lot to say, and leapt too quickly to larger-scale questions: how is the individual influenced by the groups to which he or she belongs, groups made up of sometimes very large numbers of other individuals, such as a race, a nation, a profession, a crowd? Because it makes this leap too quickly, existing group psychology has had to invent what Freud argues is a quite unnecessary category, the *social instincts* (or 'herd instinct' or 'group mind'). It is an unnecessary term, says Freud, because what it names is in fact already explainable in terms of individual psychology, and finds its earliest beginnings in the individual and the family circle. Everything group psychology needs to explain social behaviour is already there in psychoanalysis.

Psychology, then, moves too quickly from the small scale to the large, and in doing this it misses, between the two, the very thing it is after. But could we not say just the same thing about Freud's argument? Here, social psychology is essentially group psychology, and group psychology is a variation on individual psychology; it is essentially additive: groups are nothing but a large number of individuals and the interpersonal relationships among them. But if that is all, have we not then missed precisely the dimension of the social bond, the double bind which, as a logical, structural condition, is quite irreducible to the level of the individual and the interpersonal? The social bond is not a matter of the fact that we are all born into families made up of other individuals, or that those individuals have all sorts of relationships amongst themselves; *family itself* pre-exists us, as a very particular type of *structure* quite independent of any particular family or the individuals who make it up. It is a structure which individuals and particular families find themselves already in, and within which choice necessarily has the retrospective logic of affirmation and the contradictory imperatives of the double bind.

But would not such an argument be a somewhat dangerous universalisation? Is it really just a way of saying that whatever the huge historical and cultural variation may be in the ways in which families work, the functions they have in the societies in which they arise, and the very individuals they tend to produce, they are all at base the same – and (the obvious extension would be) that this base is essentially the sort of family Freud knew so well, the middle-class family of early twentieth-century Vienna? Is it, in the words of a complaint one often hears about Freud, to be deeply unhistorical and culture-blind?

That would indeed be so if what we are referring to as *structure* took the form of a model for a particular sort of family – if it were, in effect, a set of stipulations on what a family does and is, and where a family which is or does not fall into that description would be correspondingly immature, regressive, perverse or pathological; if it said, that is, that all families are the same, and those which aren't are a problem. Putting it like that should remind us of an earlier argument, the far-reaching one Freud made about sexualities in 1905. For nineteenth-century sexology, reproductive heterosexuality is the moral norm against which all other forms are to a greater or lesser degree pathological. Freud's argument on the infant's polymorphous perversity, however, turns this on its head: given that the drive's aims and objects are formed only in the contingencies and vicissitudes of a life history, the real problem is how reproductive heterosexuality comes to occur so frequently.

The argument to be made here has precisely the same shape: rather than postulating a particular type of normative family from which everything else is to be measured, the question implied by Freud's argument is instead precisely one of how *the family* in all of its divergent forms comes to be. Instead of a set of structures and fixed relationships at the heart of the family telling us *This is what a family must be*, we have the double bind as the characteristic and necessary form of the social bond, in which every such demand is accompanied immediately by *This very same thing is what a family must* not *be*. Far from being a template, the double-bind's contradictory demands ensure that there can be no template at all, no single true *family*, the right way of being a family; there is only a multitude of families, all of which work *and* do not work in some way or another.[13] Just as the absence of any general form of the relationship between the sexes means that every actual sexual relationship is in a sense to be played out for the first time, played by ear without guarantees of success, so too with the absence of any template to *the family*.

All human beings are born from a mother; all are premature, in that we have a long period in which we are utterly dependent on others for our survival; all are born with a particular genital conformation; all go through a complex and pro-tracted process of separation from the maternal body. These are not simply biolo-gisms, for two reasons. The first, and more obvious one, is that they are already social facts. To put it more accurately, if slightly awkwardly, they are *nowhere not* already social facts. It would be a mistake to buy into that perpetual and fruitless dis-tinction between nature and nurture, as if the human being could be seen as the sum of some attributes which belong solely to the hardwiring of its biological inher-itance and are thus relatively fixed, and others which have been learnt through the routines of a culture, and are thus relatively mutable and capable of being unlearned and reconfigured. One obvious problem with that would be that the two poles offered as explanation are completely imaginary: we never meet them in the wild. No human being, and no aspect of any human being, is ever purely either: every apparently purely biological facet of our existence is already a cultural datum, and there is no apparently cultural facet which does not somewhere touch on the facticities of the organism. But beyond that, two such poles cannot be simply addi-tive. To try to explain a certain aspect of human behaviour as partly nature, partly nurture is trying to explain the properties and consequences of water (its density and specific gravity, its ability to flow, and to wet some things and not others, its colour in large quantities, its necessity to life, its effect on the weather cycles, its sup-port of marine life, the history of navigation and trade routes, the economics of famine, the invocations of poetry …) by ascertaining which part of each is due to hydrogen and which to oxygen.[14]

The second and more far-reaching reason that such propositions are not biologisms is that they are not statements of a positive content from which cer-tain consequences would follow with a clear and repeatable logic: the double bind ensures that that sort of continuity is not possible. Far from being the assertion of some sort of essential given human nature that would be the premise from which everything would follow, these are moments from which *nothing necessarily follows*. What happens as a consequence of our birth, our pre-maturity, our genital configuration, our slow and often incomplete negotiations of Oedipus, is that the chains of cause and effect are massively invaded by the accidental and the contingent. We enter history. From now on, we shall never leave it, as it opens up everywhere at our core as that gap of the contingent ensured by the double bind. The double bind is not sort of trans-historical essence of being human; it is the moment from which the very possibility of a history opens out, with all of the variations it may take.

Something does not follow; everything follows from that.

Metasociology

What status are we to give to this odd story of the primal horde and its over-thrown father, that projection of Oedipus so unlike anything taken seriously in contemporary cultural theory?

As we have seen, castration is a childhood theory of sexuality before it is a psychoanalytic theory. Castration is the child's way of making sense of the inexplicable fact of sexual difference. As primal fantasy, it has no need at all of being an event which could be located at a particular time in the child's life (not surprisingly, the child never remembers a moment at which she *was* castrated). Its function is to give consistency: everything happens *as if* it had taken place, and this is its explanatory power.

But how then does the psychoanalyst's theory differ from the child's? How does it differ from the stories of origin we think of as myth? Like the child's theories, the psychoanalyst's give consistency to what, without them, would lack consistency. We cannot observe the unconscious, but once we have hypothesised its existence we are able to construct a clear and powerful chain of logic connecting and accounting for all sorts of things which before that postulation seemed scattered and without connection. Is the psychoanalyst's theory then simply a more mature, refined version of the child's? Is psychoanalysis itself at base a childhood theory of sexuality?

Psychoanalysis is good at listening. That is, after all, its founding gesture. Where nineteenth-century psychiatry observed the hysteric, or submitted her to drenchings, prolonged baths, extremes of cold, in order to see how this object of investigation reacted, psychoanalysis begins with the injunction, *Talk to me. Tell me about yourself.* Rather than stating a diagnosis for the patient to accept and act on, the analyst withdraws judgement and quietly refuses the position of the expert. The disturbances that bring the patient to analysis are formed out of the contingencies and singularities of a history, as indeed are the very form the symptoms take as they both express and mask that disturbance. Disturbance and symptoms alike become intelligible only in the light of that history, which is in the analysand's possession, not the analyst's. In that light, no matter how unintelligible they may appear from the outside, even in the delusions of the psychoses, the symptoms appear as a logical, even rigorous – if unsuccessful – response to the situation, an attempt to negotiate its contradictions and impossibilities.• The skill of the analyst is in a controlled not-knowing, an insistence that the *analysand* be the one who knows all along – even if, as is always the case, the analysand does not yet know that he knows.

Something similar happens with Freud's approach to the child's theories of sexuality. It would be banal and pointless to treat the

> The [psychotic] patient has withdrawn from the people in his environment and from the external world generally the libidinal cathexes which he has hitherto directed on to them. Thus everything has become indifferent and irrelevant to him, and has to be explained by means of a secondary rationalisation as being 'miracled up, cursorily improvised'. The end of the world is the projection of this internal catastrophe; his subjective world has come to an end since his withdrawal of his love from it.
>
> ...And the paranoic builds it again, not more splendid, it is true, but at least so that he can once more live in it. He builds it up by the work of his delusions. *The delusional formation, which we take to be the pathological product, is in reality an attempt at recovery, a process of reconstruction.* ('Psychoanalytic Notes on an Autobiographical Account of a Case of Paranoia' (1911a), pp. 70–71; emphasis in original)

child's theories as no more than mistakes, with all that would imply (such as the need to correct, and the assurance that one's own position, from which one does the correction, is indeed uncontaminated by the errors one corrects). Instead, Freud asks what follows from such theories. How do they help organise the child's life and knowing, what the child does and how it acts with others and the world? Far from being things which adulthood and its knowledge sweep into oblivion, these childhood theories may survive into and be the very basis for the adult's behaviour.• Disavowal, as we have seen, allows the survival of such a theory long after it has been refused: *I know that X is not the case, but nevertheless, I behave as if it were ...*

> A knowledge of infantile sexual theories in the shapes they assume in the thoughts of children can be of interest in various ways – even, surprisingly enough, for the elucidation of myths and fairy tales. They are indispensable, moreover, for an understanding of the neuroses themselves; for in them these childish theories are still operative and acquire a determining influence upon the form taken by the symptoms. ...
>
> Neurotics are people much like others. They cannot be sharply differentiated from normal people, and in their childhood they are not always easily distinguishable from those who remain healthy in later life. ('On the Sexual Theories of Children' (1908b), pp. 211, 210)

Psychoanalysis's theories of sexuality are thus also, at the same time, necessarily *theories about how theories of sexuality work*. There is a certain *meta*-dimension indispensable to them, which is inseparable from the dimensions of the unconscious and the contingent. To say that psychoanalytic theories are *metatheories* is to indicate not just a folding back onto themselves (a theory about theories), but also the way in which all theories, the psychoanalyst's as much as the child's, are acts in the world. More than a representation of the world, they are a set of complex strategies for living in it. Like those of any act, the consequences of any theory are never fully calculable, for they open out into a future. A theory is always a knot: some knots, those theories of the neurotic, may be agonised stalemates it is extremely difficult to break; others, like the psychotic's, are valiant attempts to remake a world which has disintegrated; some, such as those of psychoanalysis as a clinical practice, aim at reducing hysterical misery to ordinary unhappiness.

That *meta*- has a second sense, connected to this knot. Where psychology is classically concerned with modelling consciousness, Freud describes psychoanalysis as a *metapsychology* in as much as it models a psyche that is never entirely conscious. The term sounds like and inevitably recalls *metaphysics*, which Freud sets against metapsychology. Metaphysics, he argues, is the projection onto the world of what are in fact the dramas of the psyche; metapsychology, on the other hand, has as its task the recogn tion and mapping of this process of projection. • But as we have seen, the distinction between the two – metaphysics and metapsychology,

> In point of fact I believe that a large part of the mythological view of the world, which extends a long way into the most modern religions, *is nothing but psychology projected into the external world*. The obscure recognition* (the endopsychic perception, as it were) of psychical factors and relations in the unconscious is mirrored – it is difficult to express it in other terms, and here the analogy with paranoia must come to our aid – in the construction of a *supernatural reality*, which is destined to be changed back once more by science into the *psychology of the unconscious*. One could venture to explain in this way the myths of paradise and the fall of man, of God, of good

and evil, of immortality, and so on, and to transform *metaphysics* into *metapsychology*.

*[Freud's footnote] A recognition which, of course, has nothing of the character of a recognition.[15]

(*The Psychopathology of Everyday Life* (1901), pp. 258–59; emphases in original)

superstition and science – is not at all that one is saturated in myth and the other is free from it, for psychoanalysis has its own myths in Oedipus and the primal horde. Freud's term for these is precise: they are *scientific myths*, and he insists on their necessity.•   What then, if anything, distinguishes that strange oxymoron *scientific myth* from *myth* pure and simple? Does myth have the same brief, and the same structure, as the hypotheses of psychoanalysis itself?

We have said that it would be possible to specify the point in the mental development of mankind at which the advance from group psychology to individual psychology was achieved by the individual members of the group.

For this purpose we must return for a moment to the scientific myth of the father of the primal horde. (*Group Psychology and the Analysis of the Ego* (1921), p. 135)

We cannot get away from the assumption that man's sense of guilt springs from the Oedipus complex and was acquired at the killing of the father by the brothers banded together. (*Civilization and its Discontents* (1930), p. 131)

What all theories must share with childhood theories of sexuality is their status as secondary revision. A theory selects, orders, connects, forgets. We recall how the first rule of dream analysis is to look at the detail rather than the whole. • The free associations through which dream analysis works are developed from the elements of the dream rather than from the whole, because whatever unity the dream possesses will always have come from the

[W]hat Schiller describes as a relaxation of the watch upon the gates of Reason, the adoption of an attitude of uncritical self-observation, is by no means difficult ...

Our first step in the employment of this procedure [dream analysis] teaches us that what we must take as the object of our attention is not the dream as a whole but the separate portions of its content. If I say to a patient who is still a novice: 'What occurs to you in connection with this dream?', as a rule his mental horizon becomes a blank. If, however, I put the dream before him cut up into pieces, he will give me a series of associations to each piece, which might be described as the 'background thoughts' of that particular part of the dream. (*The Interpretation of Dreams* (1900), vol. 4, pp. 103–04)

ondary revision: the dream-work itself is profoundly unconscious and knows nothing of unity, coherence or consistency. Psychoanalysis is always an *analysis*, trying to reach the disparate, conflictual, irreconcilable components that have been brought together into a seeming whole only by the strategies of secondary revision.

Psychoanalysis cannot do without those processes of secondary revision, for they include all the things necessary to an argument, reason and understanding: cogence and coherence, intelligibility and rigour, connection and consequence. But they are not its object. Its object – which will thus hardly even bear the term *object* – is prior to those, their very condition of possibility: the unconscious costs and frayings and breakages which subtend all things conscious.

Psychoanalysis tries to accept, as fully and as rigorously as it can, the paradox of this object. As we have seen, there is thus always a sense in which all of the concepts of psychoanalysis are simply, knowingly and necessarily *wrong*: they can lay no claim to represent or resemble, but only to reconstruct, elsewhere, those unreachable non-concepts which are its true, oblique object – and around which, like childhood theories and myths, psychoanalysis must circle.[16] This attempt to think through the paradoxical and impossible status of an object *before* secondary revision is what distinguishes psychoanalysis from metaphysics, superstition and childhood theories[17] – and also on the other hand, what ties it to them.

The empty core

This central, constitutive impossibility of the social is how we can read the central thesis of *Civilization and its Discontents*, Freud's major work on the trends of contemporary culture. In it, Freud introduces the concept of the death drive for the first time into his cultural criticism, to suggest that civilisation – culture[18] – is a struggle between Eros on the one hand, and on the other a death drive which manifests itself as an apparently endless capacity for aggression and destruction.• But this is a highly metaphysical opposition of abstractions which, as Freud well knows, never in fact appear to us separately and in their pure form. • As we saw in Chapter 2, the death drive is not so much a type of drive among others, one element (even if a problematic and somewhat unruly one) in a taxonomy of drives. It is instead a name for the inconsistency and division inherent in *drive itself*. Drive – any drive, Eros

... civilisation is a process in the service of Eros, whose purpose is to combine single human individuals, and after that families, then races, peoples and nations, into one great unity, the unity of mankind. Why this has to happen, we do not know; the work of Eros is precisely this. These collections of men are to be libidinally bound to one another. Necessity alone, the advantages of work in common, will not hold them together. But man's natural aggressive instinct, the hostility of each against all and of all against each, opposes this programme of civilisation. This aggressive instinct is the derivative and the main representative of the death instinct which we have found alongside of Eros and which shares world-dominion with it. And now, I think, the meaning of the evolution of civilisation is no longer obscure to us. It must present the struggle between Eros and Death, between the instinct of life and the instinct of destruction, as it works itself out in the human species. This struggle is what all life essentially consists of, and the evolution of civilization may therefore be simply described as the struggle for life of the human species. And it is this battle of the giants that our nurse-maids try to appease with their lullaby about Heaven. (*Civilization and its Discontents* (1930), pp. 122)

The manifestations of Eros were conspicuous and noisy enough. It might be assumed that the death instinct operated silently within the organism towards its dissolution, but that, of course, was no proof. A more fruitful idea was that a portion of the instinct is diverted towards the external world and comes to light as an instinct of aggressiveness and destructiveness. In this way the instinct itself could be pressed into the service of Eros, in that the organism was destroying some other thing, whether animate or inanimate, instead of destroying its own self.

itself – does not work purely in accordance with the principle of constancy. The death drive names what in Eros itself does not press towards ever

Conversely, any restriction of this aggressiveness directed outwards would be bound to increase the self-destruction, which is in any case proceeding. At the same time one can suspect from this example that the two kinds of instinct seldom – perhaps never – appear in isolation from each other, but are alloyed with each other in varying and very different proportions and so become unrecognisable to our judgement. (*Civilization and its Discontents* (1930), p. 119)

greater unities, but without which drive itself, including Eros and its syntheses, would not exist.

Freud speaks of this death drive as being pressed into the service of Eros by being directed outwards: the organism preserves itself by turning what would otherwise be self-destructive outwards into the world. But this is still to reinstall a sort of inverted principle of constancy: it postulates a certain constant amount of destructiveness in the organism, which can be deflected from one object to another but cannot itself be destroyed. It saves the hypothesis, as the Devil does for God.• Freud's example of anti-Semitism points to a more intimate relationship the death drive is not just something that can be harnessed towards

... nobody wants to be reminded how hard it is to reconcile the undeniable existence of evil – despite the protestations of Christian Science – with [God's] all-powerfulness or His all-goodness. The devil would be the best way out as an excuse for God; in that way he would be playing the same part as an agent of economic discharge as the Jew does in the world of the Aryan ideal. (*Civilization and its Discontents* (1930), p. 120)

the ends of Eros, but is strictly inseparable from Eros. The very unification has a violence as its flipside.•

What *Civilization and its Discontents* postulates, then, is a society whose core is radically and necessarily inconsistent – not in the obvious and banal sense of a moral deploration, but as a consequence of precisely the same logics we have been

It is always possible to bind together a considerable number of people in love, so long as there are other people left over to receive the manifestations of their aggressiveness. ... In this respect the Jewish people, scattered everywhere, have rendered most useful services to the civilisations of the countries that have been their hosts; but unfortunately all the massacres of the Jews in the Middle Ages did not suffice to make that period more peaceful and secure for their Christian fellows. When once the apostle Paul had posited universal love between men as the foundation of his Christian community, extreme intolerance on the part of Christendom towards those who remained outside it became the inevitable consequence. (*Civilization and its Discontents* (1930), p. 114)

tracing throughout Freud's thought. The core of the social is its impossibility. The social is inhabited by difference, just as the very idea of 'the human' is inhabited by the sexual difference that guarantees that it can have no unity.

It is tempting to say then, by analogy, that *There is no social relationship*: not in the sense of the Thatcherite fantasy of a world without a social dimension, made up of nothing but self-determining individuals and their interpersonal relationships, but in the sense in which *the social is not a whole*. It is instead a tension amongst structurally irreconcilable elements and aspects. The social is an aggregate, not a unity. Social relations follow only in the same sense in which symptom follows from cause; they are *ad hoc*, made out of the contingencies of what lies to hand – the 'residues of history', as it were, with all of their *a priori* incalculability. As with relations between the sexes, there is no general *a priori* pattern for them. The very possibility of there being a cohesive social bond is built on relations which *need not* lead to cohesion of any sort, though cohesion is not going to come from anywhere else. Eros carries the death drive as its other side: it is impossible to have Eros without the death drive, as the death drive is the name for what makes Eros possible. The social relationship is, in a word, and just like the sexual relation, *impossible*. And by that, as with the sexual relation, what is meant is not that social relations do not occur, but that they occur only because of the very things which prevent them from being perfectly general. As with any double bind, any particular way of negotiating it is never enough. Everything remains open and yet to be done.

All knowledge circles that double void at the heart of both the psyche and the social world, and which we have suggested can be summed up in *There is no sexual relation* and *There is no social relation*. And here, we find we have come back to the categories of the ethical and the political, in a quite classical, even Kantian, sense. This double bind – *something does not follow* – means that there is no way of deriving what *should* be from what *is*, or an ethics from an ontology, where the ethical would follow from the ontological with the rigour and necessity of natural law, with the inexorability of a falling body in a gravitational field. No matter how urgent, how necessary it may be in the sense that *we need it to be so*, something does not follow: in Kant's terms, practical reason does not follow from pure reason. From that, we have the very opening of the ethical and the political.

Ideology

The analogy is precise. Freud's theories of culture and the social are a *metasociology*, in just the same senses in which psychoanalysis is a metapsychology. If a psychology maps out the rich empirical data of consciousness; a metapsychology maps out its inconsistent and unconscious converse. At the heart of the psyche is its necessary failure to coincide with itself, the trauma of the contingent which structures it: in a word, the death drive. The metasociology Freud offers is a mapping-out of the unrepresentable trauma – *there is no social relation* – at the heart of the social.

Like metapsychology, Freud's metasociology is an attempt to avoid homuncularity, and to derive a theory of the social that does not, secretly or otherwise, have at its core the figure of free individuals who found the social by entering into a contract with each other. As we have seen, that argument is circular: free individuals who enter into a contract are already social creatures through and through. The story of the deposition of the primal father is non-homuncular to the extent that it leaves the centre of the social permanently and structurally vacant. This is what allows Freud to claim it as a *scientific* myth: it aims at an explanation that would not beg the very terms it attempts to explain, but develop out of what is logically prior. As with metapsychological description, what Freud offers is in effect – though he never expresses it in those terms – a description in terms of a dynamics (the drive and its incessant tension of forces), an economics (even if a ruined one, once the death drive takes us beyond the principle of constancy into the endless generation of a surplus), and a topography (the social double-bind which shares the logic of the unconscious, the social functioning of the superego).

It is of course an incomplete and inconsistent eviction, just as that performed by metapsychology, and for similar reasons. The primal father is deposed by a contract among the sons, after all. We have seen homuncularity making its way back into *Group Psychology and the Analysis of the Ego*, where *social* slides into *interpersonal*. But we also find the argument *against* homuncularity breaking out of that frame everywhere, unable to remain within its constraints. One of the features of groups which previous investigators such as Le Bon and Trotter had often recognised, and which seemed to them one of the reasons for hypothesising a 'herd instinct' or 'group mind', is the way in which groups can abrogate any individual independence from their members. What psychoanalysis sets as its problem, then, is not the predominance of the rational and contractual individual over the social, but the ways in which that can be *swept away* in the social. Neither will Freud admit the saving hypothesis that this is all done by the power of one single individual, who imposes his her will on others. It is exercised, he insists, by every individual upon every other. And that doubles the paradox: for the individual who exercises power upon others is him- or herself the subject of others' exercise of that very power, simultaneously imposing a will on others and swept away and rendered will-less by the will of others. What we are seeking here cannot be simply an individual psychology at the cause of things.•

Or again, we find a similar movement in *Civilization and its Discontents*. It begins as an argument about the high cost of civilisation to the individual. The social bond is a libidinal bond, and can be fuelled only by a deflection of libido away from objects on which it would otherwise be focused. Here, the social bond is

It might be said that the intense emotional ties which we observe in groups are quite sufficient to explain one of their characteristics – the lack of independence and initiative in their members, the similarity in the reactions of all of them, their reduction, so to speak, to the level of group individuals. But if we look at it as a whole, a group shows us more than this. Some of its features – the weakness of intellectual ability, the lack of emotional restraint, the incapacity for moderation and delay, the inclination to exceed every limit in the expression of emotion and to work it off completely in the form of action – these and similar features, which we find so impressively described in Le Bon, show an unmistakable picture of a regression of mental activity to an earlier stage such as we are not surprised to find among savages or children. A regression of this sort is in particular an essential characteristic of common groups, while ... in organised and artificial groups it can to a large extent be checked.

... We are reminded of how many of these phenomena of dependence are part of the normal constitution of human society, of how little originality and personal courage are to be found in it, of how much every individual is ruled by those attitudes of the group mind which exhibit themselves in such forms as racial characteristics, class prejudices, public opinion, etc. The influence of suggestion becomes a greater riddle for us when we admit that it is not exercised only by the leader, but by every individual upon every other individual; and we must reproach ourselves with having unfairly emphasised the relation to the leader and with having kept the other factor of mutual suggestion too much in the background. (*Group Psychology and the Analysis of the Ego* (1921), pp. 117–18) another version of both a social contract (people group together to better protect themselves from the violence of nature and to make optimal use of resources) and the reality principle (the sound economic management of libido takes it away from the immediate satisfaction of the drives to invest it in longer-term assurances). The social bond demands a certain renunciation, which Freud suggests may even be too great. But once the death drive is introduced, just over halfway through the book, this gives way to another rather different argument: even once we take that economic calculation into account, the sums still do not add up. At the heart of the social, inseparable from all of these attempts at synthesis and ever-greater accretion, we find an aggressiveness that is never wholly in their service.

Homuncularity is displaced with the recognition the death drive affords: if the human receives its explanation in terms of what is logically and necessarily prior to the human, then there can be no guarantee that these forces will lead teleologically to human ends. Not only is the death drive blind; it is a name for the blindness of drive itself, all drive. Drive is the basis of possibility of the human, but it is also the inconsistency at its heart. This is why we have to say, as we did of Freud's metapsychology, that a consistent metasociology is not possible. The *meta-* is always a stance from within these inconsistencies. The questions it asks – its metaquestions, like those metaquestions psychoanalysis asks about the child's theories of sexuality – are not just questions about the social, but also *questions about what it means to ask certain questions of the social*. How does asking certain questions of the social, seeing the social in certain ways, organise the social dimension and the relations of those involved in it?

A metasociology, then, is another name for a *theory of ideology*. To use the term in this way is not in the dismissive sense of a faulty or deluded knowledge, or in opposition with truth. (Truth and deception are never related in such a simple way for psychoanalysis, which, after all, listens to the ways in which truths can be expressed only as deceptions, and for the truths which deceptions cannot help but utter.)

Ideology is instead a name for the *investments* of knowing. All knowledge has its desires. That in itself says nothing of the truth or falsity of a knowledge: it is merely to point out that knowledge and science, like all utterances, are *addressed*. This dimension of address is always what psychoanalysis listens for (*What is desired in or by this utterance?*). The most objectified and codified knowledge, even, let us say, the most incontrovertibly true, necessarily has this dimension of address, and thus of ideology. There can, after all, hardly be a term more laden with all sorts of social freights of fantasy and desire than *science*: science is both salvation and damnation (it can be evoked in both ways in ecological debate, for example), human self-making and a hubristic playing God (both of which, similarly, are evoked in debates over gene technologies and stem-cell research). The powerful objectification involved in science is far from an elimination of the dimension of fantasy; on the contrary, it is the very support of that obverse social fantasy of the pure, inhuman power of science.

Ideology, then, is *the name for the social and cultural investments of knowledge.* The questions it opens out onto,[19] and with which this book opens out onto its end, are, *What does this let us do? What do we desire in doing this? How does it deal with that trauma at the heart of the social, the absence of a social relation? What world does it offer us as a fantasy about the social, and why might we want it?* These are, and have been from the outset, the questions of psychoanalysis.

The case histories:
'Fragment of an Analysis of a Case of Hysteria' ('Dora') (1901)

'Dora' is Freud's first major case history after the break with Josef Breuer. Its prefatory remarks point out the double-bind within which any psychoanalytic case history must operate: on the one hand, there is the professional necessity for complete confidentiality, which requires that any details that might identify the patient must be suppressed or altered beyond recognition. On the other hand, though, that singular and individual detail is precisely what psychoanalysis works with: the symptom is built from what is there, in the life, for it to use.

Given the date of the case history – Freud wrote it early in 1901, less than two years on from the epochal *The Interpretation of Dreams*, whose methods he was also at this time putting to work in *The Psychopathology of Everyday Life* – it is not surprising that the analysis relies significantly on two of Dora's dreams.

The subject was an 18-year-old girl who first came to see Freud in October 1900. She presented with attacks of *tussis nervosa* (nervous cough) which could last for several weeks or even months, dyspnoea (breathing difficulties) and a sensation of pressure on the upper thorax, hoarseness and lack of voice, migraines, depression, fatigue, unsociability, and feelings of disgust. In the course of the treatment, Freud was able to unravel a complex and sordid family story.

Dora's father was a well-to-do manufacturer in his late 40s, who had been through a number of serious and incapacitating illnesses during his daughter's life: tuberculosis, which had required the entire family to move to a better climate; a detached retina; and a number of the symptoms of syphilis, which he had contracted before his marriage.[20] Deeply attached to her father, Dora had shown signs of disturbance from an early age: bedwetting and dyspnoea from her seventh and eighth years, attacks of migraine and nervous coughing at the age of 12. Her mother stands on the margins of the drama as a stern figure obsessed with cleanliness, and a merciless critic of her daughter.

The crux occurred during Dora's family's extended stay in the town of B—, where they became friends with the K. family. Frau K. nursed Dora's father during his illness, and the two started an affair. Herr K. was at first apparently on good terms with the 16-year-old Dora: she would mind the K. children, and he would bring her presents and go for walks with her; but then she accused him of having kissed her and made an indecent proposal in the course of one of their walks. Confronted with this story, Herr K. denied it, and accused her of fantasising, a diagnosis with which her father agreed. The symptoms that brought her to Freud dated from this time. In effect, she had been placed in an untenable position by a pact between two men: the father she adored, and Herr K., for whom Dora was the implicit exchange for his wife. As well as this, and as many commentators have pointed out (see the essays collected in Bernheimer and Kahane, 1990), Dora showed a clear homosexual attraction towards Frau K. Freud was tardy in recognizing this (it shows up as the conclusion to a long footnote on 'supplementary interpretations' (pp. 104–05)). But by then, it was too late. The case history is a fragment of an analysis that was never completed: after three months, Dora announced that she would not be returning after another two weeks' treatment. She had pointedly given him the two weeks' notice one gives a servant.

The case is of great interest for a number of reasons. It is Freud's first major case history; it is incomplete, and the reasons for its incompleteness are a real source of chagrin for Freud; it is a failure for this reason, like his most famous case history, the 'Wolf-Man' case history; and like the 'Wolf-Man' it has an intricate structure of narration, in which the stakes of Freud's own counter-transference are quite clear – he wants this case to succeed, and to be the exemplar of his methods.

'Analysis of a Phobia in a Five-Year-Old Boy' ('Little Hans') (1909)

Hans was a happy, affectionate and intelligent child, from a loving family whose parents were both close acquaintances and supporters of Freud. It was in fact Hans's father rather than Freud himself who carried out much of the treatment; the case history draws extensively on the notes the father made available to Freud. Hans is the first case of an analysis of an infant, and exemplifies perfectly so many of the features of infantile sexuality Freud had been investigating around this time. He was intrigued by sexual difference, marked as he saw it by the relative size of 'widdlers' (which he noticed in zoo animals and also the horses on the streets of Vienna). Hans was familiar with the masturbatory pleasure his own widdler could give him, and had taken to heart his mother's threat that if he kept playing with it, she would get Dr A. to cut it off. His jealousy of his father as a rival for his mother's affection was doubled with the arrival of his sister Hanna when he was three and a half-years-old, and complicated by the fact that he also deeply loved his father, who returned that love. In all of this, he is almost the classic Oedipal boy. It is hardly surprising that Freud saw the case as confirmation of the second of the *Three Essays on Sexuality* (1905c), and that the case has important consequences in other writings of the time, such as the essay 'On the Sexual Theories of Children' (1908b) on which Freud was working during the treatment.

Hans first began showing signs of anxiety shortly after the birth of his sister, in the form of anxious dreams in which his mother was gone, an increase in shows of affection for his mother, and a fear of big animals (with their big widdlers). Just over a year after the birth, this became clearly phobic, with an incident in which Hans saw a large dray-horse fall over in the street and drum on the ground with its hooves: after this, the boy was afraid that a horse might bite him in the street, or even enter the house to bite him; he became afraid not only of being bitten by horses, but of moving horses, big horses, and vehicles drawn by horses – anything, in short (as Hans himself explained), which could lead to a horse's falling down. The horse, with its big widdler, is the father, and the phobia comes from the ambivalence of Hans's feelings: his desire to see his rival dead, and his guilt from this very wish.

In the 1922 Postscript, Freud tells with gratification of a later visit from a young man who introduced himself as Hans grown up, and thanked him for the success of the analysis.

'Notes upon a Case of Obsessional Neurosis' ('Rat Man') (1909c)

With the 'Rat Man', Freud had now published a case history on each of the three major forms of neurosis: Dora was an example of conversion hysteria, and Little Hans of phobias or anxiety hysteria.

The patient was a university-educated army officer, in his late 20s when he first came to see Freud. The obsessions from which he had been suffering since childhood had become particularly severe in the last four years, since his second rejection by the woman with whom he was in love, and he had had thoughts of suicide. He had intense scopophilic desires (to see women naked), and at the same time an obsessional fear that if he did not prevent such behaviour something terrible would happen to the woman he loved and to his father, even though his father had died nine years ago. This great fear is what gives the case history its tag: it refers to an Eastern torture he had heard of, in which a container of rats would be turned upside down on a prisoner's buttocks for the rats to eat their way in through his anus. His compulsive desires included one to cut his own throat with a razor, and he surrounded himself with the prohibitions and ceremonies that are so characteristic of obsessional neuroses.

The immediate precipitating cause of the anxiety attack that had brought him to Freud was a series of events that occurred while he was on manoeuvres with his unit. During the exercise, he lost his pince-nez, and wired his opticians in Vienna to send another pair. That evening, one of the officers with whom he was sitting, a man whom he dreaded for his apparent fondness for cruelty, told the story of the rat torture. A day and a half later that same 'cruel officer' handed him the parcel which had arrived express from Vienna with the new spectacles in it, the delivery fees for which he said had been paid for by a Lieutenant A. The patient's first reaction was that he was not to pay back the money, for if he did the rat torture would happen to the woman he loved and to his father. This took the shape of an apparently quite contradictory vow, '*You must pay back the 3.80 kronen to Lieutenant A.*', but one which he knew the moment he formulated it to be impossible: the money was due to the trusting post-office official, not the Lieutenant who had first collected it.

As with Little Hans, we have a conflict that can be traced back to the double-bind of an unresolved Oedipal situation. The patient's father was both someone who must be obeyed (hence the patient's unconditional obedience to the 'cruel officer''s requirement that he pay back Lieutenant A.), and at the same time someone whom the son saw as standing in the way of his own happiness, and whose death he had fantasised for many years. What's more, during the last stages of the father's terminal illness, because the son mistook the doctor's words, he missed being present at his father's deathbed. The drama is thus one of an escalating and unpayable debt. It is no accident, as Freud points out, that this should have come to a head in a situation involving another impossible debt, or that the German word for 'installment', *Rate*, should be so close to *Ratte* (rat): dream-work and symptom alike work through associations of the signifying word rather than the signified meaning.

'Psychoanalytic Notes on an Autobiographical Account of a Case of Paranoia (Dementia Paranoides)' ('Schreber') (1911)

Strictly speaking, this is not one of Freud's case histories at all, as its subject was never a patient of his, but a psychoanalytic interpretation of the 1903 book, *Memorabilia of a Nerve Patient*. Its author, Daniel Paul Schreber, had been a judge who suffered a series of psychotic episodes, underwent lengthy psychiatric treatments in clinics and asylums, eventually took successful legal action for his discharge, and wrote the lucid and much-discussed memoir on which Freud based his analysis. It is Freud's only detailed investigation of a case of psychosis.

Schreber's illness was delusional. The Court Judgement that freed him from psychiatric care summed it up: 'He believed that he had a mission to redeem the world and to restore it to its lost state of bliss. This, however, he could only bring about if he were first transformed from a man into a woman' (p. 16). He experienced miracles: many of his bodily organs were destroyed in the course of his illness and restored by divine rays, as the voices with whom he conversed confirmed. These voices had also told him that the world would come to an end in another 212 years; his task over that intervening time would be the transformation of his body, which, when directly impregnated by God, would give rise to a new race of men. He believed that he was prevented in this by a plot against him, to have him declared incurably insane so that his soul could be murdered by his doctor. In the course of writing his memoir, he became increasingly convinced that this plot was in fact at the instigation of God himself, who misunderstood the nature of human beings, and would have him sexually abused.

Schreber is the only real person in this universe; all others, no matter how real they may seem, are just, in his phrase, 'cursorily improvised men' (p. 68). The psychoses, Freud suggests, are in this respect quite unlike the neuroses. Where the neuroses are characterised by a conflict between the ego-instincts and the sexual instincts (or, as he later puts it, after the second topography, between the ego and the id), the psychoses involve a profound disturbance in the relation between the ego and *the world.●* For the psychotic, as Schreber's delirium says clearly and quite literally, *the world ceases to exist*. Thus, says Freud, 'the paranoic builds it up again, not more splendid,

> ... a simple formula has now occurred to me which deals with what is perhaps the most important genetic difference between a neurosis and a psychosis: *neurosis is the result of a conflict between the ego and its id, whereas psychosis is the analogous outcome of a similar disturbance in the relations between the ego and the external world*. ('Neurosis and Psychosis (1924a, p. 149; emphasis in original)

it is true, but at least so that he can once more live in it. He builds it up by the work of his delusions. *The delusional formation, which we take to be the pathological product, is in reality an attempt at recovery, a process of reconstruction'* (pp. 70–71; emphasis in original).

This failure of the world brings the psychoses very close to narcissism, where object-libido is turned back from objects in the world to the ego itself: the sexual drives take the ego as their object. (Like the psychoses, narcissistic disorders are difficult to treat through psychoanalytic methods, and for very similar reasons: analysis works through transference, which presupposes that libido can be directed onto other persons in the world.) In fact, the Schreber case suggested just that link to Freud: out of it came the paper on narcissism some four years later,● and then, in the mid-1920s with what grows out of that,

> [The psychotic] seems really to have withdrawn his libido from people and things in the external world, without replacing them by others in phantasy. When he *does* replace them, the process seems to be a secondary one and to be part of an attempt at recovery, designed to lead the libido back to objects.*
>
> *[Freud's footnote] In connection with this see my discussion of the 'end of the world' in [Section III of] the analysis of Senatspräsident Schreber... ('On Narcissism: An Introduction' (1914a), p. 74)

the entire second topography.

'From the History of an Infantile Neurosis' ('Wolf Man') (1914)

This is Freud's most celebrated, complex and inconclusive case history, and the one of greatest interest in the history and practice of psychoanalysis.

The patient, a young Russian from a wealthy land-owning family, came to Freud in 1910, completely incapacitated after a breakdown sparked by a gonorrheal infection some six years earlier, when he was 18-years-old. He had suffered from a severe anxiety hysteria when he was four-years-old, which became an obsessional neurosis that lasted until he was ten. These form the 'infantile neurosis' of the title, and to which the case history restricts itself.

The patient's sobriquet comes from the dream whose recounting is central to Freud's analysis, as it allows him to reconstruct the primal scene at the heart of the neurosis. In it, the child dreamt that his bedroom window opened, and he could see that six or seven white wolves were sitting in the walnut tree outside – at which point he screamed and woke up. The two things which impressed themselves on him were the complete immobility of the scene (the only motion was the opening of the window) and the intensity of the wolves' gaze at him. The primal scene Freud draws from this, through a complex and ingenious analysis which draws on a wealth of detail recounted by the patient, is the classic one of the very young child's sight of the parents copulating. That the Wolf Man was unable to recollect such an event is hardly surprising, for it must have happened, if it happened at all, in what is usually the period of childhood amnesia: few people have any consistent or cogent memories of their life before the age of four. From this, Freud draws the important, if reluctant, conclusion that the primal scene need not have taken place as an actual event: even before *The Interpretation of Dreams*, he had insisted that fantasy can be just as effective in producing psychical consequences as actual events.

The case history was intended as a triumphal demonstration of Freudian methods against the various heresies of former stalwarts Jung and Adler, but things were never to be so neat. The course of treatment it recounts lasted until 1914, just before the outbreak of the Great War. The Wolf Man returned to Vienna in 1919, after having lost his family home and assets in the Revolution, and underwent further analysis with Freud until early 1920, as Freud said, 'to deal with a piece of the transference which had not hitherto been overcome' (p. 122). In the years immediately after this, he had intermittent contact with Freud, but in 1926, now an obsessive hypochondriac, he again sought analysis. Freud referred him to one of his pupils, Ruth Mack Brunswick. But in 1938, two disasters occurred: Vienna came under Nazi annexation, and the Wolf Man's wife committed suicide. Brunswick's pupil Muriel Gardiner arranged for him to have analysis again with Brunswick, who was now in Paris. He continued analysis for the rest of his life, with Brunswick and others, and with Muriel Gardiner as a friend and informal analyst who eventually encouraged him to write the memoirs which, in 1972, she published with other documentation by herself and Brunswick as *The Wolf-Man* and *Sigmund Freud* (Gardiner, 1972). Gardiner concludes that 'There can be no doubt that Freud's analysis saved the Wolf Man from a crippled existence, and Dr Brunswick's reanalysis overcame a serious acute crisis, both enabling the Wolf Man to live a long and tolerably healthy life' (Gardiner, 1973, p. 366). The Wolf Man died in 1979, aged 93.

'The Psychogenesis of a Case of Homosexuality in a Woman' (1920)

This case history is Freud's last, his briefest, and his least commented-on. It is the report of a treatment he had made almost 20 years ago, now written up and published at the beginning of the decade in which he would revise many of his ideas of female sexuality after the realisation of the asymmetry of the Oedipus complex

The patient was a young, beautiful and intelligent woman of 18 who had shown an open, public and unapologetic pursuit of a woman some ten years older, whom the younger woman's parents alleged was known to be both bisexual and promiscuous, but who did not return the affection. The relationship particularly incensed the father, whose sternness had largely estranged his children; the mother was far less troubled by it, and even enjoyed her daughter's confidences. The daughter made no attempt to disguise the relationship, though when the father passed the two women together in the street for the first time and cast his daughter an angry look, she responded by rushing off and flinging herself off a wall onto a suburban railway line. The undoubtedly genuine suicide attempt did no permanent physical damage, although the young woman spent a long time recuperating. Its longer-term effects were that the woman who was the object of her affections treated her with more warmth after such a proof of her passion, and her parents did not dare to oppose her to the same extent.

Freud's analysis comes to the conclusion that her negotiation of the usual revival of the Oedipus complex at puberty was derailed by the birth of a younger sibling: instead of her bearing a child in unconscious fantasy to the father whose affection she wished to win, a real child was borne by her rival, her mother.

Notes to Chapter 3

[1]This is the famous example Louis Althusser uses to illustrate how the ideological mechanism of *interpellation* works (Althusser, 1994, p. 130–36).
[2]The 'Thelma and Louise' episode of *The Simpsons* ran this scenario. Marge and a woman friend are heading across country in an open-top car, and stop at a diner somewhere in the desert. The parking lot to the diner is full of open-top cars, and every table in the diner has two women sitting at it, leaning across and talking earnestly to one another. Suddenly

a siren sounds, and instantly the diner empties, with everyone rushing to their car and leaving. Outside, a child is riding a tricycle with a siren attached to it, and the diner attendant says, 'Darn kid! That's the third time this week he's done that'.

[3] Here and in the title of *Civilization and its Discontents*, Freud's German word is *Kultur*. The Editor's Note to the Standard Edition of *The Future of an Illusion* points out the decision to translate this as 'civilization', and the adjectival form as 'cultural' (1927a, p. 4).

[4] Hence the title of one of Freud's best pieces of expository prose on psychoanalysis, *The Question of Lay Analysis* (1926b), where the question is one of whether a person without a medical degree should be allowed to treat patients. Contemporary Austrian law, with the general support of the medical profession, said not.

[5] Other writings draw different relations between psychoanalysis and the study of the social and cultural. In a number of other places, as diverse as '"Civilized" Sexual Morality and Modern Nervous Illness' (1908a), 'Thoughts for the Times on War and Death' (1915a), *The Future of an Illusion* (1927b), *Civilization and its Discontents* (1930), and the 'Why War?' exchange with Albert Einstein (1933), Freud argues that modern European societies are neurotic in ways all their own, not just because of some 'resurgence of the primitive'.

[6] In his earlier writings, Freud generally, if not always, suggests that the child's 'first, grand problem of life' is the question '*Where do babies come from?*' ('On the Sexual Theories of Children' (1908b), p. 212). From the mid-1920s on, though – which is when he is struck for the first time by the sheer asymmetry of the sexes and their development – he suggests that sexual difference actually has that role (in 'Some Psychical Consequences of the Anatomical Distinction between the Sexes' (1925b), he adds a footnote correcting those earlier statements, p. 252–53). But if, as we have argued here, the whole question of sexual difference is inseparable from that of difference in general, difference as origin, by which there is a world, then the two questions become variations of one another.

[7] Here, we can perhaps qualify the thesis of Claude Lefort's *Democracy and Political Theory* (1988), that it is only with the invention of democracy that the locus of power becomes permanently and structurally empty, to take into account the profound retrospectivity of that invention, which is to reveal that the locus of power has been essentially empty all along.

[8] This is an objection often made to Foucault's concept of *capillary power*, from *Discipline and Punish* (1975) and the first volume of the *History of Sexuality* (1976). If capillary power is not the infusion of power relations downwards from dominator to dominated, but instead *saturates* the social space, how can there be any space for the contestations of power? The obvious answer to this is the one we have been rehearsing here: power itself is never consistent or homogeneous, as the very condition of its being power. One *can* never fully obey power.

[9] Slavoj Žižek has written much about this: a king is not treated like a king because he is a king; he is a king because he is treated like one. See, for example, Žižek. 1991a, pp. 253–60.

[10] Žižek takes the argument further. The political leader whose flaws are publicly exposed may also be the figure who carries out an action which has popular approval but must be publicly disavowed. The example Žižek gives is of Kurt Waldheim, revelations of whose probable war crimes did not only *not* damage his 1986 Austrian presidential campaign, but possibly even helped it: in a country with a traumatic history of Nazi collaboration, the refusal to confront the past may have been precisely the point of identification for many voters (Žižek, 1989, p. 105).

[11] It is more accurate to say that this is a set of *masculine* relations: it is not that women do not enter into these relationships, but in the asymmetry of sexual difference they do so in ways which are already characterised as masculine. See, for example, Sedgwick, 1990, and Derrida, 1997.

[12]This is the logic Žižek identifies in anti-Semitism as an attempt to come to grips with the split nature of the social by means of paranoid fantasy. If the world does not treat me with justice, if I and those like me are impoverished while others flourish, if I see the enjoyment which should be mine out of my reach but not of others', then one explanation fantasy offers is that someone has stolen what is rightfully mine. See, for example, Žižek, 1989, pp. 125–28.

[13]By the same token, we should not read this as yet another version of the vague relativism which seeks to assure us that all families and all forms of family are as good as one another, that my choice is as good as anyone else's simply because it is mine. Every family may be structured around an insoluble knot, but some knots and some families can be lethal. The sheer error of logic in this assurance is the leap it makes from *There is no single true form of X* to *All forms of X are equally true*. In that 'equally true', the whole question of a common measure which it had appeared to want to put out of play returns again, this time as the disavowed basis for the very argument. (The disavowal is even more obvious when the 'equally true' is replaced, as it often is, by a euphemism such as 'equally valid', which makes it quite clear how the argument wants and indeed needs to invoke all the effects of truth while conjuring away what are felt to be its universalising or imperialising tendencies.)

[14]This is also a reason for taking a step back from the all-too-familiar distinction between biological *sex* and cultural *gender*. That avoidance is one of the reasons for Lacan's coinage, *sexuation*, which fits on neither side, but whose suffix retains the implication that it is not a given.

[15]In the English translation of the Standard Edition, Freud's footnote has an editorial addition: 'A recognition which, of course, has nothing of the character of a [true] recognition.' Presumably this is because the paragraph goes on to speak of how 'It is only in our modern, scientific but as yet by no means perfected *Weltanschauung* that superstition seems very much out of place'. Yet the paragraph also speaks of the similarities in the reasoning of the superstitious person and the paranoic, and how in their 'draw[ing] conclusions from insignificant signs' both of these are 'just like all normal people, who *quite rightly* base their estimate of their neighbours' characters on their chance and unintentional actions' (pp. 258–59; emphasis added) – and, we may add, thus just like the psychoanalyst, and in particular the psychoanalyst concerned with the psychopathology of everyday life. What the paragraph does is not confirm but blur the distinction between a 'true recognition' and one that is not. Freud's point is perhaps not that this recognition has nothing of truth in it, but that it has none of the character of *recognition*: it is a recognition which does not recognise that which it recognises.

[16]See Abraham, 1994. Abraham's essay is an elaboration of Freud's metaphor of the unconscious as kernel, and the way in which this necessitates what Abraham calls the *anasemia* of all the terms of psychoanalysis, which 'do not strictly speaking signify anything, except the founding silence of *any act of signification*' (Abraham, 1994. p. 84; emphases in original).

[17]And, we may add, Jungian psychology, which, in its mistaking the unities of secondary revision for the workings of the primary process, belongs with metaphysics rather than with a metapsychology of the unconscious.

[18]See note 3, above.

[19]This is where we find the work of Slavoj Žižek, who develops Althusser's theories of ideology as interpellation in the light of a thorough and inventive reading of Lacanian psychoanalysis. This is a theme throughout Žižek's work, but particularly in Žižek 1989,

1991a, 1993, 1999. For an introduction to Žižek's work, see 'Taking Sides: A Self-Interview' in Žižek, 1994, and Žižek & Daly, 2004.

[20]The writer Stefan Zweig estimated that at that time, in a large city such as Vienna, somewhere between 10 and 20 per cent of all young men had some form of venereal infection (cited in Decker, 1991, pp. 42–43).

REFERENCES

Freud

This list gives, at a glance, the chronology of all the major works, and all works mentioned or cited in this book. The date in the left-hand column is the year of publication. A date in square brackets in the second column is the year of composition, if this is different from the year of publication.

All page numbers in the text are to the Standard Edition, except where otherwise noted.

Abbreviations used:

SE   *The Standard Edition of the Complete Psychological Works of Sigmund Freud.* General ed. James Strachey. 24 vols. London: Hogarth Press, 1953–74.

PFL   *The Penguin Freud Library.* General eds. Angela Richards and Albert Dickson. 15 vols. Harmondsworth: Penguin, 1976–86.

1894   The Neuro-Psychoses of Defence. *SE* 3, 41–67.

1895   Freud, S. and Breuer, J. *Studies on Hysteria*. SE 2; *PFL* 3.

1900   *The Interpretation of Dreams*. *SE* 4–5, 1–642; *PFL* 4.

1901   *The Psychopathology of Everyday Life*. *SE* 6; *PFL* 5.

1905a [1901]   Fragment of an Analysis of a Case of Hysteria. *SE* 7, 1–122; *PFL* 8, 29–164. [The 'Dora' case history.]

1905b   *Jokes and Their Relation to the Unconscious*. *SE* 8; *PFL* 6.

1905c   *Three Essays on the Theory of Sexuality*. *SE* 7, 123–245; *PFL* 7, 31–169.

1908a   'Civilized' Sexual Morality and Modern Nervous Illness. *SE* 9, 177–204; *PFL* 12, 27–55.

1908b   On the Sexual Theories of Children. *SE* 9, 205–26; *PFL* 7, 183–204.

1909a [1908]   Family Romances. *SE* 9, 235–41; *PFL* 7, 217–25.

1909b   Analysis of a Phobia in a Five-Year-Old Boy. *SE* 10, 1–145; *PFL* 8, 165–305. [The 'Little Hans' case history.]

1909c   Notes upon a Case of Obsessional Neurosis. *SE* 10, 151–249; *PFL* 9, 31–128. [The 'Rat Man' case history.]

1910a [1909]   *Five Lectures on Psycho-Analysis*. *SE* 11, 7–56.

1910b   A Special Type of Choice of Object Made by Men (Contributions to the Psychology of Love I). *SE* 11, 163–75; *PFL* 7, 227–42.

1911a [1910]   Psychoanalytic Notes on an Autobiographical Account of a Case of Paranoia (Dementia Paranoides). *SE* 12, 1–82; *PFL* 9, 129–223. [The 'Schreber' case history.]

1911b   Formulations on the Two Principles of Mental Functioning. *SE* 12, 213–26; *PFL* 11, 29–44.

1912   The Dynamics of Transference. *SE* 12, 97–108.

1912–13   *Totem and Taboo*. *SE* 13, 1–161; *PFL* 13, 43–224.

1914a   On Narcissism: An Introduction. *SE* 14, 67–102; *PFL* 11, 59–97.

1914b	On the History of the Psychoanalytic Movement. *SE* 14, 1–66; *PFL* 15, 57–128.
1915a	Thoughts for the Times on War and Death. *SE* 14, 273–300; *PFL* 12, 57–89.
1915b	Instincts and Their Vicissitudes. *SE* 14, 109–140; *PFL* 11, 105–38.
1915c	Repression. *SE* 14, 141–58; *PFL* 11, 105–38.
1915d	The Unconscious. *SE* 14, 109–140; *PFL* 11, 139–58.
1916–17 [1915–17]	*Introductory Lectures on Psychoanalysis. SE* 15–16; *PFL* 1.
1917a [1915]	A Metapsychological Supplement to the Theory of Dreams. *SE* 14, 137–51; *PFL* 11, 223–43.
1917b [1915]	Mourning and Melancholia. *SE* 14, 109–40; *PFL* 11, 245–68.
1917c	On Transformations of Instinct as Exemplified in Anal Eroticism. *SE* 17, 125–33; *PFL* 7, 293–302.
1918 [1914]	From the History of an Infantile Neurosis. *SE* 17, 1–122; *PFL* 9, 225–366. [The 'Wolf Man' case history.]
1919	'A Child is Being Beaten' (A Contribution to the Study of the Origin of Sexual Perversions). *SE* 17, 175–204; *PFL* 10, 159–93.
1920a	The Psychogenesis of a Case of Homosexuality in a Woman. *SE* 18, 145–72; *PFL* 9, 367–400.
1920b	*Beyond the Pleasure Principle. SE* 18, 1–64; *PFL* 11, 269–338.
1921	*Group Psychology and the Analysis of the Ego. SE* 18, 65–143; *PFL* 10, 91–178.
1923	*The Ego and the Id. SE* 19, 1–66; *PFL* 11, 339–407.
1924a [1923]	Neurosis and Psychosis. *SE* 19, 147–53; *PFL* 10, 209–18.
1924b [1923]	A Short Account of Psychoanalysis. *SE* 19, 189–209; *PFL* 15, 159–82.
1924c	The Dissolution of the Oedipus Complex. *SE* 19, 171–79; *PFL* 7, 313–22.
1924d	The Economic Problem of Masochism. *SE* 19, 155–70; *PFL* 409–26.
1925a [1924]	An Autobiographical Study. *SE* 20, 1–74; *PFL* 15, 183–259.
1925b	Some Psychical Consequences of the Anatomical Distinction Between the Sexes. *SE* 19, 241–58; *PFL* 7, 323–43.
1926a [1925]	*Inhibitions, Symptoms and Anxiety. SE* 20, 75–175; *PFL* 10, 227–333.
1926b	*The Question of Lay Analysis: Conversations with an Impartial Person. SE* 20, 177–250; *PFL* 15, 277–363.
1927a	Fetishism. *SE* 21, 147–57; *PFL* 7, 345–57.
1927b	*The Future of an Illusion. SE* 21, 1–56; *PFL* 12, 179–241.
1930 [1929]	*Civilization and its Discontents. SE* 21, 57–145; *PFL* 12, 243–340.
1931	Female Sexuality. *SE* 21, 221–43; *PFL* 7, 367–92.
1933a [1932]	*New Introductory Lectures on Psychoanalysis. SE* 22, 11–82; *PFL* 2.
1933b	Why War? *SE* 22, 195–215; *PFL* 12, 341–62.
1937	Analysis Terminable and Interminable. *SE* 23, 209–53.
1939 [1934–38]	*Moses and Monotheism: Three Essays. SE* 23, 1–137; *PFL* 13, 237–386.
1940 [1938]	An Outline of Psychoanalysis. *SE* 23, 139–207; *PFL* 15, 369–443.
1950 [1887–1902]	Project for a Scientific Psychology. *SE* 1, 281–397.
1966 [1912–36]	*Sigmund Freud and Lou Andreas-Salomé: Letters.* Ed. E. Pfeiffer. Trans. W. and E. Robson-Scott. London, New York: W. W. Norton, 1970
1985 [1887–1904]	*The Complete Letters of Sigmund Freud to Wilhelm Fliess* 1887–1904. Ed. Jeffrey Moussaieff Masson. Cambridge, Mass.: Belknap Press

A set of abstracts to the Standard Edition is available online from the New York Freudian Society, at http://nyfreudian.org/abstracts

Other

Abraham, N. (1994) 'The Shell and the Kernel: The Scope and Originality of Freudian Psychoanalysis. In N. Abraham and M. Torok, *The Shell and the Kernel: Renewals of Psychoanalysis, Volume I*. Ed., trans. and intro. Nicholas T. Rand. Chicago: University of Chicago Press. (pp. 79–98)

Althusser, L. (1994) Ideology and Ideological State Apparatuses (Notes Towards and Investigation). In S. Žižek (Ed.), *Mapping Ideology*. London and New York: Verso. (pp. 100–40)

Appignanesi, L. and Forrester, J. (2000) *Freud's Women*. Harmondsworth: Penguin.

Badiou, A. (2004). *Theoretical Writings*. Ed. and trans. R. Brassier and A. Toscano. London and New York: Continuum.

Bernheimer, C. and Kahane, C. (Eds.) (1990) *In Dora's Case: Freud—Hysteria—Feminism*. Second edition. New York: Columbia University Press.

Boothby, R. (2001) *Freud as Philosopher: Metapsychology after Lacan*. New York and London: Routledge.

Borch-Jacobsen, M. (1988) *The Freudian Subject*. Trans. Catherine Porter. Foreword François Roustang. Stanford: Stanford University Press.

——. (1991) *Lacan: The Absolute Master*. Trans. Douglas Brick. Stanford: Stanford University Press.

——. (1993) *The Emotional Tie: Psychoanalysis, Mimesis, and Affect*. Trans. Douglas Brick *et al*. Stanford: Stanford University Press.

Borges, J.L. (1970) Funes the Memorious. *Labyrinths*. Trans. D.A. Yates and J.E. Irby. Harmondsworth: Penguin. (pp. 87–95)

Bourdieu, P. (1990) *In Other Words: Essays Towards a Reflexive Sociology*. Trans. Matthew Adamson. Cambridge: Polity Press.

Butler, Judith (1990) *Gender Trouble: Feminism and the Subversion of Identity*. London and New York: Routledge.

Butler, J., Laclau, E., and Žižek, S. (2000) *Contingency, Hegemony, Universality: Contemporary Dialogues on the Left*. London and New York: Verso.

Copjec, J. (1994) *Read my Desire: Lacan against the Historicists*. Cambridge, Mass. and London: MIT Press

——. (2003) *Imagine There's No Woman: Ethics and Sublimation*. Cambridge, Mass. and London: MIT Press.

Crews, F. (Ed.) (1999) *Unauthorized Freud: Doubters Confront a Legend*. New York: Penguin.

Decker, H. S. (1991) *Freud, Dora, and Vienna 1900*. New York: Free Press.

Derrida, J. (1987) *The Post Card: From Socrates to Freud and Beyond*. Trans. Alan Bass. Chicago: University of Chicago Press.

——. (1995) *The Gift of Death*. Trans. David Wills. Chicago and London: University of Chicago Press.

——. (1997) *Politics of Friendship*. Trans. George Collins. London and New York: Verso.

Foucault, M. (1977) *Discipline and Punish: The Birth of the Prison*. Trans. Alan Sheridan. London: Allen Lane.

——. (1979) *The History of Sexuality*. *Volume I: An Introduction*. Trans. Robert Hurley. London: Allen Lane.

Frow, J. (1997) *Toute la mémoire du monde:* Repetition and Forgetting. *Time and Commodity Culture: Essays in Cultural Theory and Postmodernity*. Oxford: Oxford University Press. (pp. 218–46).

Gardiner, M. (Ed.) (1973) *The Wolf-Man and Sigmund Freud*. London: Hogarth Press.

Grosskurth, P. (1991) *The Secret Ring: Freud's Inner Circle and the Politics of Psychoanalysis*. Reading, Mass.: Addison-Wesley.

Hertz, N. (1990) Dora's Secrets, Freud's Techniques. In C. Bernheimer and C. Kahane (Eds.) *In Dora's Case: Freud—Hysteria—Feminism*. Second edition. New York: Columbia University Press. (pp. 221–42).

Jones, E. (1964) *The Life and Work of Sigmund Freud*. Ed. and abridged Lionel Trilling and Steven Marcus. Harmondsworth: Penguin.

Lacan, J. (1977a) *Écrits: A Selection*. Trans. Alan Sheridan. London: Tavistock.

——. (1977b) *The Seminar. Book XI. The Four Fundamental Concepts of Psycho-Analysis, 1964*. Ed. Jacques-Alain Miller. Trans. Alan Sheridan. London: Hogarth Press and the Institute of Psychoanalysis.

——. (1988) *The Seminar. Book I. Freud's Papers on Technique, 1953–1954*. Ed. Jacques-Alain Miller. Trans. John Forrester. New York and London: W.W. Norton.

——. (1992) *The Seminar. Book VII. The Ethics of Psychoanalysis, 1959–1960*. Ed. Jacques-Alain Miller. Trans. Dennis Porter. New York and London: W. W. Norton.

——. (1998) *The Seminar. Book XX. On Feminine Sexuality, the Limits of Love and Knowledge, 1972–1973 (Encore)*. Ed. Jacques-Alain Miller. Trans. Bruce Fink. New York and London: W. W. Norton.

Laclau, E. and Mouffe, C. (1985) *Hegemony and Socialist Strategy: Towards a Radical Democratic Politics*. London and New York: Verso.

Laplanche, J. (1976). *Life and Death in Psychoanalysis*. Trans. and intro. Jeffrey Mehlman. Baltimore and London: Johns Hopkins University Press.

——. (1989) *New Foundations for Psychoanalysis*. Trans. David Macey. Oxford: Basil Blackwell.

——. (1999) *Essays on Otherness*. Ed. John Fletcher. Trans. Luke Thurston, *et al*. London and New York: Routledge.

Laplanche, J. and Pontalis, J.-B. (1973) *The Language of Psycho-Analysis*. Trans. Donald Nicholson-Smith. New York and London: W.W. Norton.

Lefort, C. (1988) *Democracy and Political Theory*. Minneapolis: University of Minnesota Press.

Masson, J.M. (1984) *The Assault on Truth: Freud's Suppression of the Seduction Theory*. New York: Farrar, Straus and Giroux.

Salecl, R. (1994) *The Spoils of Freedom: Psychoanalysis and Feminism after the Fall of Socialism*. London and New York: Routledge.

——. (Ed.) (1998) *(Per)versions of Love and Hate*. London and New York: Verso.

——. (Ed.) (2000) *Sexuation*. Durham: Duke University Press.

Salecl, R. and Žižek, S. (Eds.) (1996) *Gaze and Voice as Love Objects*. Durham: Duke University Press.

Sedgwick, E.K. (1990) *Epistemology of the Closet*. Berkeley: University of California Press.

Vaihinger, H. (1935 [1911]) *The Philosophy of 'As If': A System of the Theoretical, Practical and Religious Fictions of Mankind*. Trans. C.K. Ogden. London: Routledge and Kegan Paul.

Žižek , S. (1989) *The Sublime Object of Ideology*. London and New York: Verso.

——. (1991a) *For They Know Not What They Do: Enjoyment as a Political Factor*. London and New York: Verso.

——. (1991b) *Looking Awry: An Introduction to Jacques Lacan through Popular Culture*. Cambridge, Mass. and London: MIT Press.

——. (1993) *Tarrying with the Negative: Kant, Hegel, and the Critique of Ideology*. Durham: Duke University Press.

——. (1994) *The Metastases of Enjoyment: Six Essays on Woman and Causality*. London and New York: Verso.

——. (1997) *The Plague of Fantasies*. London and New York: Verso.

——. (1999) *The Ticklish Subject: The Absent Centre of Political Ontology*. London and New York: Verso.

Žižek, S. and Daly, G. (2004) *Conversations with Žižek*. Cambridge and Malden: Polity.

Zupančič, A. (2000) *Ethics of the Real: Kant, Lacan*. London and New York: Verso.

INDEX

Page numbers in **bold** indicate a major discussion of the term.
Page numbers in *italics* indicate a citation from Freud.
SMALL CAPITALS indicate a text by Freud.

Vaihinger, Hans, 57 fn. 2

Waldheim, Kurt, 153 fn 10
'war neuroses', 79–80, 86–87
WHY WAR?, 115, 153 fn 4
'WOLF MAN' (case history). *See* FROM THE
    HISTORY OF AN INFANTILE NEUROSIS
word-presentations, *35*

Žižek, Slavoj, xi,-xiv fn 2
    castration, 111 fn 16
    interpellation, 154–55 fn 19
    logic of anti-Semitism, 154 fn 12
    object of desire, 110 fn 4
    political bond to leader, 153 fn 9 & 10
Zupančič, Alenka, xi
Zweig, Stefan, 155 fn 20